next-step selling

a new sales
approach to create
and deliver value
for your customers

next-step selling

a new sales
approach to create
and deliver value
for your customers

John Barker

Pearson Education Australia
Unit 4, Level 2
14 Aquatic Drive
Frenchs Forest NSW 2086

Publisher: Nella Soeterboek
Commissioning Editor: Mark Stafford
Project Editor: Jane Roy
Cover and internal design: Ingo Voss
Typeset by Midland Typesetters

Printed in Australia by Griffin Press

1 2 3 4 5 05 04 03 02 01

ISBN 1 74009 623 1

National Library of Australia
Cataloguing-in-Publication Data

Barker, John (John Robert), 1953– .
    Next-step selling: a new sales approach to create and
    deliver value for your customers.

Includes index.
ISBN 1 74009 623 1

1. Selling. I. Title

658.85

An imprint of Pearson Education Australia

contents

Part 3   Bringing the Process to Life— The Essential Sales Skills

introduction

Why was this book written?

T hose people contemplating reading this book will probably ask themselves, 'Is there anything in this book that I can use to improve my professional selling career?' I believe the answer is a most definite and resounding '*Yes!*'.

But it could be said that I am somewhat biased. In which case, let me suggest that the answer to this question is perhaps a conditional 'Yes'. I believe this book will provide new insights and practical, proven and successful approaches to the sales process of complex sales *if*, and only *if*, like countless other salespeople, you are truly looking for an approach to selling that places your prospective, or possible, customer ('prospect') at the very heart of the exchange. And after all, isn't that what selling really is—an exchange?

With this in mind, and in answer to the question 'Why was this book written?', one could say that it was written for four primary reasons.

First, this book was written out of sheer frustration—frustration at being unable to find a simple, workable system or view of selling that spoke about the process of complex selling in clear, realistic, logical and practical terms; a system of selling that focused on viewing the sale as a process which recognised that the whole basis of the complex sale depended on the prospect. I believe that without a very clear and definite selling philosophy, no salesperson will move beyond first base, when it comes to succeeding in the world of complex sales.

Second, this book *evolved* naturally over a period of time as a counterpoint to all the books, articles, seminars and tape series that claim to teach those fixed selling 'techniques' that view the sales process as being something the salesperson *does to* the customer. These selling techniques seem to me, on the most basic level, to promote selling tricks and traps to the many misguided, but nevertheless potentially good, salespeople who feel that to succeed in sales they *must* learn to be able to spring these techniques on their unwary prospect.

Third, the book was written for all those salespeople who think they are ready for advanced selling skills. My experience is that few of these salespeople are ready for, nor indeed do they even need, *advanced* skills (whatever 'advanced' implies). I have generally found that what they *do* need is a review of the sales *basics*. This involves the salesperson truly understanding and rejecting many of their old notions of the sale and coming to grips with a totally new perspective of the selling process—a *value-based* perspective.

Finally, this book came into being as a direct response to what I saw as a challenge to put in print a better way of presenting the fundamentals of the sales process, as it relates to complex selling. In essence, my primary objective in writing this book was to challenge your thinking and, in so doing, to mount such a compelling argument for a well-conceived and implemented value-based selling approach to your particular type of sales process that you would embrace this approach completely.

Who was this book written for?

Quite simply, this book was written for those salespeople who are seeking a way of moving beyond the traditional reactive approach to sales to a more proactive approach, focused almost solely on building value for their prospects. These salespeople, or 'value builders' as one might term them, really do understand the true nature of complex selling. This book, then, is for those salespeople who have tried the traditional selling methods and systems and found them wanting.

This book is very much for those salespeople who are tired of the old ways—for those who are ready to embrace a new approach to selling. This approach to selling would reinforce the professionalism required to execute it and reward those who are prepared to demonstrate a clear capacity to both display the determination to look at the sale from the prospect's perspective and to recognise and display the discipline necessary to step outside their normal behavioural comfort zone for long enough to view first-hand the rewards that will surely come from creating value for their prospects.

This book is for those who believe that the relationship you build with your prospect, both interpersonal and professional, is fundamental to the sales process.

Finally, this book is for those of you who have been looking for something that is relevant to today's more complex sales environment, where the prospects are more knowledgeable, more aware and more determined to obtain the best value for their hard-earned money.

How was this book written?

I have presented this new *value-based approach* to selling in three parts. This approach has been adopted because I felt it essential to clearly delineate this very different focus on selling by differentiating the philosophy of the complex sales process from the framework of the more traditional sales process. It was also, in my view, essential to propose a fairly basic model for a 'typical' complex sale, involving specific sales elements; then, in the third and final part, to address a selected range of personal sales skills considered necessary to bring the framework to life.

Each part of the book may be read separately without the need to read the preceding part first; having said that, I believe that it would be preferable if you were to read the three parts in sequence, and would encourage you to do so. A quick overview of the three parts follows.

Part 1

To many, what is proposed will represent a startlingly new approach to selling—an approach I have loosely termed 'value-based selling'. This approach will require a complete shift in focus and methodology in their beliefs, attitudes, selling style and overall sales philosophy. It may not be stretching the boundaries too far to suggest that such a shift indeed involves that much-used but little-appreciated concept of a 'paradigm shift'. That is, as a result of considering the philosophies and model proposed in the first part of this book, many salespeople will view the sales process and their role in it from a totally new perspective.

To some, what I have called a 'new approach to the sale' will provide a sense of relief, in that their view of selling as a process is shared by others. With this will come a reassurance that their beliefs, attitudes and methodologies regarding selling are both acceptable and in demand, and that their view of the overall structure of the sales process is valid and workable. To those of you to whom this applies, I hope there are issues raised in this first part of the book that reinforce your current approach and perhaps provide additional information and encouragement to continue developing your value-based sales approach.

If you have difficulty accepting my premise of a buyer-centred sales approach, or *value-based selling*, I encourage you to step beyond your comfort zone and try it. Not just once. Try it a number of times. I believe you will be a more relaxed, more natural and more successful salesperson as a result.

Part 2

The second part of the book looks in detail at the major sales elements involved in all complex sales processes. Each sales element is an important part of the sales process, the relative importance of which varies with differences in you the salesperson, your organisation, your product and your prospect.

As you will see as you advance through this part of the book, it is my contention that, in the world of complex outside sales, there are no specific sequential steps to a sale. Rather, I believe that there are elements in the sales process that are common to most (and perhaps all) sales situations, and I discuss each element as proposed in my sales model, which I have called the 'anatomy of a sale'. This model proposes 10 key sales elements and five key phases in the overall complex sales process.

When it comes to steps in a sale, only in simple sales do I believe it might be argued that selling is a simple matter of following preordained steps. Even in this simple sales scenario, I believe this learned step-by-step approach to selling is potentially flawed and, worst of all, provides no sustainable basis or platform upon which to build an approach to the more complex sales process.

I prefer to believe that successful selling isn't about following predetermined steps but about understanding, recognising and appreciating the elements of a sale and effectively responding to each. A clear understanding of each element is, I believe, the essential first step to a successful professional selling career.

Part 3

Sales texts seem often to be guilty of confusing the personal sales skills required to effectively execute selling strategies with the so-called sales steps they advocate. Nothing could be further from the truth, in my experience of complex selling.

For example, many authors suggest 'prospecting' as a distinct and discrete *step* in the sales process, and will talk of 'prospecting skills'. In my view, they appear to confuse the step they call 'prospecting' with a skill by the same name. This part of the book sets out to address those personal 'soft skills' (some might say sales competencies) that are required to kick-start and then progress and manage the sales process.

The skills I refer to are the combination of learned behaviours, attitudes, knowledge and experience that allow you, the salesperson, to breathe your own individual brand of life into the sales elements and, hence, the sales process itself. These skills are what makes the sales process come alive, and are what you as a salesperson often aspire to acquire and improve; it's what you bring to the sales process as your unique contribution to the profession of selling.

Throughout the book, when referring to products and services being sold, I will refer only to *product*. If, for instance, you sell intangibles such as consultancy services, please consider this to be your 'product' in the sales process.

I often refer to buyer's, customers or clients as 'prospects'. I do so because this book is primarily targeted to selling new accounts and as such they will remain prospects until they have been sold; even then, for each new sale they could continue to be regarded as prospects.

Finally, I wish you well and sincerely hope that you gain new insight into the complex sales process as a result of absorbing the myriad thoughts, observations and experiences threaded throughout this book.

PART 1

A NEW APPROACH TO SELLING

chapter 1

The basics: What is selling?

To be effective in any role involving human endeavour you must have a clear, unambiguous and realistic view of the environment in which you are operating and the objectives or outcomes towards which you are striving. And so it certainly is in the world of selling.

To be effective as a salesperson it is absolutely imperative that you have a clear understanding of exactly what constitutes 'selling' in your particular sales environment and, accordingly, understand clearly and specifically what your role is as a salesperson in that environment.

So, in very general terms, can you answer each of the following three questions?

1. What is your role as a salesperson?
2. What is 'selling'?
3. What are you selling?

What is your role as a salesperson?

Are you absolutely clear about your role in the sales process in your particular sales environment? Why don't you take a few moments right now to explore the generic role of a salesperson; having done that, explain in, say, 20 words or less what you believe is your particular selling role. You should be absolutely clear about your role in the sales process as a salesperson, and I believe it is imperative that your ideas are in alignment with those of the organisation whom you represent. In my experience, a great deal of stress in sales organisations is caused by the apparent but nevertheless unexplored divergences in the selling model adopted by management (which is often vague, ill-conceived and rarely well communicated) and that adopted by the salespeople (which is also usually vague and rarely well articulated). Where there is little or no clear sales culture reinforced by management, I usually find that the salespeople are left to their own devices to interpret management's signals and have little or no clear picture of their role in the organisation; nor do they understand what is required of them by the organisation. As a result, many salespeople don't see where they fit into the organisation's 'big picture' and experience difficulty seeing their role as one of value.

So, what is the generic role of 'salespeople' adopted in many selling organisations? I believe that the role of most salespeople could be stated as follows.

> *The role of salespeople in many sales organisations is to recruit and retain customers.*

Far too simple, you think? In that case, I challenge you to come up with a brief statement that better encapsulates the generic role of a salesperson!

What is selling?

Think about the activity of selling in your sales environment. Are you absolutely clear what is meant by the term 'selling'? I suggest the following as a relatively simple, all-purpose, one-size-fits-all explanation of the activity of selling.

> *Selling is helping a prospect to make a positive buying decision—one that is in their best interest and that, without the assistance of the salesperson, they might not make.*

Let's be clear right from the outset. I am not talking here about manipulation. I am talking about assisting the prospect to make a buying decision that is in *their* best interest. Manipulation is about win/lose; it's about taking advantage of the relationship; it's about thinking, acting and selling primarily, if not totally, from the point of view of the *seller's perspectives*, not the *prospect's needs*.

Professional value-based selling doesn't involve manipulation. Professional value-based selling is all about finding out what the prospect really needs and wants, and then working towards helping them to get it.

Having considered the questions of 'What is selling?' and 'What is the salesperson's role in it?', it's time to look at a third and closely related question.

Are you clear about what it is you are selling?

I suggest that, basically, there are only three things you as a salesperson have to sell!

- *The product*
- *The organisation* } = *What the salesperson has to sell*
- *You*

The order in which I have listed these is significant. In my experience, this is the order in which they are presented by most salespeople in response to questions from the prospect, or indeed when planning a presentation before even meeting the prospect. It also represents the priority of focus that most salespeople consider applies to each.

Furthermore, it usually reflects the order in which these answers are given to the above question. What I find alarming, however, is that a large proportion of salespeople who answer the question 'What am I selling?' nominate only the first—and perhaps the second—of these: it is an extremely small number of salespeople who nominate all three components. That is to say that by far the majority of salespeople are clear that the foremost thing they have to sell is the 'product'. (As explained in the introduction to this book, for the sake of simplicity I am including such intangibles as services as a product, rather than writing the words 'product or service' in every instance.)

It would appear from responses to the question that fewer salespeople are aware that they are also selling their 'organisation'. That is, they have difficulty in explaining why the prospect should do business with their organisation and not with their competitor's organisation.

Finally, only a minority of salespeople seem to understand that they are really selling themselves, or even understand *how* to sell themselves. These salespeople recognise that how they sell themselves to the prospect is something the prospect factors into the buying process.

So, are *you* clear about what you are selling? My experience indicates that the majority of your sales colleagues are not. They focus largely, if not solely, on the *product* and, it often appears, look for every opportunity to dump product information. The product dump usually occurs in an ad-hoc, undisciplined presentation that has very little relevance to the prospect's actual perceptions and specific situation.

While we are discussing these three key components of what it is you have to sell, it's also worth considering that each component includes both tangible and intangible parts. What might some of these tangible and intangible supporting parts be?

- *Your product*—A tangible would obviously be the physical product itself. But what about an intangible? Would a letter from a customer expressing endorsement of and satisfaction with your product qualify as intangible evidence? What about what the product might do in terms of improving return on investment, morale, quality control etc.?
- *Your organisation*—A tangible might include evidence of its actual physical presence (buildings, trucks, signage, personnel etc.). Intangible aspects of this component might include the time the organisation has been in business, its past track record, past history, client or customer lists, and achievements.
- *You*—In some respects this should be the easiest of all for the salesperson to discuss, but in practice it's very rarely the case. What tangible evidence can you produce to sell the 'you' component of the sale? Well, obviously there is the physical you, your presence, your proposal, copies of your awards, photographs of your past projects or work etc. Now what of the intangible evidence you are selling about 'you'? There's your experience, your expertise, your commitment, your enthusiasm, your attitude, your reputation and so on.

My experience is that the second and third components of what is being sold—the 'organisation' and 'you'—are those that are least often presented to the prospect as part of the sales package offer. It's almost as if the majority of salespeople have difficulty recognising, accepting or articulating the importance of these components of the sale. And, let's face it, if the salesperson cannot comprehend and articulate these two vital components, then why should the prospect accept, understand or appreciate their significance?

Given the highly competitive nature of selling, and given that prospects often have difficulty seeing and/or accepting what you might believe to be patently obvious evidence in support of your product, your ability to effectively sell yourself and your organisation to a prospect is one of the major potential means of differentiating yourself from the competition, and the primary input for developing an irresistible and compelling sales story centred around you and your prospect, your respective organisations and the product.

The missing links

I imagine that anyone reading this book wants to acquire knowledge, improve their selling skills and succeed as a professional salesperson. This may be self-evident: why else would anyone take the time to read what I have to say if they weren't in some way committed to achieving success in selling?

But are you, the reader, clear about what it will take to succeed?

In my experience, most salespeople aren't clear about what must be done. Many want quick fixes, tricky closes, clever phrases and, most of all, simple, no-risk systems that involve little or no change in their current behaviour. Many salespeople want a system of selling that requires little or no thinking or proactive independent action on their part or that doesn't challenge their existing philosophy of selling, if they do indeed possess one.

Unless you are prepared to challenge some of your beliefs about selling, and are committed to reviewing your attitudes, skills and habits, you are unlikely to succeed in the more complex selling game, where stakes are high and the potential rewards unlimited.

So, back to the original question.

What do you need to succeed in the world of the complex sale?

Evidence points to just four main items, which are in many respects inseparable in the sales process mix:

1. product knowledge;
2. selling skills;
3. sales process knowledge; and
4. the right attitude.

The fourth item, 'the right attitude', is indirectly the focus of Part 1 of this book. As you might well appreciate, your attitudes to selling, and to the prospect, are determining factors in your approach, or let's call it your philosophy of selling. The old adage 'It isn't your *aptitude* but your *attitude* that determines your *altitude*' remains essentially correct. To some this may seem trite, but in my experience it is nevertheless true. And when it comes to attitude, it's your attitude to three things that will primarily determine your potential for success. Expressed as a formula, these are as follows.

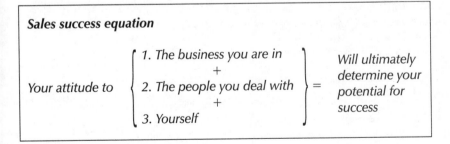

Sales success equation

Your attitude to
{
1. The business you are in
+
2. The people you deal with
+
3. Yourself
}
= Will ultimately determine your potential for success

This book isn't primarily concerned with attitude per se, although now is probably the right time, and here the right place, for one final word on attitude.

Remember that our prospects don't often see what we as salespeople might consider or view (either rightly or wrongly) as 'blindingly obvious' when it comes to the differences between competing similar products on offer. In fact, our prospects often suggest, or at least behave as if they believe, that there appears little or no discernible difference between our and our competitor's products, presentations and prices. My belief, based on countless reviews with buyers, is that there are really only two factors they might consider that tend to differentiate the product from the inevitable variety of options and alternatives. I call them the *separation factors*.

Separation factors

Factor no. 1: The level of service provided
                    +/or –
Factor no. 2: The quality of the relationship built } = The separation factors

---

If you think this is a simplistic observation, you will likely not accept the following statement: in order to effectively differentiate your product, you must first differentiate yourself. And to do this, you must first be prepared to assume professional control. That's right—you, not the prospect, should be in control of the sales process. And, guess what? Most prospects tell me they not only want this, they expect it!

chapter 2

The changing ages of selling

M̲ost salespeople grow and mature as salespeople through a combination of the right attitudes, experiences, skills, education and training, the appropriate mentors, and the right resources and encouragement.

I suggest that there are possibly four distinct stages that salespeople might develop and mature through. And it would appear that where we start, and how we progress and develop as professional salespeople, depends largely on our focus.

Consider for a moment two possible distinctly separate dimensions that could be used to measure the focus of a salesperson. Let's call the first the 'salesperson–customer', or 'us or them', dimension. This might be used to measure whether your focus prior to and during the sales call is on the other person, your prospect, and on their needs; or alternatively on you, the salesperson, and your own needs.

The second dimension we will call the 'product–process' dimension, or the 'what or why' dimension, because it succinctly summarises a choice available to the salesperson. 'Product'-focused salespeople continually revert to focusing on *what* it is they have to sell, and as a result consistently dump product information on the prospect. Those salespeople who are concerned primarily with the sales 'process', rather than the product, focus on the relationship, which leads naturally to continually asking *why*, or indeed *why not*?

Now let's suppose that we combine these two dimensions: we might then create a simple four-quadrant model that looks something like Figure 2.1. Each quadrant represents a very different approach to selling. We call these four quadrants 'persuasive presenters', 'product pushers', 'problem solvers' and 'value providers', based solely on the four different hypothetical combinations of focus adopted by the salesperson as represented in Figure 2.1. I propose a theory of evolution that goes roughly as follows.

In the very early stages of selling, most of us start in the profession as students in quadrant 1 (Q1), the junior school of salesmanship. Life is

Figure 2.1   *The four quadrants sales approach*

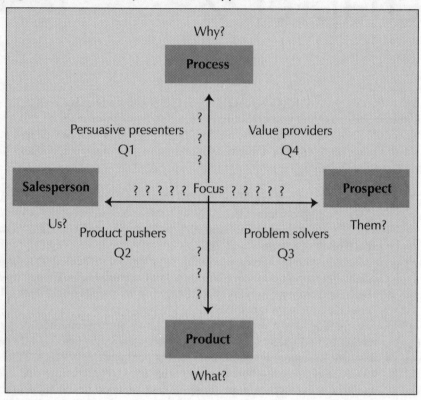

fascinating, we see ourselves as bulletproof, and there is nothing that we feel cannot be achieved with a little initiative and a healthy dose of the right attitude, such as enthusiasm and perseverance. In short, we are in the formative stages of learning, often termed the 'unconscious incompetent' phase. Which means we simply 'don't know what we don't know'. With this approach to selling we rely heavily on memorising our lines, including predetermined learned responses to our prospect's questions and various common objections. That is, we are very focused on both ourselves as salespeople and the sales process that we believe we need to instigate and follow. I have termed this the 'persuasive presenter'.

Having flirted briefly with this approach, the vast majority of salespeople realise, as they experience the real world of sales, that there is more to selling than this, and consequently seek to advance to what they see as a more sophisticated approach. They move from Q1 to Q2—the approach I have termed 'product pushers'. They have moved away from the reliance on the mechanics of the sales process to being primarily product-focused, believing that the key to a successful sale is the product's features, yet remain committed to maintaining the focus on their own objectives. That is, they focus on what *they* want to happen.

(By way of anecdotal example, I know of one situation where a new salesperson acting in 'product pusher' mode in the company of his sales manager inflicted a severely 'product'-focused and 'salesperson'-focused presentation on a prospect, only to have that prospect place a very large order with him—it would seem in spite of the salesperson's presentation, rather than because of it. As you can imagine, the salesperson was pleased as punch and couldn't resist telling everyone what a great sale he had just made. Late the next day, the sales manager, a 30-year sales veteran with the company, thought it was time to take the new salesperson aside and put him straight. He told the young recruit in no uncertain terms that, contrary to what he believed, he hadn't 'made a sale'. In fact, the sales manager went on to explain, he just happened to be the person to whom the customer had communicated his order and the sale had been made well before the salesperson even opened his mouth.)

Someone once described this 'product pusher' style of selling as the terrible 'teenage' years of selling. Most of us, whether we have children or not, have heard of the dreaded teenage years. As it applies to selling, it would appear that we either mature and grow out of it in time or leave the selling profession—the latter outcome usually being an involuntary decision. It's in this second approach to selling that salespeople embrace the objective of pushing hard for a favourable decision. We have grown from our formative years into an adolescent. As a result we have discovered the 'characteristics' of our product, adopted them as our own, and we are on a 'mission'—a crusade—to tell anybody who we imagine shows even the slightest interest what it is we have to sell. Our stock in trade are the 'features' of the product, and the skills we bring to the party and on which we depend heavily in these formative sales years are based around our ability to ask for the order, to 'overcome' objections and, of course, to demonstrate competent presentation skills. If we bothered to ask, the majority of our prospects would probably describe us, at this stage of our growth, as naive, self-centred, adolescent salespeople, which in the sales world equates to a product and salesperson-centred persuader, hence 'product pusher'.

The next phase in the ongoing maturing process of a salesperson is the development of Q3—the 'problem solver' approach to selling. Here the salesperson understands and accepts that persuading or pushing for the order isn't the way of the future in selling. The young salesperson has progressed beyond the teenage years into early adulthood, and with this comes a realisation that they don't necessarily know everything about anything.

In this 'problem solver' mode, our intrepid salesperson has learned from their knowledgeable and experienced peers that they are in the business of providing 'solutions' for their customers. On the face of it, this is often a revolutionary concept for a young salesperson and appears a laudable goal. However, the delivery doesn't quite match the lofty ideal of the objectives, and our hero becomes consumed by 'advantages'. My experience indicates that if you took the time to acquaint the salesperson with this fact, you would almost certainly be met with a vacant stare. 'What do you mean . . . advantage?' they might say. 'What's an advantage?' I have even heard something like this: 'Don't be ridiculous, I'm dealing in benefits, just ask my prospects.' So I followed the salesperson's suggestion and asked his prospects whether they really were hearing about benefits from the salesperson. And the majority said, 'No!' They said that they were hearing about ways in which the product *might* be used, but that the majority of these possibilities didn't apply in their particular circumstances. They also told me that those potential positives identified by the salesperson that did apply weren't dealt with effectively. Basically, these prospects suggested that the salesperson was engaging in a form of 'hit and miss' salesmanship. Something akin, they told me, to 'throwing mud at a wall in the hope that some will stick' and thereby influence or make the sale.

As I see it, in Q3, the 'problem solving' mode, most salespeople are only concerned with *how* their product can be presented as a solution to any problem or problems that the prospect might have. The potentially disturbing part is that the salesperson's perception in this mode of selling often centres around the view that the prospect has exactly the same problem as many of the salesperson's other prospects and, while the prospect may have trouble expressing their needs succinctly, it really doesn't matter because the salesperson knows exactly what they really need or want. Basically, problem-solving salespeople believe that with their experience they know what is best for the prospect, based on their past experience and product knowledge. Our Q3 salesperson has heard the buzzwords *trust*, *rapport* and *interpersonal communications*, and believes they herald the dawning of a new age in selling. As a result, they now believe they have the keys to unlock (read *manipulate* or *manufacture*) a successful outcome (read a *yes* from the customer), and it is only a matter of time (read *inevitable*).

What our young adult salesperson fails to appreciate is that they are still very much centred on product mode. As such, they do most of the talking and, while perhaps less dependent on the product than in their previous life as product pusher, they have engineered the primary focus to remain on them, by standing centre stage with the spotlight on their product and on them as the saviour of the prospect. They simply translate their own needs into language that appears to speak to the prospect about the prospect's problems.

The bad news with the first three sales approaches or quadrants, the 'persuasive presenters', 'product pushers' and 'problem solvers', is that these styles of selling are likely to be increasingly irrelevant, certainly in the arena of complex sales, and especially in the new millennium. Why?

Simply because computers and the Internet can provide this type of order taking, product pushing and 'solution'-based selling in a more consistent, more accurate and more graphic manner, seven days a week, 24 hours a day. And they can do it for far less money, with much less aggravation, and with a great deal less exposure or risk for the sales organisation. Salespeople who stay mired in the first, second or even third quadrants of salesperson development and maturity will be replaced by systems that do this type of traditional selling far more efficiently. For that matter, they will also be in quadrants overpopulated by other salespeople and, as a result, will have few if any clear advantages for being hired over their equally competent colleagues.

The good news is that the demand for salespeople who can continue to grow and mature and develop skills that allow them to operate on the next level, the Q4, 'value provider' level, is enormous. These will be the new and sought-after breed of successful sales professionals. These salespeople, who strive to operate on a consultancy level, truly understand how to build value for their clients and appreciate how to build it in a way that the computerised sales system cannot emulate—at least not in the foreseeable future.

This new 'value provider' approach to selling requires the salesperson to be acutely 'benefit'-focused: after all, this is the only way of demonstrating true value to your prospect. To focus on real 'benefits', our salesperson must have a broad range of skills above and beyond those required for the previous three sales approaches. These new skills are centred around such things as *relationship building*. *Strategic thinking* and *planning* will play a major role, as will the ability to clearly propose and demonstrate true value. This isn't to say that those skills developed around other areas and mentioned in the previous three quadrants are not applicable. However, to reach this more sophisticated level generally requires a major shift in a salesperson's perception of the selling process; accordingly, all of the previously mentioned skills revolving around such areas as self-confidence, memory, presentation and closing skills, and the ability to build trust and rapport, seem to take on very different meanings.

Watching a salesperson work on this higher plateau of selling, which I termed a 'consultancy level', is to watch a true professional practise their craft. They are truly customer- and process-centred and very focused on one of their primary objectives as relationship builder.

As this may sound a little confusing, let's take a minute to review the main differences between this Q4 approach and those of the first three.

Have you grown as a professional salesperson?

Think for a moment about one of your current prospects. Consider the following questions in the context of this person. Your answers might tell us something about your current preferred sales approach. They may well give us an insight into what quadrant of selling you are currently operating from.

So, here we go. Think carefully. Consider your responses to each of the eight questions outlined below, and take the time to write down your answers.

Eight important questions

1. What do you see as your primary purpose in visiting your prospect?
2. How do you want your prospect to view your role in the sales process?
3. How do you view the role of the prospect in the sales process?
4. How do you think an observer might describe the sales process that both you, the salesperson, and your prospect are engaged in?
5. Which of you, the salesperson or your prospect, asks most of the questions?
6. What type of questions are asked?
7. How do you view the 'closing' activity of the sales process?
8. What do you see as the overall objective in the 'negotiating' activity of the sales process?

Now compare your responses to those we have set out opposite.

You can probably see that how you answer each of these questions reveals a good deal about how you view the sales process and, in particular, the role—be it 'persuasive presenter', 'product pusher', 'problem solver' or 'value provider'—you might choose to adopt as a salesperson in it.

So, how did you go? What quadrant of selling do you predominately engage in?

I have set out in Table 2.1 (p. 16) a summary of the four quadrants or approaches to selling discussed earlier, indicating the primary differences between them in a number of critical areas, such as:

- *Critical area no. 1*—the sales orientation adopted by the salesperson.
- *Critical area no. 2*—the primary sales aids used to advance the sale or bring it to a close.
- *Critical area no. 3*—the primary sales competencies, skills and knowledge required by the salesperson to effectively demonstrate the various approaches.
- *Critical area no. 4*—the level of the prospect–salesperson sales relationship that has been achieved *as viewed by the prospect*.

Questions to ask yourself	Persuasive presenters, product pushers and problem solvers	Value providers
1. Your purpose?	'To sell/tell/persuade the prospect . . .'	'To learn from the prospect . . .'
2. Prospect's view of you?	Expert, educator, teacher. A persuader.	Adviser, resource person, thinker. A consultant.
3. Your view of the prospect?	Student or novice. Someone who can learn from your experience and expertise.	Equal partner. Without them, there is no sales process.
4. Observer's view of the process?	Essentially a monologue, with you, the salesperson, doing most of the talking.	Essentially a dialogue, with you, the salesperson, doing most of the active listening.
5. Who asks?	Prospect asks the majority of genuine questions in an attempt to understand WHY.	Seller asks the majority of questions, designed to control the sales process and to understand.
6. Type of questions?	The seller's questions are self-focused and manipulative and are primarily designed to find out WHY NOT.	The salesperson's questions are genuine inquiries and are primarily designed to find out WHY.
7. View of closing?	A selected technique to be used at frequent and often predetermined opportunities to finalise the sale.	A natural process that starts at the beginning of the relationship and that you both work through towards a decision.
8. Objective of negotiations?	Win/lose, win/I don't care, or lose/win.	Win/win.

Table 2.1 *The changing approaches to selling*

The four quadrants of the sales approach

Differentiating factor	Q1 Persuasive presenters	Q2 Product pushers	Q3 Problem solvers	Q4 Value providers
Sales era	Salesperson	Product	Image	Competitive
Sales orientation	Salesperson- and process-centred	Product- and salesperson-centred	Prospect- and product-centred	Prospect- and process-centred
Primary sales aids	■ Script ■ Product brochures etc.	■ Features ■ Unique selling propositions	■ Advantages ■ Image and reputation	■ Benefits ■ Positioning
Primary sales skills, competencies and/or behaviours	■ Confidence ■ Memory ■ Attitude ■ Persistence	■ Presentation ■ Objection resolution ■ Closing ■ Demonstration	■ Interpersonal communications ■ Credibility ■ Rapport development ■ Experience and creativity	■ Relationship building ■ Strategic planning ■ Questioning ■ Active listening
Prospect–salesperson relationship level	Competitor	Commodity	Competency	Consultancy

chapter 3

Your prospect is different

I t seems to require a rather special selling philosophy and, based on my observations, one that is all too infrequently embraced, to approach the more complex sale—a selling philosophy that first and foremost involves recognising that your customer is different and, as such, unique and therefore special.

You might be tempted to argue that they are still very much a human being and share many of the various attributes we come to expect from other humans; there is, after all, a mind, a body, and so on. As such, you might believe that there is nothing unique or special about each and every customer. What does, however, make the customer unique, and therefore very special, is a whole raft of interrelated aspects. These aspects include such things as attitudes, intelligence and values, skills, education, training, life experiences and behavioural tendencies, to mention only a few.

Some of these individual aspects, let's call them 'personality traits', combine to focus and shape their thoughts and actions, sometimes very differently from ours. For example, one commonly held view is that our values and attitudes are the main factors that determine *why* we do something. It has been suggested that it is these 'hidden motivators' that form the basis of the way we view the world, or the filter, if you like, through which we interpret and value life and life experiences. I suggest that these values and attitudes are hidden because they are generally difficult to assess by simply observing someone. They might, however, be determined by a trained, experienced person through the use of skilled questioning and listening. As I have suggested, they are the *why* when it comes to what we do in any given situation. This includes why we might do what we do when it comes to making buying decisions and in selling our products.

Next, our thinking-oriented personality aspect, commonly known as 'intelligence', is arguably the greatest modifier of our actions or behaviour. It doesn't on its own direct or motivate, but it has a large impact on *what* we will do in any given situation. For example, you may have a tendency to nibble on junk food during the day. Your values and attitudes may tell you via an emotional and/or rational internal message system, for your ears only, *why* it is that this reliance on fast food isn't good (for whatever reason). As a result, you are motivated (*provided*, of course, the value or attitude creates an emotional/ rational response, or the *why* is strong enough to impel you to *act*) to do something about it.

It is your intelligence (sometimes in concert with other personality aspects, such as your skills, education, experience and training) that will often alter or even control your responses and channel them in a certain direction. Your values and attitudes might tell you a story based on *why* and show you internal pictures of possibly one or both of the following:

- *Why number 1*—how bad you will look and feel if you continue to snack on junk food; and/or
- *Why number 2*—how good you will look and feel if you control, or perhaps eliminate, this unsatisfactory behaviour.

These internal stories and pictures can be promoted by you (that is, they can be self-programmed), by others, or by your environment.

Our personality aspects of intelligence together shape the *what* of our actions—that is, what we will do now that we have decided to act. They shape the force, the *why*, that originally moved us to action, which you will recall was our values and attitudes. Together our skills, life experiences, education and training, usually led by our intelligence, decide *what* we will do given a stimulus that motivates us to action.

Like attitudes and values, these five elements are difficult to assess by direct casual observation. It generally takes a skilled practitioner to interpret each of these elements. In some instances, notably with intelligence, it is impossible to determine accurately without administering and scoring a test; whereas it may be possible to gain an insight into a person's skills, life experiences, education and training by careful probing and the use of structured interviewing techniques.

But the story doesn't end there. There is one other player yet to make its entrance—our *behaviour*. Of all the personality aspects, our behaviour (and attendant emotions) is the most easily observed. And for the skilled person, our external observable behaviours and emotions can be interpreted with a remarkable degree of accuracy. It is our prospects' behaviour—that is, the *how* of their actions—that gives us clues as to their real needs and wants as human beings.

I suggest that you enter all sales relationships with a view to carefully observing behaviour—that is, the *how* a person acts: how they walk, how they talk, how they like to buy, how they prefer to be closed, serviced, influenced etc.; even how they decorate or arrange their office. With the requisite skills you will find that these can provide very reliable indicators as to how the prospect wants to be sold.

Take the time to look deeply into the situation. Leverage your sensitivity, your experience, your urge to understand the prospect's special situation, to find out exactly what is different about this person. This requires you to shift your focus from of yourself and onto your prospect. To do this, many of us must reignite our natural curiosity about people. This natural curiosity is the competitive edge you bring to selling that will almost certainly separate your value-based approach to selling from the approaches adopted by some of your colleagues and many of your competitors. Don't do as most salespeople do. Don't content yourself with looking for indicators of commonality that your prospect might share with other customers, then jump to assuming what they need and want based on your previous experience with other customers.

If your prospect says something like 'We've always tended to operate by . . .', instead of immediately checking this statement against your perception of the accepted norm and then attempting to change the prospect's views, hold fire and listen. Instead of unconsciously responding with something like 'Our experience suggests that that approach may be somewhat counterproductive', wait: don't jump right in and attempt to stamp your interpretation on the situation. Don't try to fit the circumstances into one of your predetermined mental moulds. Instead, after your prospect has made the statement, pause, then say, 'That's an interesting approach. Why is that?', or perhaps 'That is certainly a different approach from many others in your field . . . Tell me a little more about . . .'

Most salespeople recognise that identifying and then meeting the prospect's real needs are what selling is all about. They understand that without a clear picture of those needs from the prospect's perspective, selling is going to be an uphill battle, a lottery at best, where luck plays a major role. Did you notice I suggested understanding the real needs 'from the prospect's perspective'? The old adage 'The customer is always right' may not be true in many cases, but when it comes to selling it's always true. THE CUSTOMER IS ALWAYS RIGHT. It doesn't matter what you think. It doesn't matter what you know. The prospect's perception of the situation and *their* needs are always right.

You therefore have two choices. The first choice is the one adopted by traditional salespeople—that is, those salespeople who sell from their own perspectives. Here, what the prospect really thinks and feels is irrelevant.

The second choice is the preferred one for those salespeople who are intent on a selling approach with the focus firmly fixed on their prospect. However, my experience indicates that, for most salespeople, this choice will require:

- a major attitude shift; and
- considerably enhanced sales skills and/or sales knowledge.

Two choices for responding to the prospect's perceptions

Choice no. 1—Accept the prospect's stated or implied perspective of their needs at face value and sell accordingly.

Choice no. 2—Influence the prospect's perceptions. Actively work to have them consider other perspectives. Work with them to investigate and clarify their perceptions of their real needs.

As a salesperson, in order to pursue choice no. 2, this means that you must actively engage in the following *six key behavioural initiatives*:

- *Initiative no. 1—Understand your own behaviours, attitudes and values.* Recognise those of your prospects and adapt to meet your prospects on *their* terms.
- *Initiative no. 2—Place yourself in a continuous, lifelong learning mode* with your prospects and your profession. Accept that you don't know everything, and probably never will.
- *Initiative no. 3—Accept that the prospect is unique* and therefore strive to establish and build a relationship based on that uniqueness—a relationship that will allow you to deliver real value as it is perceived by the prospect.
- *Initiative no. 4—Build on your experience of success with others.* Leverage your experience, skills and ability to stay totally focused on your prospect to outdistance your competition.
- *Initiative no. 5—Actively work to unblock your natural inquisitiveness* and begin to take a sincere personal interest in your prospects, learning from them rather than attempting to teach them.
- *Initiative no. 6—Recognise that to improve, you must be willing to take some risks*, to step outside your comfort zone, and to risk thinking and acting differently.

The sixth initiative, in particular, bears further discussion. There is an old definition of insanity that goes something like this:

Definition of insanity

'Insanity is continuing to do the same thing, day after day, in exactly the same way, and expecting a different result.'

What does it mean? It means that salespeople are, by this definition alone, in the majority, *insane*. They readily admit they want to improve, to succeed, to make more money, to build an enviable professional reputation. But, and it's a big *but*, they generally prefer to stay in their comfort zone, where it's warm and safe and secure. They prefer to remain where the outcomes are known, where they can act out of habit, with less thought and a minimum of effort. Sometimes they emerge from their circle of safety, try something new, and scurry back with scarcely a look over their shoulder. They may say 'Oh, I tried something like that once!', or 'Yeah, I did try that a couple of times but it didn't seem to work and besides . . . I was really uncomfortable'.

This response won't cut it in any professional endeavour, let alone the more complex person-to-person sales environment. We have all done it—we are all guilty of it at some time.

What would happen if babies adopted this 'comfort zone' mentality while learning to walk? They might think, 'Hey, I tried to walk a couple of times, I'm bruised, sore and I feel pretty sorry for myself. I think I'll give up trying to walk and go back to crawling. I'll try again later—maybe some time in my late teens.' But they don't, do they? They keep trying, keep stepping out of their comfort zone, keep falling over, bumping and bruising themselves *until* they can walk. They are a bit wobbly at first. They don't go far without clinging to something secure and upright, but sure enough, they keep trying, things get better and then, admittedly at different rates for different children, they improve. Soon they are walking like the best of us. We salespeople could take a leaf out of our children's books when it comes to taking a risk.

With these six initiatives in mind, why don't you select one? Then select a specific behaviour relating to that initiative that you wish to change. Write an affirmation statement about the change endorsed by your selected initiative that you are committed to pursue, and work to incorporate it into your everyday sales life.

Sound like a good idea? Most people we talk to tell us this is a good idea, but hesitate to act. When we delve deeper to find out why, we generally hear a raft of reasons that are usually nothing more than creative variations on one of three common rationales trotted out in an endeavour to justify their staying within their comfort zone. Let's look briefly at these three common rationales for not pursuing change:

- *Rationale no. 1—Resistance to change.* This generally surfaces as a repudiation of any real need to change any particular one of their tendencies that they believe has served them so well in the past. A change means practice; it means moving into unknown territory and having to work harder at person-to-person communications. Don't get me wrong. These salespeople genuinely believe they want to improve, but at the same time they clearly aren't prepared to let go of their current habits or practices. Their approach is a bit like wanting to learn to swim but never being prepared to let go of the edge of the pool.

- *Rationale no. 2—Defensiveness.* In this scenario the salesperson wants to adopt new approaches, but becomes so defensive and protective of the old ways that they continually rationalise and excuse them. In some ways it often seems that the new approaches they desperately want to follow are taken as a direct rebuttal of their current efforts—which then is taken by them as direct personal criticism.
- *Rationale no. 3—The old ways.* In some salespeople, the old ways, the ingrained traditional sales models with their learned spiels, manipulative questions, and tried-and-tested closing techniques, are just too well established to allow new ideas to seed, take root and grow. It's as if they don't seem to be able to clear their mental garden of the previous crop prior to planting new seeds. Sure, the ground looks clean and clear and ready for a new crop, but pretty soon the old plants, quietly germinating below ground, rise up, overtake and strangle the newly planted seedlings. Pretty soon they are back to where they started.

chapter 4

A word about needs and wants

What exactly, in the context of your prospect, is a need?

Simply put, in the context of selling, a 'need' is the tension that is created by the gap between where your prospect is now— that is, their current situation or 'current reality'—and their vision of where they want to be in the future, which we might call their 'results needed'. Many salespeople seem to operate in the belief that a successful sale is dependent on their ability to demonstrate just how superior their product (or solution) is to that of their competitors! That is, to use the old sales training vernacular, they create USPs, or *unique selling propositions*. This no longer applies in today's competitive sales era of 'me too' responses from competitors—competitors who all seem to claim that they also have this USP or their own unique USP. When it comes to the more complex sales environment, nothing could be further from reality from the prospect's point of view. Unique selling propositions don't cut it. The prospect will focus almost exclusively on their own needs. The only unique part of the equation is the prospect and their situation.

Are you surprised? From the prospect's viewpoint, then, this 'need' is the gap which the prospect perceives exists between what I refer to above as their current reality and the vision of their results needed. The need is the tension they feel as they become aware of and consider this gap. Graphically, the prospect's needs look something like Figure 4.1.

In this context, the true objective of any sales function should be to assist the prospect in clarifying and defining their current reality, and their vision of their future ideal situation (their results needed). If you accept this proposition, your objective is to position yourself, your organisation and your product such that they address the clearly defined current reality and offer specific targeted benefits that are appropriate to their vision of the results needed. That is, you position your product as a vehicle for assisting them in making the move from 'here' to 'there'—from where the prospect is 'today' to where they want to be 'tomorrow'. In fact, those two words, *today* and *tomorrow*, serve as excellent shorthand descriptions. Whenever you think of the prospect and their current situation,

Figure 4.1 *Needs equation*

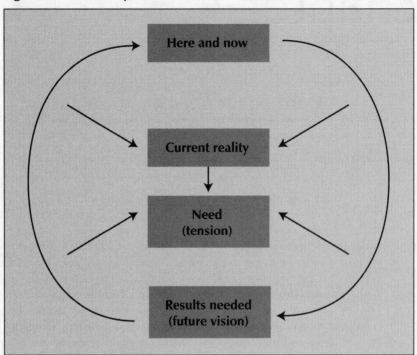

consider this metaphorically as their 'today' state. Likewise, when you are considering the prospect's required or ideal situation, their results needed, their vision of where they want to be in the future, use the shorthand term 'tomorrow' state. I have found this to be a simple yet appropriate way of viewing a prospect's needs. As such, we can restate the true objective of the sale as 'to position your product in such a way that it's not seen merely as a product but as a *vehicle for assisting the prospect in moving from today to tomorrow*'. This might look something like Figure 4.2.

And that raises another interesting issue. From the prospect's point of view, what exactly is the real objective of the move from their today state to a new position that incorporates tomorrow? There must be a clear objective from their point of view or there will be no incentive for the prospect to move at all. Remember, the prospect may not acknowledge or appreciate that their today state is unsatisfactory. So, why then do they need to do anything about it? In other words, what drives the prospect to move decisively to do something to change the status quo?

The answer is remarkably simple. The impetus for considering any change to their *today state* is seen by the prospect, in its most basic terms,

Figure 4.2   *Position your product as a vehicle.*

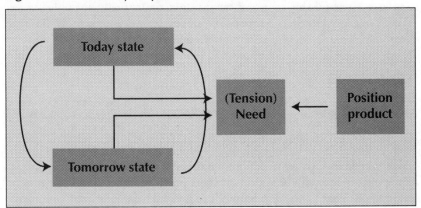

as a move away from unnecessary, real pain towards accessible, imagined pleasure. Whether pain or pleasure, or both, motivates the decision to act is academic. My experience is that, in most cases, it's a mixture of both pleasure and pain that overcomes the inertia that invariably accompanies the status quo and promotes the prospect's drive for a definite move to a vision of a new and better tomorrow from a distinctly unpleasant today.

Now, if life were as simple as the picture painted above, we would simply ask our prospects to describe in 20 words or less what their perception of their real today is, and then ask them to do the same with their vision of their ideal imagined tomorrow. But things, as I'm sure you have already experienced, are rarely that simple. Especially as the sales process escalates in complexity.

There are certainly situations where the prospect is both acutely aware of, and very clear about, the implications of the gap between their today and their tomorrow states. As a consequence, they may also be clear about exactly what is required to bridge that gap, thereby allowing them to move away from real pain and towards imagined pleasure by having you, the salesperson, assist in meeting their needs. This is the case in some specific selling situations. For example, suppose you need something from the hardware store to carry out a relatively minor repair on the coming weekend. You visit the local store, buy a packet of no. 7 brass countersunk wood screws, a bottle of glue and a hammer, and leave satisfied that your needs have been completely met.

But in the world of complex sales, this is likely not to be the case. Here the prospect often intuitively senses or knows that their real *today state* requires improving, but they are unclear about exactly what they can realistically expect to achieve or how best to go about achieving it. Their vision of the imagined *tomorrow state*? They know, or at least suspect, that the current situation is less than ideal but are unsure how to proceed beyond this point, or what might realistically be achieved.

As I suggested earlier, a prospect's needs equation may look like the following.

Needs equation

Prospect's 'tomorrow' state – Prospect's today' state = Prospect's needs

---

But remember, those needs may not be perceived by the prospect as requiring any immediate action on their part, if indeed they require any action at all. That is, the gap between today and tomorrow that generates the prospect's needs may be such that the prospect feels they can tolerate it. They feel that it doesn't justify the expenditure of time, effort and resources on their part.

This is clearly the environment that requires the approach of the value-based salesperson. This is where their skills come to the fore in working with the prospect's perceptions of their real and imagined situations, by evaluating options and implications, clarifying, influencing and shaping the prospect's thinking. This then enables the salesperson to position selling ideas that best meet the prospect's real needs.

For example, the prospect may call you in to discuss the supply of a 'faster printer', being under the impression that it is a hardware-based problem. But what do they use the printer for? What other functions are required? Is memory an issue? Is running cost important? In other words, the prospect is unclear about their current reality—that is, their today state. Until that variable is investigated, and likewise for the vision of imagined required results, you can't use the needs equation as a valid model to determine their real needs.

As previously stated, a need is the gap *perceived* by the prospect between where they are now and where they want to see themselves, or their vision for themselves, in the future; between their current reality and their results needed states; or, to use the terminology coined here, between their today and tomorrow states.

The key word here is 'perceived'. We all operate under our own perceptions, sometimes collectively labelled values, interests or attitudes. Under no circumstances should a salesperson override the prospect's perceptions and attempt to substitute their own perceptions, dressed up as 'the facts' or 'reality'. It's worth keeping in mind that, assuming that there is indeed such a thing as reality, we would all see different parts of it and attach different meanings to those parts. As you grow and develop as a salesperson, you must dispense with the notion that there exists a collection of black-and-white views of things clearly labelled as 'reality'.

The fact is, 'reality' doesn't exist—only perceptions exist, which are often wrapped in the cloak of objective language and presented as 'reality'. The 'reality' that really counts is what is already in the heart and mind of the prospect.

To use again that well-worn phrase of a past era, 'The customer is always right.' Now, it may appear somewhat trite, even cynical, to accept that when it comes to communication the receiver is right and the sender is wrong. But do you really have any choice if you want to establish your message in the mind of your prospect?

It's only by looking from the outside in, by turning the normally accepted process around, that you can simplify and clarify the process for the receiver. Only by focusing on the prospect and not the product can you gain an appreciation of the principles, thinking and concepts held by your prospect that can have a major impact on your ability to communicate with them effectively.

No matter how you, the salesperson, feel about the prospect's perceptions, the fact remains they have every right to feel the way they do. Salespeople who continually carry on about the prospect being 'irrational' or 'illogical' or 'unreasonable' fail to recognise that it's up to them to accept the perceptions expressed by their prospects—good, bad or indifferent—and to deal with them effectively.

If these are 'needs', what then are 'wants'? Wants are the prospect's needs, as viewed by them through a screen of values, interests and attitudes. It's your prospect's wants that you will undoubtedly first uncover when dealing with their perceptions. They may seem to *want* 'greater capacity', when in fact they may not *need* greater capacity but a faster output.

The simple message here is to anticipate that your prospects will deal in wants, at least initially, and to accept that it's your role as a value-based sales consultant to convert these expressed wants into specific real needs. Why *real*? Because, in almost every circumstance, wants carry with them emotional connotations that may mean little or nothing to someone other than the prospect, and usually this emotional baggage that accompanies wants works to obscure the prospect's *real* needs.

When your prospect says they *want* a reliable printer, what do they really mean? What emotion is driving this particular issue of reliability? Why? What is their *real* need?

I propose that you consider viewing needs and wants in the following fashion. 'Wants' are negative. By that I mean wants are driven by the emotion of a perceived lack of something. The prospect wants a 'reliable printer' because they perceive they currently don't have one but should. Dealing with a want tends to include the past and the present. The past because they look back to when they did have a reliable printer. The present because their need (so they tell you) is for a reliable printer *now*. Needs, on the other hand, are positive. By that I mean that the prospect views needs as something that will be a benefit and will move them forward. By meeting needs, the prospect can improve their current situation: they can move from the present into the future.

The value-based salesperson knows that they must not accept wants but must work to clearly identify the prospect's *real* need and tie this need back to the emotions that generated the original want in the mind of the prospect. The value-based salesperson understands that they must deal in the very *real* personal and business needs, as well as the more subjective personal and business wants, of each prospect.

chapter 5

Your approach determines
the available outcomes

L et me tell you a flying story. Many years ago, when a friend was learning to fly, he had real problems with landings. Quite simply, his landings were atrocious and, on one memorable occasion, so bad that the local airport control tower sent a fire engine and a crash team out to inspect his handiwork. In fact, he came perilously close to making the national news on that particular evening.

What he told me he learned from this experience is that if you want to improve in something, you need to practise—in fact, practise, practise, practise. No surprises there, I hear you say. However, what he also learned was that often practise isn't enough. He suggested that sometimes you need to adopt a totally different approach if you really want to improve, to be outstanding in something that you are currently only fair to average at and in which, despite your best efforts, little real improvement is forthcoming. What works for him, and certainly for many others, in these difficult situations is to try to stand well back from the problem, and attempt to take a very different view of it—a fresh perspective, as it were. What my friend was referring to, which might result from someone seeing something in a totally new way, is called a 'paradigm shift'.

What saved the day for my friend were two simple paragraphs in a long-forgotten flying text he found in his library. What the book apparently suggested was that a landing would only ever be as good as the pilot's approach to the runway enabled it to be. In other words, the quality of his approach to the runway, while he was still very much in the air, determined to a great degree the quality of his landing. The book went on to give advice on controlling the aircraft's approach in simple, no-nonsense terms that seemed so obvious my friend said he didn't understand why he hadn't considered it before. My friend's experience is what is often referred to in training terminology as a 'blinding flash of the obvious', hereafter referred to as a 'BFO'.

What happened to him, as he stood back and looked at the problem afresh, was that he gained a totally new perspective on landing and on how to control his approach to the runway. It just happened in a flash. He tells me he has never viewed landings the same again since that BFO. It's true to suggest that he underwent a paradigm shift. Things seemed to take on entirely different meanings, and he saw connections and linkages to other factors, which until then just hadn't occurred to him or he simply couldn't see. It was as if, in that instant, there was a partial reordering of the cosmos. Things became patently clear, and finally the whole process seemed to make sense.

Selling is much the same. Your approach to the process will, to a large degree, determine your available outcomes from the sales process. To use the flying analogy, your approach to the runway will have a major bearing on whether you execute a good landing, with all passengers on board enjoying the ride, *or* whether you kiss down hard, bounce, stand hard on the brakes as you start to slew off the strip and throw your passengers around inside the cabin. Some outcomes are even worse. To continue with the flying analogy, sometimes at the last minute you decide you're not going to make it. You push home the throttle, retract the flaps and climb to circuit height again so that you can go around to try and land once again. Unless you are performing these manoeuvres as part of practice, they are guaranteed to cause some stress to both you and your passengers. The blood pressure rises, the adrenalin flows, and when you eventually do manage to get the plane down on the ground, your passengers are out of there at the first opportunity, sometimes before the aircraft has even rolled to a complete stop. So it is with your selling approach. Sometimes your prospects can't wait for your sales approach to come to a complete stop. They bail out at the first available opportunity. The sales approach you select will, to a large extent, determine the available outcomes of your sale further down the track.

Let's look again at the more common approaches to selling we discussed earlier—the persuasive presenter's, product pusher's and problem solver's approaches to selling. We'll call them collectively the *traditional selling approach*.

Set out below is a simple flowchart of the methodology adopted, either consciously or unconsciously, by the practitioners of this traditional approach to selling.

The A, B, C and D of the traditional sales approach

A—Attract attention.
B—Build buy-in.
C—Create craving.
D—Demand a decision.

Let's quickly review each of these four steps.

First, *attract the prospect's attention*. This traditional approach requires the salesperson to do something to first get and then hold the prospect's attention. There are all sorts of ways of doing this. It could be a simple, non-verbal device in a retail environment, such as a flashing light, a cleverly designed advertisement in the local paper, or perhaps a provocative statement such as '95% of Australians aged 65 and over will be unable to survive without government assistance!'. Your aim, if you practise this approach, is to have your prospect's attention focused on your coming presentation.

The second step is to *build buy-in*. This is generally achieved by doing or saying something to build on and go beyond the first step of attracting the prospect's attention and to actually arouse interest in and excitement about the product on offer. This could be achieved by telling the prospect that 'For a minimal weekly investment, all this could be yours . . . it's really that simple. Are you interested?' During this stage the salesperson typically continues to bait the prospect with promises of a better, more secure, easier, less costly life, and usually does so by asking the style of question that can only be answered one way—with an obvious 'Yes'.

The third step sees the salesperson building their presentation to fever pitch as they attempt to *create craving* for the product in the prospect's mind. This is often accomplished by the salesperson continuing to reinforce emotional mental images of the prospect enjoying the fruits of their hard-earned labour: 'Can't you see yourself being able to take the time to sit in the sun in your favourite chair, reading all those books you always wanted to read, while your investment plan continues to funnel dollars into your private account at your local bank? With this system you can afford to do all those things you've dreamed about doing for years . . . After all, you deserve it, don't you?' Perhaps this mental picture is supplemented by posters showing scenes of people doing just that. The desired outcome of this stage of the traditional sales model is that the prospect is so emotionally attached to the wonderful vision of 'tomorrow' you are offering that it would appear silly, perhaps even irresponsible, if they didn't respond by saying 'Yes' to your sales presentation.

Which brings us to the final step, the close step—otherwise known as 'the big C'—whereby you *demand a decision* from the prospect. That part of the sale that has struck a strange mix of confusion, anticipation and fear into the collective hearts and minds of many salespeople—that part of the sale where it is often suggested that by utilising a snappy, much-rehearsed, clever closing technique you can have the prospect eating out of your hands and agreeing to your presentation. Here the stated objective for most salespeople is 'to strike while the iron is hot', while the full flush of emotion is still present and before the good vibrations have ebbed. There are many books dealing solely with the subject of closing, most of which state or infer that closing is something you *do to* a prospect.

Now, for the record, the traditional selling approach is a perfectly valid model for selling. In fact, if popularity were the deciding factor, the casual observer and many a prospect could well be excused for believing it was a mandatory, or perhaps even basic, selling approach taught to all new salespeople in 'new salesperson school'. However, in my view, it's valid only in those selling transactions that are relatively small or simple. It's not the approach of choice for successful professional salespeople engaged in larger or more complex sales. Prospects don't favour this traditional sales approach in the more complex sales environment either.

The other interesting observation I venture is that those salespeople in quadrants 1, 2 and 3—the persuasive presenters, product pushers and problem solvers—seem to gravitate naturally to the traditional selling approach. It's my opinion that *until* these salespeople undergo a total and fundamental shift in their perception of the selling process—involving recognising the shift in focus required and the methodology inherent in the value-based sales approach—they will remain mired in the traditional sales approach, blissfully ignorant of their real potential. To move to the next level, the consultancy level, involves a different understanding of the salesperson's and the prospect's roles in the sales process. This, as I have suggested in the flying story, generally requires a paradigm shift, a BFO— a completely new way of viewing selling.

In the traditional sales approach, the seller:

- *does most of the talking;*
- *adopts a 'telling role';*
- *often employs 'fear' to motivate the prospect to act;*
- *assumes the prospect wants exactly what the seller is selling; and*
- *sees the sales transaction as adversarial, thereby requiring a victor and a vanquished.*

For all the above reasons, and many more I haven't touched on, traditional selling will fail in those selling areas where decisions aren't made quickly, where options abound, where there are substantial costs at stake, where the decision-making process isn't straightforward, or where the prospect doesn't clearly recognise or accept their tomorrow or their today states, or have trouble assessing what is required to bridge the gap (that is, meet their needs) between the two. This is distilled as two distinct propositions below.

Selling proposition no. 1

If the prospect is aware and clear about their needs—that is, they are clear about the gap between their tomorrow and their today states and about what is required to bridge the gap,

THEN

the situation requires minimal selling skills and the relationship may not be as critical as customer service.

BUT

Selling proposition no. 2

If the prospect knows or senses that their today state is unacceptable, but is unclear about their tomorrow state and/or how best to bridge the gap between the two,

THEN

the situation requires a skilled salesperson, who can build value and establish relationship as a foundational element.

A little earlier I outlined the modus operandi of the traditional sales approach by suggesting a simple four-step model used by salespeople to outline *their* four-step approach or sequential objectives. Now, understand that these are *their* objectives, and as such are unlikely ever to be discussed with the prospect or indeed to be of any interest to the prospect.

What happens instead is that traditional sales approach-based salespeople translate these self-serving steps or objectives into a simple sales model that incorporates the major activities or elements they believe they need to engage in *with* the prospect. Notice that for the first time the prospect enters the equation—but only as a means of disguising the salesperson's true intent by cloaking their sales objectives in more friendly terms.

Why don't you attempt now to draw what you think might represent a view of the traditional sales model and then see how it compares to the model we observe as being practised by those persuasive presenters, product pushers and problem solvers? It's an interesting exercise, so take a couple of minutes and sketch something in the space on the next page and look at our view of the sales model (Figure 5.1) adopted by those traditional selling approach-based salespeople.

Your traditional sales model

Draw your model here

Figure 5.1 is a simple model that represents my observations of the traditional selling approach. The model indicates how the salesperson generally views this approach by outlining the four main sales activities and the approximate proportion of time the salesperson spends on each activity. As you can see, the model takes the shape of a triangle; clearly the major thrust is on closing, and the prospect is viewed at the bottom of the triangle with the salesperson at the top or apex.

So, how did you go? Any similarities between your suggested model and mine?

Why am I suggesting that the traditional selling approach may have severe shortcomings in the arena of more complex sales? Take a moment to review the seven reasons suggested below outlining why traditional selling *can* be ineffective as the sales process becomes more complex.

Notice anything? The list schedules the sort of shortcomings you can expect to see with electronic selling. These are all issues that the electronic media, be it the Internet, television shopping or whatever, will have a great deal of difficulty in overcoming. I predict that the 'electronic bazaar', as some have dubbed it, will take on the form of the traditional selling approach, albeit with a level of sophistication, interactivity and razzamatazz that hasn't been seen or experienced to date. What I predict for the electronic-based sales process is a slick, well-designed, perhaps even manipulative sales approach that will make *Star Wars* look prehistoric. And that's both good news and bad news.

Figure 5.1   *Selling: the 'traditional' model*

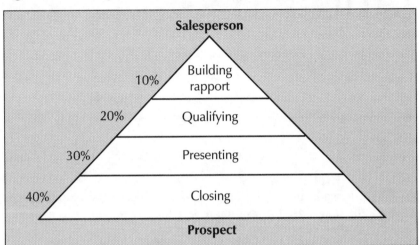

The traditional approach can be ineffective because traditional selling:

1. *ignores the prospect's agenda;*
2. *provides fixed 'solutions' without first determining the prospect's real and unique needs;*
3. *is usually internally driven (i.e. salesperson-focused) as opposed to externally driven (i.e. prospect-focused);*
4. *assumes the prospect wants and needs exactly the product on offer by the salesperson;*
5. *assumes the prospect's real needs, based on users or buyers who have gone before;*
6. *does little or nothing to help the prospect clearly identify and define their today state and understand the consequences of maintaining it; and*
7. *doesn't concern itself with exploring the prospect's future vision of their tomorrow state.*

The good news, as I have suggested, is that there will be even more demand for salespeople who have moved beyond the traditional way of selling to a value-based selling approach. The bad news is that, for those salespeople who persist in the old ways, the computer is going to do the same job cheaper, better, faster and 24 hours a day, every day.

So, is there a better way? The answer is 'Yes!'. I have chosen to call it 'value-based selling'.

chapter 6

Value-based selling

T o move from any of the various traditional sales approaches to the value-based 'consultancy' level, where you are truly a benefit-focused relationship builder, you need to recognise and accept each of the following key imperatives. Not one or two or even three of them, but *all* of them. You need to adopt a new way of viewing the whole selling process, not just convenient parts of it. The value-based approach is a complete and very different philosophy of selling from that of any of the three approaches that I have termed collectively the 'traditional sales approach'. It's an approach that is very much dependent on how you view the sales process, rather than on what you do in the sales process.

So here goes. How many of the following seven imperatives do you accept and respond to now and can therefore put a tick in the 'Yes' box for?

Value-based selling involves you, the salesperson, in recognising and accepting each of the following imperatives:

	Yes	No
1. *Selling must be viewed first and foremost as an exchange.*	❏	❏
2. *Identifying and understanding the prospect's real needs should always precede any attempt to address those needs.*	❏	❏
3. *Obtaining a commitment to advance the sales process is a win for everybody, prospect and seller alike.*	❏	❏
4. *A salesperson should stop concentrating on 'telling', 'persuading' or 'solving' and instead start focusing on 'understanding' and 'positioning'.*	❏	❏
5. *A shift away from the 'product' towards the 'process' is a basic selling fundamental for more complex sales.*	❏	❏
6. *A focus on the 'prospect' rather than the 'salesperson' must be maintained throughout the sales process.*	❏	❏
7. *A commitment from the prospect is a win for both the prospect and the salesperson.*	❏	❏

There are no trade-offs, no 'near enough is good enough'. All of these seven are imperatives. They are the basics that must be honoured at all times, with all prospects under all conditions in the more complex sales environment. Anything less is a drift back towards the traditional selling approach, which just won't cut it as the sales process becomes more sophisticated.

We looked at a suggested traditional sales model in Chapter 5, so now might be the right time to ask: What would a value-based selling model look like? Could we in fact expect any major differences from that proposed for traditional selling?

Why don't you take a moment to sketch in the space below what you think might represent a viable value-based sales model.

Now have a look at the outline of our model in Figure 6.1 on the next page and compare it to the one you drew. What strikes you immediately about this proposed model of selling (Figure 6.1) versus the traditional model proposed in Figure 5.1?

The first obvious difference between this simple value-based model and the previous traditional selling model is that the triangle has been inverted, with the prospect now up the top at the broad base, being supported by the salesperson at the inverted apex. The model, like its predecessor, divides the proposed selling approach into four primary and quite distinct areas of focus or activity, but here the apparent similarity ends.

Your value-based selling model

Draw your model here

Figure 6.1 *Value-based selling model*

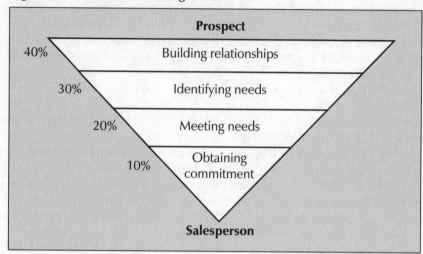

The major activity in Figure 6.1 is 'building relationships'. This is the foundation element and is returned to again and again through the value-based selling process. I see the prospect–salesperson relationship as analogous to the reefs that protect the small islands on Australia's Great Barrier Reef: the reefs serve as a form of submerged breakwater that protects the islands and adjacent mainland from the heavy seas that are blown up by storms from time to time and which threaten to damage them. However, the reef itself needs constant maintenance and revitalisation or it will die, leading it to eventually erode and then be unable to protect the land–sea interface of the islands and mainland coastline.

The relationship we build with our prospect is very similar. Like the reef, this relationship itself needs to be protected and constantly maintained, reinforced and on occasion repaired. So, our relationship with our prospect requires ongoing attention and represents a large portion of our selling focus and efforts.

The second separate area of focus in this value-based sales approach, 'identifying needs', probably comes as no surprise and requires no further comment at this point. But what about the third area of focus, 'meeting needs'? What does this mean? Well, it involves a key sales element, 'positioning'. Positioning is what you do with your product in the heart and mind of your prospect, but more on that later.

'Obtaining commitment', the fourth area of focus, is suggested as a meagre 10%. This doesn't mean it's not an important facet of the sales process, rather that it's not the *most critical facet*. Obtaining commitment or, as it is often referred to, *closing*, shouldn't be the major area of focus, as it often becomes with the traditional sales model, where we find it preoccupying the minds and focus of salespeople often *even before they have met the prospect.*

I will have more to say about these areas of focus when we explore the sales process in more detail a little later. Suffice it to say that the core ingredient of the value-based selling approach is the relationship you build and maintain with your prospect. To effectively build and maintain this relationship you must learn to exhibit or engage in the following six behaviours.

Six behaviours required to build and maintain a strong relationship

1. *Suspend personal judgement.*
2. *Observe.*
3. *Analyse behavioural and attitudinal clues.*
4. *Adapt for greater connection.*
5. *Test your conclusions.*
6. *Fine-tune your relationship strategy.*

Why is a value-based approach to selling so effective?

Value-based selling is effective because it:

1. *promotes the salesperson's competence and builds confidence;*
2. *ensures that the prospect actively participates in exploring and ultimately identifying their own real needs;*
3. *assists in uncovering the prospect's perceptions and concerns before attempting to meet their real needs;*
4. *promotes working with the prospect in a partnership by creating and proposing ideas that meet their real needs;*
5. *allows the salesperson to uncover hard targets for positioning their product; and*
6. *establishes a consultative approach to the sale.*

None of the above six reasons for the effectiveness of value-based selling has anything, in my view, in common with the traditional sales approach. The two approaches are really worlds apart in philosophy and delivery. If you are still unconvinced and find yourself sitting on the fence, one final word may convince you to consider implementing a value-based selling approach. It's simply this: with acceptance of the value-based sales approach comes a realisation that *it's not what you have to sell that is important. It's what the prospect actually needs and wants to buy that is important!*

If this makes sense to you, if you are prepared to adopt this as the cornerstone of your sales approach, I believe you will understand the strength of the value-based selling approach and adopt its philosophy and framework, seeking to implement the competencies and skills required to bring this approach to life.

You ultimately have two options in how you approach a sale. For simplicity's sake, let's call them the black door and the white door. Choose the black door and you go down the *telling* road, where you will in all likelihood continually strive to apply pressure to the prospect to accept your propositions (i.e. your product). This invariably leads to a bargaining phase, where price becomes an issue and concessions are inevitably made by the salesperson to close the deal. This is the road of the product-focused and/or the salesperson-focused seller. This is the story line of the four-act play outlined in the model of the traditional selling approach—the four acts you will recall being building rapport, qualifying, presenting and closing.

Now go back to the beginning. You have a chance to start all over again, and this time you wisely choose the white door. Here you focus on building a relationship with the prospect and exploring the prospect's needs. The product hasn't even been directly involved so far. As you work with the prospect to identify their needs and wants, you help crystallise for them their today and their tomorrow states. As you help the prospect to consider the gap or their real need, the prospect, not the salesperson, begins to apply the pressure. The prospect, not the salesperson, often begins to contribute to the *compelling sales story* by introducing your product because you are demonstrating value, and in so doing price may become a secondary issue, if not altogether irrelevant. In fact, in many cases the price will move up, as the prospect now clearly understands and appreciates the value you bring to the table and, accordingly, realigns their perceptions about budgets, applications and competitive advantages embodied in the product.

Congratulations. By selecting the white door you are now an honorary inductee of the value-based selling school. By the way, doesn't it look as if it could be much more fun, much more interesting, much less stressful? And you even learned something about someone else, about their business, about their operations, about their desires and aspirations. You will find this approach much more rewarding, much more successful and much more natural.

If you are reading this and think you are too old, too set in your ways, or if you think perhaps too much water has flowed under the bridge or you have gone too far down the road in your reliance on the traditional selling approach, you might take time to reflect on the old proverb that says, 'It's never too late to turn back if you are on the wrong road.'

chapter 7

What drives a prospect's buying behaviour?

Q uite simply, I endorse the view that all behaviour originates from needs. This includes you, and it certainly includes your prospects.

Understand that your prospects' buying behaviour is driven by nothing more sinister or magical than their own wants and needs. Further, all behaviour is directed towards the satisfaction of needs. Again, this includes your prospects. Therefore, their buying behaviour is focused on satisfying their perceived wants and needs. *Prospects buy to satisfy a want or need.* So let's talk a little more about wants and needs!

I suggested earlier that a need was really nothing more than the gap between where someone is now—that is, their current reality, or 'today' state—and where they want to be in the future, their vision of a more ideal future situation, or what I call their 'tomorrow' state. I therefore proposed a prospect's needs as being created by the gap between their today and tomorrow states. I also suggested that there were two possible sides to this need: the first, a move *away from the pain* associated with the problem situation of the today state; the second, a move *towards the pleasure* associated with the vision of a much more desired outcome, the tomorrow state.

Now, a need is one thing, but what provides the momentum to overcome the initial inertia that maintains the status quo and resists change? What provides the motivation to resist staying with what is known and safe and comfortable? What prompts us into moving towards doing something to satisfy our needs? In other words, what gets us off our butts and moving or acting to change the unsatisfactory today state by agreeing to pursue a course of action designed to produce the potential pleasures inherent in our vision of a future tomorrow?

Simple . . . I suggested the answer earlier when I said that what causes us to move into action is one or both of two things, as in the box on the next page. This scenario applies to *all of us*, whether buyers or sellers, parents or children, boys or girls.

If, as I suggested earlier, behaviour originates from our needs, and our behaviour is directed towards satisfying or meeting those needs, then it

> ***Motivators to act now:***
>
> 1. *pain associated with dissatisfaction with the current reality of today;*
>
> *and/or*
>
> 2. *pleasure associated with the vision of a more attractive and satisfactory tomorrow.*

could be said that everyone is motivated. What is generally not recognised, however, is the commonly held view that unless we see other people motivated to do what *we think* is important, we consider them to be unmotivated. This often applies to our perspective or version of reality as it relates to our prospect's buying behaviour.

To shed a little more light on this elusive animal 'motivation', let's imagine an everyday scene. You are sitting at home one evening listening to a favourite CD and reading a glossy magazine. You have the whole place to yourself for a few hours. As you turn the pages of the magazine you come across a full-colour, rather luxurious advertisement for a brand of chocolate. Until this moment you were very much at peace with yourself and your environment. Now you suddenly crave something to eat, preferably something sweet and preferably chocolate. You put the magazine down and wander into the kitchen and scan the refrigerator, shelves and cupboards, which are full of leftovers, biscuits, fruit and vegetables. Finally you spot some dark cooking chocolate. Not exactly what you had in mind, but at least it's chocolate. You take a few pieces back to your comfortable chair and go on reading the magazine while munching on the chocolate.

To analyse—the *need* for something sweet lay dormant, just below the conscious mind until the advertisement surfaced the physical need. All of a sudden you were *aware* that you needed something sweet to eat. This caused you to undergo a minor but noticeable degree of stress or *tension* when your previous subconscious *dissatisfaction* with your today state was mentally compared to your *vision* of how much pleasure you would feel in your tomorrow state. This tension built, perhaps for only a matter of seconds, until you acted upon it. A flowchart showing the psychology of this behaviour in simplified form is set out in Figure 7.1. Review it and see what you think.

Note the loop back to the *need* after the resulting *behaviour*. This is what could be described as a 'reality check'. Having consumed the chocolate, you perform an internal and often subconscious self-check to determine whether the need still exists. If the answer is 'no', then there is no further tension and no driving force for further behaviour or action concerning this particular need or motivator. The tension equals the person's motivation.

Figure 7.1 *Behavioural model no. 1*

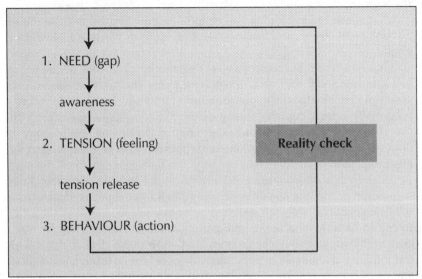

I'm sure it will come as no surprise to you that we can also use this simple model to demonstrate buying behaviour.

I suggested that the prospect's needs are really nothing more than the gap between their today state and their tomorrow state. Yet, as in the example above, is your prospect clear about their real needs? Are they even aware of their needs? Is there a sufficient gap perceived by the prospect between where they are now and where they want to be? If not, they are unlikely to be motivated to buy what it is you are offering to close the gap that exists. This is where your skills as a salesperson are required, and it is these skills that will make you a valuable commodity when it comes to the complex sale.

As a value-based salesperson it's your professional responsibility to help the prospect clearly define the current reality associated with their today state and identify the desired vision of a future tomorrow state. In doing so, you clearly assist the prospect by developing an awareness of their specific needs and providing benefit propositions that address how they can lower their tension levels and achieve a more acceptable tomorrow state by simply instigating actions and ultimately buying your product. However, life is rarely that simple and prospects rarely follow this simple model on any major purchase.

So, what element isn't present in the above model that is present in most of the more complex selling situations? Let's go back to our previous hypothetical situation. Remember that you were sitting quietly at home reading through a magazine when you came across an advertisement that sent you off in search of chocolate? Now this time there is a twist. The tension, or feeling created by your need, builds as you continue to search the cupboards and shelves for something to release that tension.

What about the kilojoules, you think? Can you afford them? You finally go back to the fridge and instead select an apple or perhaps take nothing at all.

What is different in this scenario is that thinking has entered the simple behavioural model. In essence, you have taken time out and considered your options, assessed the consequences, and as a result deferred to a potentially more acceptable future vision. The tension was tolerated while the thinking process was pursued, then the tension was focused or directed towards the perception that choosing fruit over chocolate was more acceptable.

Thinking has entered the behavioural model and the outcome is now very different. Selling has a similar parallel. Rather than, as illustrated in the first scenario, suggesting that all of our behaviour is a direct reaction to tension and results in our making an instinctive and relatively quick positive buying decision, the prospect factors in thinking as they withhold immediate action and perhaps carefully consider options, probabilities and outcomes before focusing the tension on making what they see as a more reasoned buying decision. The simple behavioural model now looks like Figure 7.2.

Figure 7.2   *Behavioural model no. 2*

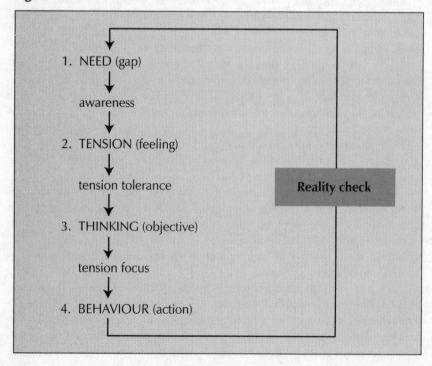

If we adapt these two behavioural models and modify the terminology, we can use them to explain the buying process that a prospect might follow, whether consciously or unconsciously, or both. Figures 7.3 to 7.5 describe the three different buying processes that a prospect might engage in.

Buying process no. 1 is the subjective, feeling-oriented buying process often observed in simple sales where the buyers quickly release the tension by behaving directly in response to their internal stimulus in order to achieve their tomorrow vision of the future.

Buying process no. 2 is the objective, thinking-oriented buying scenario, often more applicable to more complex sales, which, unlike the first process, involves factoring in thinking. This is the case with most major or complex buying decisions, where tension is tolerated for a longer period, then focused towards achieving a more beneficial decision for the prospect; something they view as the right or best decision.

Buying process no. 3, the outcome rationalisation-oriented buying process, involves all major elements as in process no. 2 but (did you notice?) in a different sequence. Here the thinking occurs *after* the decision is made. This is referred to as 'rationalisation', and we often see it in sales situations where a prospect may have made a buying decision on a subjective, emotional basis. Once made, they rationalise this

Figure 7.3 *Buying process no. 1—Subjective, feeling-oriented, simple sale*

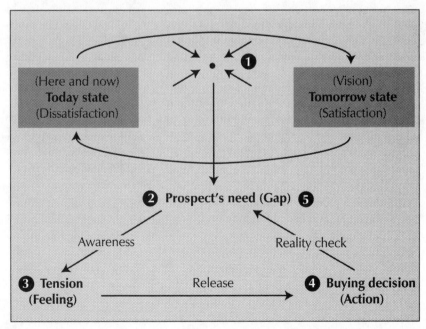

Figure 7.4 *Buying process no. 2—Objective, thinking-oriented, more complex sale*

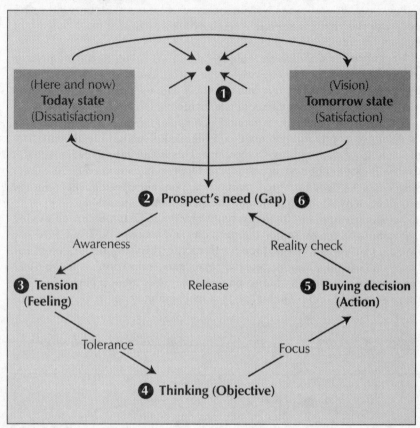

subjective decision by factoring in the thinking. This then provides the objective rationale to support the buying decision to both themselves and perhaps others. For example, most of us have a tendency to look closely at advertisements for a product we have recently purchased. We tend to do this to find means to reinforce those reasons we agreed to purchase it in the first instance. This model is one where the behaviour is primarily focused on justifying a quick or subjective buying decision.

Figure 7.5 *Buying process no. 3—Outcome rationalisation-oriented justification of decision*

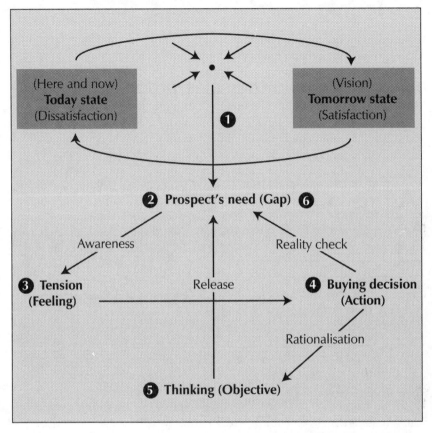

chapter 8

Your prospect and the sales process

A great many sales texts and a great deal of sales training programs appear to concentrate exclusively on the sales process *from the salesperson's side of the fence*. They seem rarely, if ever, to consider how the prospective buyer buys. And why should they? After all, isn't the salesperson viewed as selling something to the prospect? Doesn't this really translate to *doing something* to the prospect? Therefore, shouldn't we concentrate on what the salesperson is doing to the prospect? (The emphasis here, of course, being on the salesperson and their actions.)

If this then is the philosophical basis for the sales relationship, why would we need to consider how prospects view the process? Aren't their views of the sales process strictly in a nice-to-know, not a need-to-know, category? And if this is the case, isn't the prospect seen as virtually irrelevant in the sale, except to answer in the affirmative when required, agree when prompted and sign on the dotted line when asked?

But buyers aren't numbers. They aren't statistics. They aren't someone you sell something to. They are real people just like you, your friends, your colleagues, your family. Good or bad, right or wrong, doesn't enter into it. Buyers are simply people. And like all of us, they buy goods and services from their own perspective. They buy based on their *own* sense of reality, as referred to in Chapter 4.

So, with this in mind, would it help to consider what stages, if any, may be evident in the buying process of prospects? I happen to think so!

Can we find any areas of common ground with prospects when considering how they might view the buying process and how we as salespeople view the selling process? Again, I think so.

Having talked to a great many buyers, I believe that most prospects view the sale as an exchange and as requiring three distinctly different shifts in their own focus during the *buying process*. I'm not suggesting that these three shifts of focus always occupy exactly the same priority in the prospect's mind, or that they are necessarily of equal importance to all prospects, or indeed that they are always conscious considerations. Nor do I believe that each area of focus requires the same amount of input from each prospect in terms of time and effort. I most certainly don't propose that all prospects make decisions exactly the same way.

What I do know, however, and propose here, is that most prospects seem to move through at least three distinctly separate primary areas of focus on the way to making a decision. Hence my suggestion above of three different shifts of focus. We will call them *buying phases*. These buying phases are *recognition, evaluation* and *resolution*.

Why don't you see if my generic model for describing how prospects buy fits with your views of buying behaviour? Think back to your most recent buying experience, say the purchase of a major appliance for the home. Would it be true to suggest the following as a brief realistic outline of the three legitimate major buying phases involved in your buying process, as considered from your perspective as a buyer, not as a seller?

Recognition—Buying phase no. 1

Critical elements

Buyer objectives to be able to answer . . .

1.1 *Recognition of me (the buyer)!*
- A. *Do they make me feel important?*
- B. *Do they consider me and my specific situation?*

1.2 *Recognition of my needs!*
- A. *Why should I listen to the seller?*
- B. *Do they consider my needs as important?*

Evaluation—Buying phase no. 2

Critical elements

Buyer objectives to be able to answer . . .

2.1 *Evaluation of the seller and their propositions!*
- A. *Who is the seller really?*
- B. *How will the seller's proposal help me?*
- C. *What are the facts?*
- D. *What are the benefits to me?*

2.2 *Evaluation of the options!*
- A. *What are my options and alternatives?*
- B. *Does the seller have something I need?*

Resolution—Buying phase no. 3

Critical elements   **Buyer objectives**
                                         to be able to answer . . .

3.1 Resolutions of concerns?   A. *What are the problems, obstacles*
                                           and disadvantages?
                                   B. *What are the risks?*
                                   C. *What are the opportunities?*

3.2 Resolution of decisions?   A. *Do I need to decide now?*
                                   B. *What shall I do?*
                                   C. *Will I agree?*

As I acknowledged earlier, some of the buyer's questions embedded in these three buying phases won't necessarily be evident in the conscious mind of the buyer. Other questions, depending on the buying behaviour of your prospect, will be clearly demonstrated by observation of certain of their conscious behaviours and the specific objectives actively pursued by the prospect as the buying process unfolds.

Also, as I mentioned earlier, very few salespeople consider how a prospect addresses the buying process solely from their own perspective. Usually, any consideration of a buyer's behaviour, and in particular their buying style, tends to be in the light only of how the prospect's buying style might affect the salesperson's own selling objectives and behaviours. In other words, the buyer's behaviours are considered after, not before, a salesperson acts, and then generally only when the salesperson sees a problem.

For example, take the much-talked-about topic of 'overcoming objections'. Even the title suggests a very one-sided, salesperson-oriented view of selling. Since when did a prospect want their objections *overcome*? And, when suggesting techniques for addressing the prospect's objections, most texts appear to require the seller to deliver a learned script or scripts, presented in a step-by-step manner, as a way of dealing with the issues or objections raised by the prospect. A real desire to understand the *why* of the prospect's principles, thinking and feelings that often remain hidden behind stated or implied objections is rarely endorsed.

Seldom is anything addressed from the perspective of considering the prospect's buying process *from the prospect's side of the fence* in other words, seeking to understand the buyer's 'realities' as they relate to the sale. However, the information is certainly available, and in most cases all that needs to be done is to ask the prospect relatively straightforward questions, such as:

- What do you think about our suggestion?
- What do you see as other viable options?
- How will you go about evaluating the options?

However, this is rarely done. Salespeople are often too focused on pursuing their own agenda to take the time to consider others' views of reality, even if one of those 'others' happens to be their prospect.

Let me give an example (Table 8.1) of what some of the seller's key objectives *should be* versus what they *usually are*. As you might guess, this is essentially a comparison of the objectives of value-based salespeople and those objectives pursued in the approach adopted by traditional sales salespeople, using as a framework the three-phase buying model proposed earlier. See what you think.

Table 8.1 *Sales objectives*

Prospect's buying phase	'Traditional selling' approach salesperson	'Value-based' approach salesperson
Phase 1: Recognition	Convince the prospect that they are competent and are there to help them. Demonstrate that they know how to solve the prospect's problems and have something they will need.	Express their sales objectives in the prospect's terms, acknowledging the prospect and attempting to build a relationship and gain an insight with the prospect into their current situation, vision for the future and real needs.
Phase 2: Evaluation	Persuade the prospect that what they have to offer is a perfect fit with their problem or situation and is better than any of the available alternatives.	Position the product by building value and meeting the prospect's real needs. Consider the potential threats, as well as the opportunities, posed by the prospect's buying process and by the competition, and be prepared to proactively address these issues.
Phase 3: Resolution	Focus on deploying a range of learned techniques for engineering a 'Yes' from the prospect.	Carefully uncover and address barriers to the sale that may cause the prospect to withhold a favourable buying decision and work towards obtaining a commitment.

As you can see, the salesperson employing the traditional approach to selling reinforces the four-part rapport, qualifying, presenting and closing traditional model discussed earlier by considering their sales objectives only in *their* terms, relative to these sales activities. Nowhere do they seek to factor in the *prospect's* buying style.

The value-based salesperson focuses, on the other hand, on addressing the three buying phases. They do so by first building a relationship, identifying needs to address in the prospect's first phase, the recognition phase; then by meeting the prospect's needs by positioning the product in the heart and mind of the prospect, and dealing with alternative options and concerns and opportunities to address the prospect's second buying phase, the evaluation phase; and finally, by addressing the prospect's perceived barriers to the sale and obtaining commitment in the last, or resolution, phase of the prospect's three buying phases. The value-based salesperson pursues a sales strategy designed to obtain a win/win outcome for each of the participants in the sales process.

Also, it's worth noting that the traditional salesperson appears to centre the majority of their energy on getting quickly to, and dealing cleverly with, the resolution phase of the buying process, whereas our hero, the value-based salesperson, is prepared at the outset to expend a great deal of resources and energy up front addressing the prospect's first buying phase of recognition before even considering moving on to the following phases of evaluation and then resolution.

Think about it. As a buyer, which of the two sales approaches would you rather be employed when you are being sold to?

Finally, by way of providing some helpful diagnostic advice, a word about analysing problems that you as a seller may be experiencing with your prospects in what I will call the buying–selling interface—that is, the coming together of the prospect's buying phases and consequently their buying process objectives, as proposed in the three-phase buying model, and your sales objectives as the salesperson, as they relate to your approach to the sale. With the above three-phase buying model in mind, my experience is that most problems are generated by the salesperson's selling behaviour and not, perhaps surprisingly, by the prospect's buying behaviour. The seller-induced problems usually fall into the following two buyer–seller 'interface problem' categories.

Interface problem no. 1

The seller is oblivious to, or does not factor in, the prospect's buying phases.

As a result of this interface problem, what I generally observe is that:

- the prospect's preferred process of moving through each of the three separate buying phases has been ignored completely; or
- a buying phase has been ignored or rushed by the salesperson in their hurry to close the sale.

Interface problem no. 2

The seller is aware of the prospect's buying phases but doesn't respond adequately.

This interface problem also results in two major negative outcomes being created for the prospect by the salesperson. These two negative outcomes are that:

1. different paces are adopted by the salesperson and prospect, so there is a mismatch of objectives; or
2. the salesperson is mistakenly responding to a different phase from that of the buyer, again resulting in a mismatch of objectives.

So, how do you avoid these buyer–seller interface problems in the first place?

The answer is quite simple. You, the seller, need to acknowledge and respond to the prospect's unspoken, but nevertheless critical, three-phase buying approach; and, in so doing, match the preferred paces and preferences exhibited by the prospect in the way they address each of them. To implement this strategy effectively, you will need to be very aware of your prospect's behaviour, both verbal and non-verbal, and carefully consider the following eight initiatives if you are to work effectively with your prospect and avoid potential communication pitfalls.

To avoid interface problems with the prospect you, the salesperson, must:

1. consider an overall strategy for addressing the prospect's three buying phases. Plan your communication process and sales objectives around it, but stay flexible;
2. clearly identify what phase the prospect has reached in the buying process;
3. confirm that you, the seller, are there also;
4. if not, ask why not and determine how best to introduce a revised strategy;
5. check that a phase hasn't been skipped;
6. consider the pace adopted by the prospect in moving through the three-phase buying process and be prepared to accommodate it;
7. check that the prospect perceives that each phase has been adequately covered and be prepared to backtrack if feedback from the prospect indicates otherwise; and
8. confirm that your strategic sales objectives are realistic and be prepared to reassess them given how the particular prospect appears to prefer to deal internally and externally with each of the three buying phases.

chapter 9

The benefits of being able to fly on instruments

L et's talk about FABs—*features, advantages* and *benefits*. You may think you know all about these—that you learned about them years ago, and that you certainly don't need to cover them again. This is a refrain heard from many salespeople in all situations.

My experience is that the vast majority of salespeople, when asked to elaborate on what they know about features, advantages and benefits, indicate by the nature of their responses that they don't understand or appreciate the differences between the three—especially the subtle differences between advantages and benefits. So, let's look at the five most common misunderstandings when it comes to FABs.

Common FAB misunderstandings by salespeople

Misunderstanding no. 1—Cannot adequately describe what constitutes a 'feature'.

Misunderstanding no. 2—Do not understand the critical differences between an 'advantage' and a 'benefit'.

Misunderstanding no. 3—Don't understand how to connect a 'feature' and a 'benefit'.

Misunderstanding no. 4—Cannot effectively use benefits to position their own product, themselves or their organisation to the extent required to sell their ideas.

Misunderstanding no. 5—Cannot effectively use benefits to position their product, themselves or their organisation effectively against the competition.

Be absolutely honest with yourself. Can you do what most salespeople seem to be unable to do?

My advice is that you consider investing a good deal of your time in reviewing this section of the book. It is imperative that you understand the true nature of benefits; only then can you move on to appreciating how to link them to the features of the product and how to tie them to the prospect's specific needs by effectively positioning them in the heart and mind of the prospect.

So, what are the essential differences between features, advantages and benefits? Let's start with features.

The features of your product

The features of your product are essentially descriptive or technical items or facts directly connected with the product. A shorthand way of describing *features* might be as in the box below.

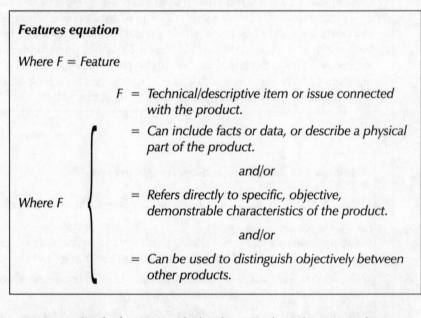

Features equation

Where F = Feature

F = Technical/descriptive item or issue connected with the product.

= Can include facts or data, or describe a physical part of the product.

and/or

Where F = Refers directly to specific, objective, demonstrable characteristics of the product.

and/or

= Can be used to distinguish objectively between other products.

An example of a feature might be the size, the colour, or perhaps even the speed of operation of the product, such as the number of pages a printer can print per minute. Features tend to be those things that could be classified as an objective fact that can be accepted as true and correct without argument. We constantly see in product brochures lists of the product's features. In fact, many product brochures contain a section called 'Features' which lists features one under the other as numbered or bullet points.

Now, features are important, *but* they need to be translated for the prospect into need-oriented 'prospect speak'. So, what does this mean that they are actually translated into?

Salespeople using the traditional approach to selling translate them into advantages. What is an advantage?

The advantages of your product

A shorthand definition of an advantage might be an explanation of what a product's features might positively mean to someone using or buying the product. As with the features equation, we can propose an *advantages* equation.

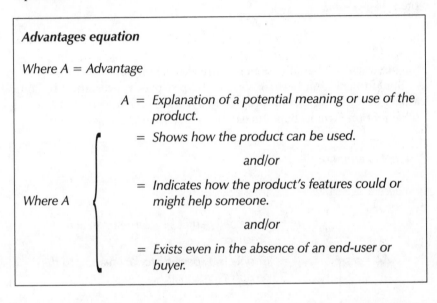

Advantages equation

Where A = Advantage

A = *Explanation of a potential meaning or use of the product.*

= *Shows how the product can be used.*

and/or

Where A = *Indicates how the product's features could or might help someone.*

and/or

= *Exists even in the absence of an end-user or buyer.*

Let's translate the three possible examples of features mentioned a little earlier into advantages.

First, size. What advantage does a feature related to size mean to the prospect? The feature might be that the product is 51 mm long. In terms of advantages, it might mean that the prospect can carry it in their pocket. Then, colour. What advantage might a feature related to colour mean to the prospect? The product is available in a range of colours. Again, as an advantage, it may mean they can choose a favourite colour, or a colour that coordinates or even contrasts with something else. Then, speed. What advantages might a feature related to speed—for example, expressed as a specific number of pages printed per minute—mean to the prospect? A possible advantage is that they can copy a set number of pages in a relatively short time. Who knows what the feature really translates to in the context of the prospect's actual situation and, ultimately, their needs?

The real problem we constantly encounter with FABs is that most salespeople seem to start with features and stop with the advantages of the product. In fact, they tend to view the product mainly through the advantages it has the *potential* to offer.

This is a shame, because such a salesperson is selling with little or no demonstrable connection with their prospect. They are not communicating in 'prospect speak'. Contrary to their often expressed belief, they are not dealing in *benefits*.

As a result, they are probably wasting the prospect's time, and for that matter their own time. In the worst-case scenario, this can be interpreted by the prospect as rudeness, arrogance and incompetence on the part of the salesperson.

Your benefit propositions

So, just what are benefits, and why are they so important?

Benefits are simply the *value* to the prospect represented by some aspect of the product as expressed in a *feature benefit idea*. Again, using the equation format, benefits can be viewed in essence as follows.

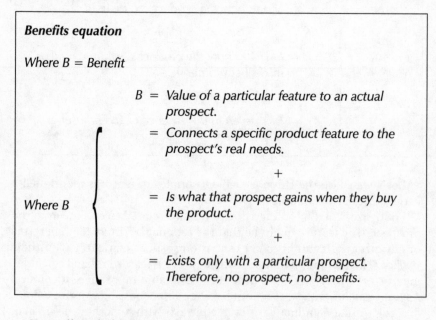

Benefits equation

Where B = Benefit

Where B

B = *Value of a particular feature to an actual prospect.*

= *Connects a specific product feature to the prospect's real needs.*

+

= *Is what that prospect gains when they buy the product.*

+

= *Exists only with a particular prospect. Therefore, no prospect, no benefits.*

You will probably have noticed that, in each of the three shorthand criteria applying to benefits, the prospect scores a mention. This is a big clue to the difference between *benefits* and *features* (and, for that matter, *advantages*), and goes a long way to answering the second part of the question ('Why are they so important?') that I asked a little while ago. If you again review the benefits equation, you'll see that in each situation a benefit is really only a benefit if it is directly linked to real prospects and their unique situation—that is, if it is linked to their real needs.

The golden rule, when it comes to using benefits, is that you can deal in benefits with your prospect only if:

- you and your prospect clearly identify the propect's real needs; and
- you position your product to demonstrate what it can do to meet those real needs.

Now to the second part of our question . . . Why are benefits so important?

Benefits are so important because the only medium you can use to build value with your prospect is to deal in benefits. We will deal with this in more detail in a minute, but first let's look at some hypothetical examples of features, advantages and benefits to help clarify the critical differences between them.

Let's take the topical product of car airbags. Using some licence and making a number of assumptions, I suggest the following FAB might apply.

Product: car airbags

Feature: *Fully inflates within three milliseconds of certain specific scheduled types of vehicle impacts.*

Advantage: *Prevents driver's head from coming into contact with interior equipment and panels in the event of serious impact with another vehicle.*

Benefit: *Will prevent serious head and neck injuries to you and your passengers in the case of the all-too-common frontal collision.*

What about sales training? You might suggest that our sales training product demonstrates the following FABs.

Product: sales training

Feature: *Competency-based.*

Advantage: *Improves selling capability levels across a broad range of identified sales skills by targeting specific sales competencies identified by the national industry body.*

Benefit: *Will measurably increase your sales team's effectiveness during face-to-face sales calls.*

I suggested that a benefit can't really exist without a real live prospect, so the examples above assume, for the sake of the explanation, that we are talking to a real prospect. They also assume that when discussing the benefit, we are linking the feature to the prospect's stated real need by outlining what they might gain.

Let's try one more example—a new artwork software package.

Product: artwork software package

Feature: *Over 10 000 different symbols and other graphics.*

Advantage: *Able to produce in-house advertisements and newsletters easily rather than needing to outsource this work.*

Benefit: *Saves time and money by using your own layout department to create finished artwork and, when appropriate, make changes on the spot as you review the layouts with your clients.*

Got the message? It's quite simple. True selling professionals engage in the following two specific objectives concerning FABs.

FAB objective no. 1

They work to understand the differences between features, advantages and benefits as they apply to their product.

FAB objective no. 2

They create opportunities to minor in advantages and major in benefits with their prospects.

Professional value-based salespeople know that the only way to differentiate themselves from the competing pack of salespeople snapping at their heels is to create real demonstrable value for the prospect. They also know that the only way to do so is to deal in benefits. They recognise that benefits are the only way to link the prospect's real needs to their product's features.

chapter 10

More about features, advantages and benefits

Y ou will recall that I spoke about the importance of understanding the differences between features, advantages and benefits in Chapter 9.

Some of you might be tempted to conclude from the earlier discussion that I was suggesting that benefits, and only benefits, were important and that features were less so or that advantages have no place in selling. Nothing could be further from the truth.

Features, advantages and benefits are all important, and each has a place in value-based selling. The danger is that they can be confused and thereby abused and misused. *Features* are important because, among other things, you must be able to demonstrate to the prospect exactly how the product delivers the proposed benefits. *Advantages* are important because, as a salesperson, you must know your product inside out, and know the marketplace in which it is or might conceivably be used so well that you are absolutely clear about the potential benefits, in the form of advantages, your product can offer. Note: I said *potential benefits*. When it comes to positioning your product, however, you should deal exclusively in features and benefits, with the primary focus on *benefits*.

In fact, it's been suggested that the real focus in complex selling isn't on your objective of engineering a quick 'Yes', but rather on determining the links between two things: the first being what you and the prospect have identified as the real needs; the second being, with the first in mind, the relevant features of your product. Having determined these, the next phase is positioning—that is, establishing connections clearly in the prospect's mind by linking these two components in terms of benefits that the prospect will receive as a result of accepting the *feature benefit ideas* that form the basis of your *compelling sales story*. It's really pretty much that simple.

So, as someone once so succinctly put it: don't sell the mousetrap; look at the prospect's needs and sell the absence of mice. Sell the benefits by focusing on the prospect's future vision of their tomorrow state.

If you think this is easy, I've got news for you. If it were easy, everyone would be doing it. However, it's relatively simple once you know enough about what you are selling, have adequate and appropriate experience, and know what you should be doing in the presence of your prospect.

To position the product effectively in the heart and mind of the prospect by linking the prospect's real needs to product features through focusing on the benefits that will accrue to the prospect, you will need to demonstrate a degree of skill and discipline, a solid base of preparation, a willingness to innovate and a pinch of creativity.

If you're having some difficulty with this concept of needing to work proactively and consciously to link features to needs using benefits and are tempted to return to dealing mainly in features, think for a moment how prospects may interpret or translate features as they relate to their situation if left to do so on their own.

From talking to buyers, my experience is that they can, if left to their own devices, misinterpret the stated features of a particular product, which can create several problems. These feature-based problems include the following.

> *Feature problem no. 1—The prospect doesn't necessarily see the benefits associated with a particular feature.*

That is, they are often benefit-blind in not naturally appreciating how the feature can be applied in their particular situation to their particular real needs. This should come as no surprise. After all, the prospect doesn't usually have the experience with a complex product to be able to understand the full implications of a particular feature as it might apply to their particular situation.

Another and less appreciated reason for avoiding dealing solely in features is that the prospect often doesn't fully appreciate their own current situation, their today state. They don't fully comprehend the implications of their own current reality; if this is the case, they will never be in a position to link product features to their needs and therefore create benefits in their own minds. It's up to the sales professional to explore these issues with the prospect and assist them to understand what the specific issues are.

Another commonly observed 'feature-related' problem has the potential to create even more problems for the salesperson.

> *Feature problem no. 2—The prospect may translate certain product features into disadvantages.*

Here the prospect not only doesn't understand the positive implications of the feature for their situation; in fact, they see the feature as a distinct negative. When this happens, you are in real trouble. So don't engage in *product dump*, leaving the prospect to translate the features into benefits that apply to them and their situation.

Two of the other outcomes associated with talking only or mainly about features are as follows.

> *Feature problem no. 3—The prospect becomes confused and may stop approaching the sale with enthusiasm and an open attitude.*

This is relatively straightforward, requiring no further comment. Let's move on to the fourth problem.

> *Feature problem no. 4—Features often are provided only as a response to a fairly superficial analysis of the prospect's needs, and as a result are rejected by the prospect as being irrelevant to their needs.*

When this happens, it's not uncommon to find that the prospect doesn't or won't share how they think and feel about your product and are less likely to give you their opinions and perceptions. As you can imagine, this is the kiss of death for a sale.

All of the above feature problems are caused by too much feature-focused talk, usually as a result of premature dumping of product information, and can be the direct cause of real barriers in the sales process.

FAB theory

The theory I propose and, for want of a better name, will call *FAB theory*, is that dealing principally with only one of the three (features, advantages or benefits) tends to lead the prospect naturally to different conclusions about your product.

What prospects have told me suggests that when salespeople talk almost exclusively and at length about the various features associated with a particular product, the prospect inevitably concludes that they don't need or want most of them. If faced with a long list of features in the form of characteristics, descriptive items, facts and data, the prospect invariably thinks, 'How much is all of this going to cost?' 'Why am I paying for all of this, especially the bits and pieces I don't need or even understand?' You can actually see the reverse of this feature-based reaction in clever marketing strategies for a relatively low-cost product. Here the advertisement pushes first the unbelievably low price, then goes on to list a host of features of the product, one after the other. Again, the low price is reinforced. And then still more features are presented. In the end, you think, 'What a cheap whatsit. I get this huge list of features for that amazing low price.' The bottom line is that throwing features at the prospect will be viewed by them as a barrier to the sale unless part of your distinctive competency is that you are the cheapest supplier of a product that has all of those features.

Contrary to what you might be thinking, our overreliance on advantages has its downside also. When salespeople start spraying advantages around, either in the mistaken belief that this is what the prospect wants to hear, perhaps out of laziness, or in the belief that if they throw enough advantages at the prospect some must stick, they run the very real risk that the prospect, faced with what seems to be inappropriate or 'disconnected meanings' or 'unclear explanations of a feature', will react negatively. When salespeople assume their *prospect's real need*, they often then compound the mistake *by assuming they have just the product that will fill this assumed need or want*. Salespeople who engage in these behaviours often go on to put not one but two feet in their mouths by telling the prospect all the advantages their product has to offer. However, much of what the salesperson describes as advantages is based on nothing more than assumptions about the prospect's real situation and is the hallmark of the traditional selling approach.

My experience indicates that this is the major 'turn-off' prospect experience. Prospects tell me that all too often, by the time they have had a truckload of advantages dumped on them by an enthusiastic but wayward salesperson, they start thinking, 'Hey, that so-called advantage doesn't apply to my situation!' and 'There's another one that means nothing to me!' or 'That isn't what I need at all', and so on. The result of this line of thinking is that the salesperson actually inadvertently creates objections: the so-called advantages cause the prospect to begin to think, 'That doesn't apply to me or my situation—I object.'

Now, benefits, prospects consistently tell me, are an entirely different proposition. When salespeople take the time to identify the prospect's real needs and then, as I said earlier, make the effort to employ their sale skills in linking their product's features to the prospect's real needs by positioning benefits, the prospect instinctively sees value being built. Almost by default, the prospect might think, 'I agree, that sounds just what I really need!' or 'Yes, that definitely applies to my situation!' or 'I can really see that working for me!'

So, in the end, it really is your choice. Why risk raising price issues and product objections when, with a little more effort, preparation, discipline and creativity, you can have the prospect agreeing with your propositions? Why am I so sure? Because the prospect told you by responding to your exploration strategies what they wanted, what they needed and what they would agree to. All you need to do is link your product to the prospect's real needs directly by positioning the product using feature benefit ideas.

Below are some concrete suggestions for preparing to work with benefits to build value for your prospects. I present them in the form of three relatively simple steps.

Three steps towards working with benefits

1. *Identify product features.*
2. *Identify potential advantages.*
3. *Internalise them.*

Let's look briefly at each of these three steps that you need to engage in in order to kick-start your ability to effectively use benefits.

- *Step no. 1—Identify product features.* Take the time to clearly identify all your product's features. List them, comb the product manuals, look at your competitor's offerings, talk to your service and parts department, and come up with an exhaustive array of product features.
- *Step no. 2—Identify potential advantages.* Now, taking one feature at a time, try to come up with at least three and preferably four or five potential advantages for each. Bear in mind that you can have similar or the same advantages for different features. However, be creative, be innovative, think about some of your current customers. How do they use your product? How do they use other similar products? What have they said? What have they found?
- *Step no. 3—Internalise them.* You're now halfway there. You need to internalise these advantages your product can offer and mentally review your list as you begin to explore and identify your prospect's needs. You will then be in a position to build value by selecting advantages that can be positioned as specific benefits that meet your prospect's needs, by designing questions around these advantages or potential benefits.

This is a worthwhile exercise to engage in—one that is sure to surprise you for a number of reasons. Advantages of this three-step approach to working with benefits include:

- *Advantage no. 1*—This is almost guaranteed to dramatically improve your product knowledge. You'll be surprised at what you learn about your product that you weren't aware of previously.

- *Advantage no. 2*—You'll be amazed at what some of the features built into your product have the potential to mean to a prospective purchaser. Remember, they don't have to mean anything to anyone but a potential end-user.
- *Advantage no. 3*—You'll be better able to formulate feature benefit ideas and effectively position them by linking them directly to your prospect's real needs.
- *Advantage no. 4*—You'll be able to analyse your competitor's offerings much more effectively *and*, from a user's point of view, sell against them by positioning even more compelling feature benefit ideas.

All these will separate you from the competition.

One more thing before we leave FABs. You need to be able to create simple propositions that build value for the prospect. I have referred to these as feature benefit ideas (or FBIs), which are made up of three basic elements or ingredients—the prospect's real *needs*, the *benefit* itself, and the *feature* that supports or validates the benefit. You can combine the last two in any order and link them to the prospect's need by positioning them in the prospect's head.

So, a positioned feature benefit idea might go something like this:

With this particular automatic collating feature you will be able to dispense with a great deal of the time you are currently taking to put the copied reports together. As I recall, this was something you mentioned you found time-consuming, frustrating and prone to mistakes, wasn't it? With this feature you just press this single button, and bingo! The machine does the rest and then buzzes you when it's finished.

Or how about this, using a question format:

This product has a selectable editing feature. What that means in your particular business situation is that you can select from a large menu of preset options and simply program the most frequently used ones into the on-screen menu of the phone. This means that your most used functions are automatically displayed on the screen at all times without the need to scroll through all those other less often used features. How useful would a feature be that puts you in control with the push of one button and avoids the frustration, delay and confusion you suggest you are currently experiencing with your existing equipment?

It's not hard. In fact, this whole subject of features, advantages and benefits, and FAB theory, is remarkably simple. And there lies the danger. The majority of salespeople struggle to define them, many can't explain their relevance, and most simply fail to comprehend the possible negative consequences of their misuse.

Don't believe me? Try it yourself. Take this simple test.

FAB test

1. *How many features and their allied advantages can you list for any single product you currently sell?*
2. *Can you construct six or so simple potential feature benefit ideas using different forms and language?*

I am constantly amazed at just how many salespeople consider themselves experienced professionals and skilled operators looking for advanced selling techniques who simply don't understand these basic FAB principles and cannot effectively demonstrate them in a selling situation.

Feature benefit ideas and your ability to construct them are the cornerstones of your selling career. They are the basics of positioning your product in the third phase of selling, the 'meeting needs' phase of our value-based sales model.

chapter 11

The ABC of the sales process

When I work with groups of salespeople I often ask them to sketch a simple diagram of what they consider might represent a basic outline of the sales process as it applies to their industry. I ask them to show the process as a combination of names or terms that they feel best represents their typical sales process.

In response, I usually see diagrams that vary from the ridiculously simple through to the enormously complex. What disturbs me most, however, is that it would appear that many salespeople view the more complex sales processes as involving a fixed format which needs to be dealt with in a strict sequence, rather than containing quite discrete sales elements that each need to be addressed during the sales process, although not necessarily in any specific order.

Most salespeople generally agree that the sales process they are involved in looks something like Figure 11.1, which clearly shows the sales process as containing at least four sequential steps.

Looking at this diagram, you will immediately see that most salespeople see the process as a basic linear flow, similar to the traditional sales model proposed earlier. Thus, when they reach the last stage, which is invariably designated as 'closing', they believe they have reached the 'end of the

Figure 11.1 *Steps in the sales process*

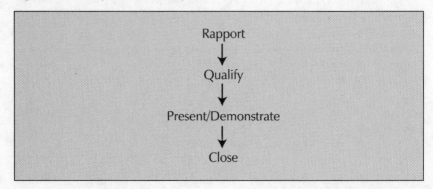

road'. They are now stuck and keep hammering away at this 'close' step until something cracks. This something is usually the relationship between the salesperson and the prospect.

I then ask them if they see their role as salespeople differently from that of, say, a salesperson in another industry, and I mention a couple of specific non-associated industries. The majority of salespeople seem to view their particular selling situation or sales environment as unique. They believe that their particular product–industry combination makes them sufficiently different from many, if not most, other salespeople. As a result, they tend to adopt a rather parochial approach to their sales processes. This invariably leads to the four conclusions below.

Four conclusions shared by many salespeople

1. *Their sales environment requires a different type of industry/organisation-specific sales process.*
2. *They have special sales-related problems unique to their selling environment.*
3. *They require different training programs, tailored specifically to their special selling circumstances.*
4. *They believe they need a trainer/consultant who understands the special needs of selling in their particular industry.*

What these salespeople fail to accept is that the key elements in the sales process are the cornerstones in selling and remain very much the same right across the selling spectrum (whether that involves the more complex or less sophisticated sales), despite their perceptions to the contrary.

My view is that when salespeople view selling as requiring rigid adherence to a series of steps, they almost certainly see themselves as doing something *to* the prospect. They are almost certainly traditional selling-based salespeople. They tend to concentrate on what *they* want to happen, in what order and when. They are certainly not value-based salespeople.

These traditional sales-based salespeople view the steps to a sale as a means to an end in themselves. For example, they almost inevitably see 'closing' as the final, all-important step in the sales process. They view this same step as describing their actions, and if you question them further they talk about 'closing the buyer' or 'closing the sale'. They see this step as also fully describing what must be done *to the buyer* before moving on to any subsequent action step they believe follows.

In summary, the more traditional selling-based sales approach favoured by many salespeople hinges on the mistaken belief that their own particular selling situation is very different from that of other salespeople. They believe that, to succeed, their particular selling process must be, by its very nature:

- *Unique*—It therefore involves a variety of very different selling strategies and initiatives from those employed by other salespeople in different organisations and/or industries.
- *Flexible*—It thereby is situationally dependent on various external factors, and is seen as requiring a number of very different tactics and methods, depending on who the salesperson is dealing with, whether they are existing customers, where they are in the sales cycle and, in particular, the product being sold. As a result, sales planning is rarely viewed as an essential element in the sales process.
- *Sequential*—It thus requires the salesperson to follow a sequence of preordained steps in order to achieve a 'Yes'.
- *Inward-looking*—By this they suggest that the steps themselves are the beginning and end of the sales process or sequence. As such, the name they give to each step usually describes what they must 'do' to the prospect to meet their own sales objectives.

Nothing could be further from the truth. When it comes to anything other than a very simple sale, I believe the truth of the situation to be very different.

Diametrically opposed to this view, truly professional salespeople view the selling process as:

- *Shared*—They recognise that there are indeed common key sales elements (they don't say 'steps') that are present in most selling situations and that continue to apply even in these allegedly very 'different' sales environments.
- *Predictable*—They realise that, when all is said and done, people are people and customers are customers, no matter what they are selling. Also, they understand that *what* they are selling makes no difference to the sales process itself—only *how* they might deliver their sales strategy. The process itself is predictable in terms of the elements it contains and the various phases it embraces.
- *Elemental*—Here, professional salespeople understand that the selling process contains not sales steps, but discrete sales elements. They understand that, unlike the step approach favoured and followed by their traditional selling colleagues, selling involves their addressing a number of elements, and these elements don't necessarily follow in any predetermined sequence or order other than that determined by common sense and logic. Furthermore, they understand that some of these elements may need to be visited only once during the process. Others may need to be continually revisited as the sales process unfolds.

■ *Outward-looking*—They understand that the elements in the selling process are simply descriptive terms and not in themselves a means to an end that necessarily describes what they must do or say. They understand that it is their individual skills that kick-start the sales process and continue to breathe life into what is, after all, only a behavioural model. The individual, personal and professional skills are the means by which each salesperson makes their selling style unique as they respond to each prospect's particular situation.

You will notice, if you compare these four responses to those given by traditional sales-based salespeople, that they provide exactly the opposite view of the sales process. A comparison of these two views is shown in Table 11.1.

So, what is the valued-based sales process? Is there any consensus as to how successful value-based salespeople view the selling process?

What these value-based salespeople tell us is that they view the sales process as involving a variety of both prospect-focused and process-focused elements that are aligned with a number of specific sales phases.

These 'elements' are exactly that, in that they correspond to or describe the major prospect- and process-oriented key elements to be addressed by the salesperson during the sale. The 'phases', in contrast, represent the separate overall key sales objectives that a salesperson needs to consider in setting an overall sales strategy, call objectives and tactics.

Table 11.1 *Comparison of views of traditional and value-based salespeople*

	View of sales process by	
Beliefs about the nature of the sales process	**Traditional sales approach salespeople**	**Value-based sales approach salespeople**
How does their sales situation or environment compare to that in other industries?	Unique	Shared
In response to differing sales environments, the sales process is by its very nature . . .?	Flexible	Predictable
How would they describe the relationship between distinct parts of the sales process?	Sequential	Elemental
Their response to the sales model, their view of the process, is to be . . .?	Inward-looking	Outward-looking

I think there is a very real consensus; as a result, the value-based sales process model, or what I call the 'anatomy of a sale', tends to look something like Figure 11.2. The elements, as you can readily see from the figure, are nothing startlingly new—nor, for that matter, are the phases proposed entirely unheard of. What the elements and phases represent, however, are those descriptive terms for the various key areas of a successful sale. They describe the critical issues and therefore form a valid foundation for the realistic determination of a salesperson's sales objectives when considered *from a prospect's perspective*.

I propose to discuss in much more detail in Part 2 each of these first nine key sales elements. The first four key phases that I propose are present in every successful valued-based sale process.

Figure 11.2 *Anatomy of a sale—five key phases in the life of a customer relationship*

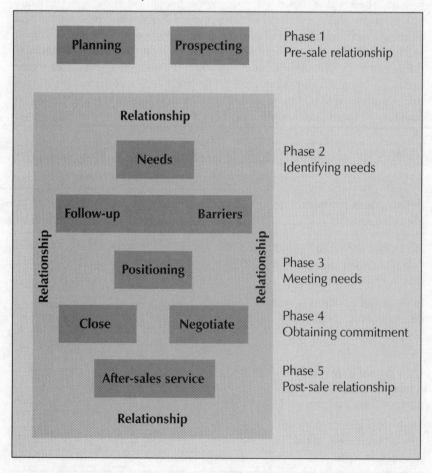

PART 2

THE SALES PROCESS—
THE 9 KEY SALES ELEMENTS

chapter 12

Planning

D espite the conventional wisdom that suggests sales is a numbers game, I have yet to see conclusive evidence in support of this proposition. Quite to the contrary, given a reasonably active salesperson who displays an acceptable degree of initiative, I have found that more sales calls doesn't necessarily translate into more sales, any more than repeated practice at something, say your basketball skills, will ensure that you win more often or perhaps get picked to play in a representative side. In fact, more sales calls can lead to *fewer* sales!

What more sales calls may mean is that there is, hypothetically at least, *more potential* that you will make a sale in any given period, or *more potential* that you will make more sales. However, there is no direct guaranteed mathematical link between sales calls and sales orders. In undertaking this analysis, you might, for instance, establish that on average you make a sale about every five sales calls. You therefore decide you have a strike rate of 1 in 5, or 20%, and think that, as sales is a 'numbers game', by doubling your sales calls you will, almost by default, double your sales orders.

This thinking can be dangerous because it directs the focus of competent and motivated salespeople onto quantity at the expense of quality. It causes them to concentrate on *activity* rather than focusing on *productivity*.

What does that mean? It means that to succeed today in the environment of complex sales, I believe you require a well-conceived sales strategy for each and every one of your prospects—a strategy that doesn't arise from the overly simplistic view of sales as a 'numbers game'. This sales strategy needs to address both of these areas, of activity and productivity. In fact, *each* one of your prospects needs a tailored sales strategy that has been crafted to the activity and productivity factors relevant to that particular sales environment.

What are these twin areas of activity and productivity, and how should we address each?

> **Twin areas to be analysed in planning your sales strategy**
>
> Area 1 *Activity—Analyse your sales environment by determining how best to get yourself in the right places, with the right people, at the right times.*
>
> Area 2 *Productivity—Analyse your sales environment by determining how best to maximise the potential of the selling opportunity once you are there.*

Too much focus on sales being a 'numbers game', usually from management, often results in a flurry of activity. However, does this activity necessarily equate or translate to a real improvement in the overall results, in either the short or long term?

Often not! And what I observe is that if there is an improvement at all, it is short-lived, usually only for that particular period during which the pressure is maintained by management to increase sales activity. In other words, it tends to last until the next managerial sales initiative is handed down from on high, and the result is that this 'activity'-directed total sales focus can often damage prospect–salespeople relationships in the process, causing much bigger, longer-term problems.

The other problem of concentrating solely on activity—that is, getting in front of the right people at the right time—is that it doesn't factor in whether you have the skills or resources to convert these opportunities to a sale. The 'numbers game' approach to sales doesn't take account of whether you can maximise the sales potential of the opportunity once you are, as they say, 'belly to belly' with your prospect.

Unlike sales activity, which tends, as we saw, to be externally driven from the top (i.e. management) down, productivity tends to be driven from an internal desire to be all you can be—a desire to acquire and implement the attitudes, skills and behaviours required to achieve your maximum potential. This is rarely the focus of high-level management initiatives and is often instead dependent almost solely on the salesperson's personal initiatives and their interaction with colleagues and their direct sales team manager or coordinator. Hence, I often refer to this facet of sales success as being driven from the bottom (i.e. salesperson) up.

Why? Because often in sales organisations there appears to be little in the way of a meaningful budget for this type of consistent, continuous, 'non-product' sales approach and soft skills training. As a result, improvement of productivity has, to date, it seems, been traditionally left to the salesperson to pursue.

If you think I'm being somewhat pessimistic or conservative, consider this question: How many medium to large sales organisations do you know of that have invested in a reasonable-sized library of sales training aids, be they books, audio and video tapes or computer programs, and which actively promote and encourage its continued use? Can't think of any? You're certainly not alone! Go and ask to see these same sales organisations' accounting library. Their legal reference library. Their product library. Then watch the expression on their faces when you ask to see their sales training library.

Why plan ahead?

A question rarely voiced but often considered in the minds of salespeople is, 'Why bother with sales planning? Why not just go out there swinging and see what I can connect with?' Two principal reactions to this type of question come to mind.

First, planning helps you to develop a well-constructed, long-term strategy and assists in the subsequent reviews of each of your potential/ prospective customers and sales accounts. Using activity as a specific area to be addressed, a good sales strategy first provides you with the focus to do those things that you as a salesperson need to engage in to identify and contact prospects. That is, your activity planning should primarily provide strategies to *put you in a position* to be able to uncover and unlock sales *opportunities*.

Second, when it comes to productivity, planning encourages you to consider, *in advance*, those things you need to do during the sales process, and in particular during each sales call, that will result in you and your prospects advancing the sale and ultimately in their buying your product.

So, planning first enables you to maximise the number of prospects you are able to introduce into your sales pipeline; second, planning enables you to maximise the number of prospects you retain in your sales pipeline and to move efficiently towards the overall objective—which is, of course, the sale.

Another major initiative—one that is often overlooked—is that a good strategy or sales plan allows you to take a degree of planned control in the sales process. Note that I say 'planned control'. This reference to control refers to an overall strategy you have for conducting and directing your sales calls, not what you are attempting to do to the prospect.

An interesting observation concerning planning is that most of those salespeople I talk to who appear to accept the importance of sales planning only focus on the relatively low levels of the planning tree. They concentrate almost totally on the immediate tactics and individual or relatively isolated specific sales activities. They often lose sight of the bigger picture because they fail to consider the larger overall goals, objectives and strategies required. In other words, they concentrate on the micro-level and tend to ignore the macro-level. It could be said that they lose sight of two critical planning laws.

> ### Planning law no. 1
>
> *Their tactics, and the resulting sales activities, are only ever as good as their overriding sales strategy and goal for the account or product. To be truly effective, planning must be driven from the top down, not from the bottom up.*
>
> ### Planning law no. 2
>
> *To really succeed in complex sales, they need to understand what should be done, and why, for every individual account and prospect.*

Many salespeople, convinced of the merits of taking the time to plan their sales campaign—often in the heat of the battle, or so it would seem—lose sight of the need to adequately consider and plan from the big picture and thereby fall into the trap of running a guerrilla campaign of 'hit and run' based on ill-founded tactics. The single most telling point about sales planning is that it forces you to crystallise your thinking, enabling you to convert your more general sales goals into a number of specific, relevant and measurable targets for the particular account. Once these targets are established, you have a clear and intelligible point at which to aim your more immediate professional energy, effort and time. Planning is what enables you to make your own luck, rather than waiting for divine providence to take pity on your efforts to date and to intervene by handing you some 'low-hanging fruit', those sales anybody could have made who was around to take the prospect's order.

Do you tend to be more activity-focused, or more productivity-focused, or perhaps both? Try this quick quiz.

> ### Activity- or productivity-focused?
>
> ■ Question 1—*Do you concentrate on your sales objectives, or do you concentrate on your sales activities in generating inquiry?*
> ■ Question 2—*Do you tend to think at the end of a busy day, 'Gee, I achieved some of my sales objectives today but I'll need to revise others' or 'Gee, I sure saw a lot of people today and made an awful lot of calls.'*
> ■ Question 3—*Do you think, overall, you are more effective than you are efficient?*
> ■ Question 4—*Do you focus on achieving your sales goals, or do you focus on making your sales commissions?*

- Question 5—*Do you direct your efforts towards maximising your sales opportunities and letting the money take care of itself, or do you direct your efforts towards maximising your money and letting opportunities take care of themselves?*
- Question 6—*Do you focus your energies on maximising the quality of your sales calls, or do you focus your energies on the quantity of your sales calls?*
- Question 7—*Do you think of yourself as working smart or hard?*
- Question 8—*Do you spend more time planning each call or planning each day?*
- Question 9—*Do you focus on achieving a planned number of sales per prospect, or do you focus on achieving a planned number of calls per day?*
- Question 10—*Do you plan to fully investigate your prospect's situation in each call, or do you plan to maximise the distance travelled each day?*

Most salespeople, from my observations at least, tend to behave as if they were selecting the second option in each question rather than the first. That is, they concentrate on seeing as many potential customers (or 'suspects') as possible in the hope that the mathematics of selling—that is, the 'strike rate', conversion rate or whatever it is termed—will produce results. They don't recognise—and neither (it appears) does management, which usually pushes this particular line—that this is only half of the story.

When it comes to measuring the activity of salespeople, what we are looking to calculate, in the majority of sales situations, is the ratio of *bona fide prospects* we are dealing with to the total number of *suspects* we started out with. To put it another way, activity measures are generally all about counting definite and quite distinct 'opportunities'. We often do this by calculating a percentage or ratio using the number of 'potential' sales opportunities divided by the number of 'possible' sales opportunities.

The *activity ratio* formula might then look something like this:

$$\text{Activity ratio} = \frac{\text{Potential customers}}{\text{Possible customers}} = \frac{\text{No. of Prospects}}{\text{No. of Suspects}}$$

$$= \text{Strike rate for opportunities uncovered}$$

When it comes to measuring productivity, we are looking to calculate how effective salespeople are in *managing* their sales pipelines. How well do they keep the prospects flowing freely down the pipeline towards the outfall? How effective are they in maintaining their pipelines in good working order, free of blockages, obstructions and even disastrous backflows?

Productivity measures are all about how effective the salesperson is when face to face with the prospect. Productivity is concerned primarily with working smarter and being more effective—that is, *making the most of the opportunities that are uncovered and available* when face to face with the prospect. Working harder isn't generally part of the productivity equation.

The *productivity ratio* formula might then look something like this:

$$\text{Productivity ratio} = \frac{Actual\ orders}{Potential\ orders} = \frac{No.\ of\ sales}{No.\ of\ prospects}$$
$$= Strike\ rate\ for\ sales\ made$$

For those salespeople genuinely interested in achieving their full potential, the real challenge in selling is to teach themselves to maintain an activity focus—that is, to work just that little bit harder, to be committed to improving their focus, and to work an awful lot smarter. And the only way to do that is to understand that sales planning is an important element of the complex sales process.

The next logical question is, what exactly is this thing we call *sales planning*?

What is sales planning?

In general terms, I tend to view the act of planning in the sales context in a relatively simple light. I view it as nothing more complicated in essence than preselecting a course or courses of action.

The key here is probably the word 'preselecting'. Planning intimates some form of forethought and careful professional analysis. Planning is about considering long-range visions and factoring in required outcomes, alternative courses of action, and the impact of external factors based on your understanding of any given situation and then selecting what you consider to be the most appropriate courses of action for that point in time.

Keep in mind that plans can and must be capable of review, and therefore are subject to change. They shouldn't be treated as if they were chiselled in stone. However, don't be tempted to use the fact that plans can and should be somewhat flexible to rationalise or excuse not taking the time to undertake planning in the first place!

Set out opposite is a simple overview of a generic form of planning hierarchy as it might apply to complex sales. You will see that I have called the model a 'sales planning tree'.

Sales planning tree

For each prospect/account

Level 1: *Overall sales goals*

$\downarrow$

Level 2: *Sales objectives for each goal*

$\downarrow$

Level 3: *Sales strategies for each objective*

$\downarrow$

Level 4: *Sales tactics for each strategy*

$\downarrow$

Level 5: *Sales activities for each tactic*

Let's take a minute to look at each one of the five levels that make up the tree. The five key levels are:

- *Level 1—Overall sales goals.* Goals are the big picture (or overall mission) for a particular account. They should be expressed as an intent in specific, result-oriented language relating to a particular position or outcome you want to achieve. The question you ask yourself is: *What do I want to achieve?*
- *Level 2—Sales objectives.* Your objectives are separate, concise statements of smaller or more quantifiable subgoals, which go together to achieve the overall mission or account goal. The question you ask yourself is: *What will it take to get it done?*
- *Level 3—Sales strategies.* These are the specific individual methodologies you plan to use to pursue your sales objectives. The question you ask yourself is: *How do I best go about pursuing each of my stated sales objectives?*
- *Level 4—Sales tactics.* These are the specific sales initiatives that allow you to implement your selected strategy. The question you ask yourself is: *What are the individual steps I need to take in order to implement my sales strategy and move towards my objective?*
- *Level 5—Sales activities.* These are usually the smallest measurable units of action required and, as such, nominate the specific activities you propose to engage in. They should be expressed in prospect-oriented terms. The question you ask yourself is: *What is my plan of action for marshalling and activating me and my organisation?*

Before we go any further, perhaps we should take a minute or two to look at some of the key ingredients that go into making a good sales plan.

Six key ingredients of sales planning

As I mentioned earlier, there are sufficient books, tapes and seminar programs solely devoted to the subject of planning, goals and goal setting to fill a large library. I don't propose to restate specific goal-related issues, other than to suggest that you bear in mind what I view as the six key ingredients required to ensure that your sales planning, and hence sales goal setting, is as effective as it has the potential to be.

Key ingredient no. 1

Keep in mind that each of your planning activities and initiatives should always be clearly linked to those planning levels at the top of your planning tree.

Your planning sessions must always start by setting your sales goals and then sales objectives. Subsequent activities must always be directed towards the achievement of those sales objectives. Resist the temptation to be sidetracked, no matter how tempting the offer.

Key ingredient no. 2

Generate clear, specific and concise sales objectives for each prospect.

Once you have done this, and only then, are you in a position to use these objectives to organise your plans of action and to break these plans into smaller, achievable and measurable bite-sized chunks.

Key ingredient no. 3

Be prepared to demonstrate tenacity and patience in pursuing your sales objectives.

Keep in mind that tenacity doesn't necessarily equate to stubbornness or being blind to other opportunities or to changing situations. Neither does patience necessarily translate into 'going with the flow' or waiting for, or agreeing to, inordinately long or ridiculous time frames. You be the judge. You're the one there making the decisions. Just understand that to achieve your overall sales goals, you will at times need the tenacity of the proverbial junkyard dog and the patience of Job.

> **Key ingredient no. 4**
>
> *Understand that, at times, even the best-laid plans of mice and men . . .*

Remember, not everything may go according to plan. Be prepared for it. Be prepared to decide whether to stick to your guns, no matter what, or whether to reassess your position and review your sales plans in the light of subsequent information.

> **Key ingredient no. 5**
>
> *Plans don't actually do anything themselves.*

Keep in mind that your sales plans need *you* to implement them, and they need *you* to keep them on course. Remember, planning is only the start, not the end, of your sales road. It's the first step you make in a well-considered sales process, not the last.

> **Key ingredient no. 6**
>
> *Make sure you express your sales objectives in prospect-oriented terms.*

You must express your sales objectives in terms that address what the prospect is gaining and how they will possibly benefit, not how you, the salesperson, will benefit or gain. This is a frequently misunderstood key ingredient. I see so many salespeople considering their sales planning and determining their activities in terms of the outcomes *they* want to achieve, with absolutely no acknowledgement of the outcomes their prospects might want to achieve. This is particularly a problem with salespeople who don't plan from the top down with the prospect in mind at all times. They simply don't take the time to consider the prospect's big picture as part of their own big picture.

The first objective

Let's talk for a minute about objectives. I suggested earlier in our sales planning tree that an objective was a smaller or more easily quantifiable 'subgoal' that answers the question, 'What will it take for me to achieve my overall sales goal?' When it comes to sales objectives, and in particular the initial objective, there appears to be varied opinion as to what the very first sales objective should be and, more importantly, what it shouldn't be.

Surprisingly, I find that many salespeople simply don't have an initial objective. And of those salespeople that do, the majority have a far too complex initial objective, one that is overly optimistic often to the point of being unrealistic. When I talk to salespeople who can confirm they have clear, account-specific sales objectives, and ask them to outline them, I usually hear something like 'My objective is to sell them!' or 'I'm going to . . .!' or perhaps 'I need to . . .!'

These may certainly be laudable sales objectives in the overall scheme of things (especially in the eyes of your sales manager), but they are unlikely to provide a great deal of direction in the initial phases of the sales process. In my experience, this longer-range form of sales objective as stated by many salespeople turns out to be a simple statement of desire, or a sales 'wish'. And this sales wish causes more problems than most salespeople realise. This 'wish' causes most salespeople to focus on selling, or more accurately 'telling', at the very first contact, which is often by telephone.

In this scenario, what the salesperson fails to recognise is that this first telephone contact with the prospect should generally have a *sole* sales objective, that objective being to influence the prospect, as to the value to the prospect, of a face-to-face appointment. This initial objective doesn't involve selling the product in any way, shape or form.

You could argue, as many salespeople do, that selling the value of the appointment and selling the product are the same thing. Believe me when I suggest that they most certainly are not!

You will recall that in Part 1 of this book I proposed that complex selling involves 10 distinct sales elements and five separate sales phases. We also proposed that these elements and phases combine to create a sales process that you *work through with the prospect* to arrive at a successful outcome for both you and the prospect, otherwise known as a win/win situation.

With this in mind, it would seem to me that suggesting that a valid initial sales objective is to 'sell the product' at any available opportunity is a gross oversimplification of the situation, and serves to give no real useful guidance or direction.

As an initial sales objective, 'sell at every opportunity' will fail, as many other similarly expressed sentiments will fail, because it ignores, confuses and disguises the primary sales objective. Why do I suggest this is the case? Consider for a moment that they:

- *ignore* the actual sales process as a process and the significant number of preceding smaller advances in a complex sales process that will go into achieving the bigger-picture sales goals;
- *confuse* a desire or a wish by the salesperson to achieve some particular outcome with those specific actions that describe exactly what is actually needed to be *done together with the prospect* to achieve the outcome; and

■ *disguise* objectives in subjective, vague, emotional terms, rather than allowing them to stand as independent, unambiguous, black-and-white, measurable terms that describe the real outcomes that are required to assure definite progress in the sales process.

> The simple fact is that every prospect contact should comply with the three Rs, in that each contact should:
> 1. be realistic and have clear objectives that can be assessed and measured;
> 2. be reassessed in the light of subsequent events, facts and observations; and
> 3. remain the centre of the salesperson's current focus prior to advancing to the next objectives.

If you're not absolutely clear, chances are you will simply be blown about on the sea of sales opportunity, taking what drops into your lap, with little or no control or choice over your direction or the outcomes. You may well be working very hard and being very active, but at the same time you are likely to be guilty of *not* working very smart and *not* being particularly productive.

The first contact by telephone

In many complex sales the first contact with a prospect is by telephone, and in that scenario your initial sales objective should be to sell the value to the prospect of a face-to-face appointment.

Instead of focusing on influencing the prospect as to the value of an appointment, most salespeople are guilty of demonstrating one or more of the following six fatal errors in their first telephone contact with the prospect.

Six fatal errors in the initial telephone contact with a prospect

> *Fatal error no. 1   Giving too much information too soon.*

This is characteristically lapsing into 'tell mode and trying to sell the product' over the telephone from the outset. This often necessitates discipline, perseverance and patience if the salesperson is to avoid this fatal error.

> *Fatal error no. 2   Talking to the wrong person.*

By not getting initial information about the prospect and their organisation and trying to get decisions from the wrong people, the salesperson is seriously jeopardising the potential sale and, for that matter, the chance to even get that first face-to-face appointment.

Fatal error no. 3   Not addressing the prospect's WIIFM factor.

This involves failing to adequately provide the prospect with a clear indication of the potential value to them of making the time to meet you as soon as is practical. Remember, their WIIFM ('What's in if for me?') factor and yours as the salesperson may be poles apart, so resist the temptation to focus on yours at the expense of the prospect's.

Fatal error no. 4   Failing to realise the opportunity to check information or ask initial questions.

Many salespeople don't recognise the opportunity present in the first telephone contact to get preliminary information about the prospect and about what makes them different. If the prospect is available and interested in continuing to talk to you, use this opportunity to ask questions and to heighten their anticipation of your meeting.

Fatal error no. 5   Neglecting to check the time available.

Not asking the prospect for permission to continue with the contact *now* after the initial discussions can be a major miscalculation on the part of the salesperson in anything other than a very brief conversation. Don't hesitate to confirm with the prospect that they wish to pursue the discussion right there and then.

Fatal error no. 6   Not being clear about what it is you want the prospect to agree to.

This involves not having a well-organised and clear message that leads naturally to a close with the objective of obtaining an appointment as soon as possible. I am constantly amazed at just how many salespeople fail to structure their initial telephone contact so that it flows naturally to having the prospect agree to a face-to-face meeting. It's as if many salespeople seem to lose their way in this critical first call.

While you might think these 'fatal errors' are fairly obvious and rarely made, you would probably be surprised at just how often I observe salespeople make them during the first, and sometimes even several subsequent, telephone contacts with prospects.

In considering the contents of this chapter on the sales element *planning*, you might think this telephone contact topic is more closely related to the chapter dealing with the *prospecting* sales element, which is the subject of Chapter 13. My reason for including these telephone-related issues here is that these initial telephone contact-related problems appear to stem more from a lack of understanding of the need for effective planning than they do from a misunderstanding or the poor execution of prospecting practices, although I would agree that both reasons may have an impact.

From my analysis of hundreds of coaching sessions with salespeople, there appear to be a number of important approaches or key criteria that I might leave you to consider as we prepare to sign off on this critical element of sales planning.

I see the following six key criteria as those you will most likely need to bear in mind as you approach and implement the sales planning element of your complex sales process.

Six key criteria for effective sales planning

Key criterion no. 1	*Be prepared to approach the planning process iteratively.*

Initially, at least, be prepared to start somewhere—almost anywhere. Correct your assumptions and revise your plans as you input more facts, collect data, include feedback and review your plans.

Key criterion no. 2	*Create clear action plans.*

Check that these action plans are unambiguous, logical, and capable of being implemented by you without needing to depend on others.

Key criterion no. 3	*Check that your action plans consider the prospect's decision-making process.*

To do this, ensure that your objectives are stated in prospect-oriented language and address their decision-making process.

> *Key criterion no. 4*   *Clearly link the activities in your action plans to your sales objectives.*

By nominating clear checkpoints and specific outcomes to be achieved for each and every face-to-face meeting with your prospect, you are more likely to work towards these and ultimately meet this key criterion.

> *Key criterion no. 5*   *Be prepared to revisit your plans.*

Review and revise your sales plans as required. Don't consider them set in stone: they are merely your route map for the sale and may need to be reviewed and reassessed as more information becomes available.

> *Key criterion no. 6*   *Follow the KISS (keep it simple, stupid) principle.*

Keep your sales planning simple. Stick to the basics. Keep it workable. Keep it relevant.

chapter 13

Prospecting

What I am attempting to do in this chapter is to demonstrate to you how easy and natural prospecting should and can be. Rather than visualising prospecting as that endless row of dark and perhaps unsettling doorways to be knocked on, or a hefty local telephone book to be methodically worked through, I would encourage you to think of prospecting as a critical sales element that can involve a wide variety of activities, from which you might choose to select only those that blend with your own personal style of selling.

Let's start with a relatively simple statement for you to consider.

> *'Your success as a professional salesperson is directly related to the quantum and quality of your prospecting.'*

To restate this maxim as it relates to your prospects, 'Your success in selling is directly connected to the number and nature of your prospects.' Your sales skills are certainly important, but did you notice that they weren't mentioned in the statement above? Your approach, how you view your prospects, your professionalism and you yourself are all critical to your success in sales, but again these didn't rate a mention.

Why? Because skills, attitude and behaviour, as I have said before, are certainly all essential ingredients in successful selling. But they are inconsequential if you as a professional salesperson have no prospects on which to demonstrate these approaches, personal attributes and talents. As a salesperson with no prospects, you are 'all dressed up with nowhere to go'.

Consider the situation where your sales skills are adequate, although still developing, your attitude and behaviour are less than ideal but nevertheless improving, *but* you have a good number of high-quality prospects to see every day. Even in this situation, where your colleagues and sales manager might rate you as 'barely competent but with scope for improvement', you can succeed in selling in spite of your shortcomings, given enough prospects with which to work. In fact, it may not be stretching the story too far to suggest that even an incompetent salesperson can make sales if they have a sufficient number of quality prospects to work with.

In some professional sales environments, such as segments of the real estate industry, even those technically proficient, highly skilled sales-people in the face-to-face sales encounters with buyers will fail unless they are continually dealing with a consistently adequate number of quality prospects.

I suggest that, in many sales environments, your ability to effectively and consistently prospect will place you well ahead of many of your colleagues, who may arguably be more proficient in the face-to-face sales situation than you but who don't view prospecting as a critical sales element.

Let's take a minute to look at this key element in the sales process. And to do this we need to start right at the beginning by asking, 'What is prospecting?'

What is prospecting?

Obviously, prospecting involves a prospect! So, perhaps this begs the more basic question: 'What is a prospect?'.

Unless you are absolutely clear and correct about what constitutes a prospect in the context of your particular sales environment, you are in serious danger of doing little or no proactive prospecting and, worse still, of not being able to recognise whether you are dealing with a 'prospect' or not.

In my experience, and depending on your situation, a prospect is a person, not an organisation or group or committee, that first of all has or will have a *need* for your product. Now, the story doesn't end there, as many salespeople think. To qualify as prospects they must furthermore be prepared to acknowledge or *recognise* that need. They must be prepared to make themselves *available* to listen to you. They must also have the willingness and ability to make a decision at some time in the reasonably foreseeable future.

If we convert this to an equation, we have the following.

Prospect equation

Prospect = Someone who has Need + Recognition + Capacity
+ Intent + Time + Availability

In most complex sales, if any one of these six key ingredients is missing when considering the people with whom you are dealing, then I would suggest that in all probability you aren't dealing with a prospect—you are dealing with what might best be described as a suspect.

Notice, that in my initial description of a prospect, I talked about a *need* and *recognition*. You, as a salesperson, must understand that having a need isn't enough. To qualify as prospects they must have an *awareness* of their needs, even if it's just a glimmer of recognition, prior to your considering them as a bone fide prospect.

If you think this is being a little extreme, consider the following scenario.

You are a salesperson dealing with a prospect, or so you think, who appears to need your product badly. They are in a bind and need what it is that you sell to get them out of the pickle they appear to be in. What's more, what you are offering is a perfect fit for their needs and that your selling proposition is a fair and reasonable one. Everyone, even the security guard at the front gates and his dog Fido, knows that what you are offering is needed. Everyone, that is, except the people in the organisation making the buying decision. So far they aren't aware of the need, and as such they haven't acknowledged it. Sound familiar?

Based on the above definition of a prospect, the person in the organisation you are dealing with isn't a prospect. Sure, things might change. They might, at some future date, see that what you proposed was indeed excellent. They might some day even represent a truly great prospect and, who knows, turn out to be among your best customers. However, at this stage they represent only a suspect. Why? Because the 'recognition' part of the six-part criteria hasn't been met.

Now, from a strategic viewpoint you may decide that the potential of the sale justifies your continued time and effort in attempting to build a relationship. It may, to your mind perhaps, even justify attempting to influence their perspective of the situation and change their thinking some time down the track when it's more appropriate.

Fine! That's a strategic decision you should make, but that potential future situation still doesn't define them as a prospect now. You may have made a conscious strategic decision and decided to spend some of your limited resources (your time, effort and money) in making sure you are around when 'reality kicks in' and your suspect recognises their need, and in doing so elevate their status from suspect to prospect.

Don't kid yourself. No matter what the potential of the people you are dealing with, the fact is that they are not true prospects unless they are, to some extent, aware of their need, are prepared to recognise it as such, and are willing to work with you to clarify and define those needs.

The next two variables in the prospect equation are *capacity* and *intent*. These two often go hand in hand. Once you have established that your potential buyers have a genuine need and are aware of that need, common sense would tend to indicate that unless you are convinced they also have the capacity to make or arrange the necessary decisions and the intent to implement them or make them happen, you are still dealing with suspects. In other words, do they have the ability or influence and authority to make things happen? Do they have the will to make decisions?

They may be absolutely convinced that what you have to offer is exactly what they need, but if they're not in a position, or not able, to communicate this to the other key players—their superiors in the decision-making hierarchy, for instance—then your proposal is probably doomed. Likewise, if they don't have the ability to make the necessary things happen, which may vary from arranging meetings with other key stakeholders to providing the resources they said they could deliver (e.g. money), then by our definition they're not true prospects. No matter how good their intentions, or how positively they endorse you, your organisation and your product, if these two key criteria aren't met they remain suspects. What you can, of course, consider is a strategy for having them assist you in arranging to meet the true prospects.

Finally to the two remaining criteria. To qualify as a bona fide prospect, your potential buyer must understand that *time* is important. That is, they must accept that the time to make a decision is now, or at least in the reasonably foreseeable future, and they must be prepared to make themselves available to listen to you. This last criterion, *availability*, is almost unnecessary to mention, you might think. But in the overall scheme of prospecting, when considering who are your suspects and who are your prospects, unless you are able to talk to your potential buyers, preferably face to face, they are highly unlikely to be real prospects, no matter how much they need or want what you are offering. Let's face it: in today's fast-paced, often aggressive, 'take no prisoners approach' to business, there would be hundreds, if not thousands, of businesses out there that would contain very real potential prospects, *if* you could only get them to take your calls or *if* they would agree to an appointment to see you.

Unless they do so, they are suspects, not prospects. Again, you may decide to invest your time, effort and resources into getting them to speak with you, and/or see you, but unless you do they will remain suspects.

The same for the time criteria. Unless your potential buyer has decided that the time to decide is now, or in the reasonably foreseeable future, you are dealing with a suspect. The concept of the 'reasonably foreseeable future' will vary depending on the sales cycle, the decision-making process etc. However, ask yourself this: 'Is this potential buyer prepared to work with me right now towards making a decision, either yes or no, about my proposition?' If you don't answer with a resounding 'Yes!', you need to do some more homework. You need to find out why. It could be any one of the previous six criteria or, for that matter, a range of other internal issues preventing any urgency being felt.

Don't kid yourself that you are dealing with a real live prospect just because you believe you have found a potential buyer. It can be dangerous for your long-term professional and financial health.

So, if we now agree on what a prospect is, we might define prospecting as nothing more than 'identifying and contacting prospects'.

Do you have a healthy prospecting attitude?

I suggested earlier that one aspect of your success as a professional is your attitude to, and your approach in, actively prospecting. In fact, what I actually said was that your success was directly related to the quantum and quality of your prospecting efforts.

As a salesperson, your prospects are the lifeblood of your profession. Without them, whether they walk in your door or whether you need to go out and find them, you won't succeed.

Think of the selling process as a pipeline—a concept most salespeople have little difficulty with, given the oft-used expression 'I've got several deals in the pipeline!', or perhaps 'What have you got in the pipeline?' Now, the pipeline should be full of only bona fide prospects, whom you as a salesperson are managing down the pipe towards the outlet. The outlet to which I refer represents nothing more sinister or complicated than the natural conclusion of a well-managed journey—that is, a successful sale. As the management of any pipeline requires constant vigilance and ongoing maintenance to keep it operating at peak effectiveness and optimum efficiency, you need to remove all blockages and reduce the potential for losses by working to plug any leaks that will appear from time to time and carefully maintaining the pumps and other vital equipment that keep the contents of the pipe flowing efficiently towards the outlet. The length of your sales pipeline equates to your sales cycle. So, the longer your sales cycle (the longer your sales pipeline), the more risk involved in the journey and subsequently the more vigilance and effort required to manage those assets in your pipeline.

As you might imagine, in addition to all of this, what is absolutely critical is the screening of what goes into the pipeline in the first instance. From all the available or potential 'deals' that could find their way into your pipe, you need to guard against allowing the inadvertent passage of those deals that have the potential to cause damage to critical pipeline equipment, such as pumps and valves, as well as those deals of suspect quality, contributing to blockages and leaks. You need to ensure that only the right assets get into your pipeline in the first place. In other words, the choice of what goes into your sales pipeline is a critical one and one that is very much up to you. You must recognise that as your resources are limited, time spent dealing with problems created by liabilities robs you of time better spent effectively managing the flow of your true assets.

This is why it is critical that you understand what a prospect is.

Prospects are the only things you should allow in your pipeline. You do have a choice. If you are less than vigilant, or don't care or perhaps can't tell the difference between real prospects and other suspects or similar liabilities, you'll end up with suspects, or worse, in your pipeline.

So, to use the pipeline analogy, prospecting is the activity of selecting and introducing the right assets, what I defined as 'prospects', into your pipeline and by default keeping all others out. Managing the flow of these prospects once they are in the pipeline is addressed by other key sales process elements. These other elements are analogous to the various pieces of critical equipment and processes that are needed to keep the pipeline functioning efficiently.

Where, then, do your sales skills fit in? Quite simply, consider your sales skills as the force that, when applied to these sales elements, energises them and thereby keeps the flow of prospects *moving* steadily along the pipeline towards the outlet. Think of the five phases of the sale as those individual sections of the pipeline that the prospects move through towards the outfall, the sale. But, remember, there are no fixed steps to the complex sale, so your prospects don't necessarily always move smoothly down the pipeline. It may be necessary for you to backtrack, to move back up the pipeline if you get ahead of your prospects, or they have been rushed through a part of the sales process they feel they need to revisit.

I believe that to prospect successfully requires an attitude where you understand and unreservedly accept each of the following seven prospecting truths.

Seven prospecting truths

> *Prospecting truth no. 1   Prospecting is forever.*

In sales, prospecting must continue until the day you die or leave sales, whichever comes first. In saying this, I'm not suggesting that your approach and methodology cannot change. It not only *can*, it probably *should*. For instance, as you work longer and become more successful in a sales position or environment, you may find you are more efficient at prospecting by employing referrals and cultivating repeat business than, for instance, undertaking cold calls and direct mail, which were the prospecting strategies you adopted in the infancy of your career. However, the fact that you must actively pursue prospects to keep your pipeline full hasn't changed. Prospecting is very much 'forever' in most outside sales environments.

> *Prospecting truth no. 2   Prospecting must be a top priority.*

There are no ifs or buts here. Prospecting must be very high on, if not at the very top of, your daily 'must-do list'. Why? Because if it isn't, you will find a reason, which you will no doubt rationalise as fair and reasonable at the time, to postpone, delay or even delegate your prospecting. I call it the 'busy-line syndrome'. This can't be allowed to happen.

You rationalise this by suggesting you were busy doing, well, work—selling, organising, confirming—making money for the organisation. The first chance you get to relax a little, you get up in your pipeline maintenance helicopter and carry out an aerial inspection of your pipeline. You find that while the outfall is still flowing reasonably well, although not gushing as it was a little while ago, things are looking bleaker further up the pipeline.

When you get to the input end of the pipe you see only a bare trickle of prospects entering—or worse, your screening system is broken and is allowing suspects into the pipeline. You know this is bad. No matter what you do now, at some stage (possibly not too far away depending on your sales cycle), your outlet will also turn to a trickle or be clogged completely by the 'liabilities' you let into your pipeline. No amount of prospecting activity now will fill your pipeline quickly. It takes time to identify and contact prospects and shepherd them into the pipeline. And it takes time to manage each prospect individually down the length of the pipe, especially in the longer, more complex sales cycles.

Avoid making this mistake. Make prospecting a top-priority activity every day.

Prospecting truth no. 3 *Prospecting is only, after all, effective communication.*

Prospecting is, when all is said and done, only a matter of communicating with other people. Many sales trainers, sales books, audio and video sales training tapes, and, for that matter, sales managers, are guilty of portraying prospecting as a black art that requires you to coerce, trick and manipulate suspects into agreeing to talk to you. These same publications and people seem to suggest that, in prospecting, the personal requirements required to succeed are primarily a very thick hide and the gift of the gab.

Nothing could be further from the truth. Prospecting involves first and foremost your ability to design and implement relatively simple communication strategies. These strategies can be undertaken in any form or medium that involves the communication process, because prospecting is, after all, simply a specific form of effective communication.

> *Prospecting truth no. 4   Prospecting requires systems.*

No effective structured prospecting strategy is based on an ad-hoc approach. Every good prospecting initiative has had at its heart an engineered systems approach to this sales element. The systems employed may assist in the design of the prospecting activities. They may run the implementation and will almost certainly maintain records for all prospecting activities.

> *Prospecting truth no. 5   Prospecting strategies must fit your own personal style.*

You need to select, from among the vast range of alternative prospecting possibilities, only those strategies that fit the real you—those you feel comfortable in implementing. Just because cold calling five days a week, every week, works for someone else, it doesn't necessarily mean it will work for you. There is a plethora of prospecting activities that you can engage in, varying from public speaking or letterbox drops, to direct mail, sponsorship and so on.

The first thing to remember is to do something every day, if possible. Don't wait for the perfect fit, the best option, the guaranteed sure thing to materialise before you start your prospecting initiative. Prospect every single day.

Second, track your results. In other words, measure the response or success of your various prospecting initiatives. Learn what works and what doesn't. What gets quick short-term results? What takes longer? What delivers good prospects? What delivers time-wasters? What requires considerable personal effort to implement? What can be effectively delegated to others?

Prospecting, especially in this computer-based, highly technological and information-focused age, has never been so easy to systematise, so set up a prospecting system right at the outset.

> *Prospecting truth no. 6   Prospecting has no boundaries.*

How and where you could possibly prospect is limited only by your imagination. Prospecting methods and strategies have no fixed boundaries. Ethical and moral issues aside, you could conceivably prospect anywhere, at any time, by almost any means.

Your creativity, resources, attitudes and behaviour will tend to be the major deciding factors shaping your approach to prospecting. Don't short-change yourself when it comes to your ability to prospect effectively. Don't accept internally or externally imposed boundaries. Keep challenging them.

Prospecting truth no. 7   Prospecting involves planning.

As I mentioned in Chapter 12, it's been suggested by many that 'sales is a numbers game'. I believe this is a potentially misleading statement, and if it applies at all then it applies more to prospecting than possibly any other elements of the sales process. Planning your prospecting goals and the applicability and relevance of applying 'numbers' to them will very much depend on the sales business and the sales environment in which you are operating.

These numbers-based objectives will also be peculiar to you and your organisation. However, in general terms, when you consider your sales environment, the resulting prospecting numbers might *include* the following *potential prospecting objectives*:

- number of suspects targeted;
- number of telephone contacts made;
- number of face-to-face contacts made;
- number of prospects identified;
- number of referrals obtained;
- number of appointments made; and
- number of referrals converted to prospects.

Of course, you could select two of these numbers to calculate just about any given ratios. For example, the number of suspects contacted by mail in a letterbox drop divided by the number of prospects this yields after a given time produces your prospecting strike rate for this form of prospecting, given a specific timeline.

So, why might 'prospecting numbers' be useful? Because, as has been suggested again and again, goals produce results. Stories are legion about the setting of goals and the subsequent achievement of them. And if one accepts this premise—that is, the fact that goals inevitably produce results—the only question that should occupy most salespeople's minds is not 'Why *should* I use them?', but rather 'Why *don't* I use them?'

There have been various definitions, explanations and exaggerations of what constitutes a good goal or objective, and the acronym SMART is often used to outline those characteristics that must be evident for any statement to be called a goal or objective—'simple and specific', 'measurable', 'achievable', 'realistic' and 'timed'. Although I don't intend to discuss goal setting in any detail in this chapter, I have found that what might help when thinking about your own prospecting objectives is to imagine them as nothing more complex or sophisticated than a description of a dream, albeit a very clear dream with a specific measurable outcome and a definite timeframe.

So, one final word on goal setting as it applies to prospecting. When it comes to setting and reviewing your prospecting goals and objectives, take a leaf out of the generally accepted goal-setting practices and make sure that:

■ your prospecting activities are directly linked to your prospecting objectives and goals;
■ your prospecting systems are structured to help you avoid being sidetracked;
■ you break your prospecting objectives down into smaller 'bite-sized chunks' on which you can base practical plans of action;
■ you continue to approach your prospecting goals with a degree of tenacity, patience and self-discipline;
■ you realise that goals don't do the work, *you* do. You, and you alone, must put your plans into action. The responsibility to implement your goals is solely yours; and
■ you are prepared for the good, the bad and the ugly when it comes to prospecting. Indulge in self-talk and manage yourself as you would any valuable team member, to keep yourself prospecting-focused. Don't let the bad or the ugly keep your eye from the ball. Don't let the good outcomes convince you that you can afford to rest on your laurels, on your past successes.

Seven simple tips for improving your prospecting

Below are seven tips I have found very helpful in improving salespeople's prospecting attitude and activity. See if they make any sense to you.

Tip no. 1   Set prospecting goals.

We looked at this in some detail in prospecting truth no. 7. Only the setting of smart prospecting goals and objectives and the implementation of good prospecting systems will assist you in maintaining a strong prospecting mentality.

Tip no. 2   Use a contact management system.

With the relatively low price of computer hardware, the wide choice of contact management software programs and the technology available for different and varied communication options, there is really no excuse for not starting out by using a computerised contact management and database system for storing, systematising and managing all the prospect and contact information available.

If you must use a paper-based system such as a card or tickler file index, do so. My message is pretty simple: to be an effective prospecting system, it must have a system of capturing and recording data and being able to access and retrieve that information in various useful formats when required. A contact management system goes one step further: it allows you to plan and implement future contacts.

Tip no. 3   Capture complete information.

Take the time and trouble to capture complete prospect information. This complete information might include the names of your prospect's immediate family, important dates such as birthdays and anniversaries, hobbies and sports. If you expect to build a relationship with your prospect, be prepared to become interested in them as a person and to demonstrate that interest from time to time.

Tip no. 4   Form a clear picture of your ideal prospect.

Think for a minute about your best and worst customers. Can you describe the characteristics or define particular aspects for each? For example, when it comes to your ideal customers, can you answer questions like:

- What do they do?
- What is their job description?
- What do they read?
- With whom do they associate?
- What common characteristics do they have?
- What do they look like?
- Who do they talk to?
- Where do they live?

The answers to these and questions like them, based on an analysis of your current ideal customers, should give you an insight into exactly where you might focus your prospecting energies. Likewise, an examination of your not-so-ideal customers should give you clues about where you might be wasting your prospecting efforts. Also, by describing your worst or non-ideal customers, you can often draw conclusions by reverse inference about your ideal prospects.

For example, you notice your less-than-ideal customers all have separate purchasing departments that almost always pursue an aggressive cost-based buying decision. As a result you may decide that one of your ideal prospect characteristics is that the organisation *not* have a separate purchasing department. Once you have a snapshot of your ideal customer you have, by default, a good picture of your ideal prospect.

Now, without narrowing your focus to such an extent that you might be blind to other opportunities, you can concentrate on implementing strategies for finding and contacting people with these characteristics. Armed with this profile of an ideal prospect, you can ask such questions as:

- Where do these people hang out?
- Where do I get lists of people with these characteristics from?
- What do these people read?
- Who gives these people advice?

Tip no. 5   Do the prospecting numbers.

While I am not entirely comfortable with the notion that selling is a 'numbers game', it can be applied with some degree of success to your prospecting. Using your particular sales cycle and working backwards from your target income, you should be able to determine well in advance, from your sales records, how many prospects you will need to see in order to generate the required sales, which in turn is required to generate your specified target income. Regressing further steps will allow you to estimate how much and what prospecting you need to engage in to uncover the number of prospects you calculated you require to generate the income you nominated.

Too hard, you think? That's usually the reaction I initially get. But when I work with salespeople to look at their sales processes and then break it down and when, as a consequence, the salespeople are asked to make simple educated guesses about conversion rates, strike rates and inquiry rates based on a number of simple processes that each lead ultimately to a sale, they are generally amazed to be able to see and feel the direct connection between their prospecting activities, the various desired outcomes and, eventually, the impact of all this on their target income. For the first time, they can directly relate their efforts in the early prospecting activities that are concerned primarily with putting prospects in one end of their sales pipeline and the potential income available by managing their sales process in such a way as to encourage a percentage to flow out at the outlet as sales.

For the first time in many salespeople's careers, often very experienced careers, by doing the prospecting numbers, they feel they are in control of their destiny and don't need to wait until the end of the year to assess whether they are on target or to determine what went wrong. They realise that if they don't stick to their prospecting plan every week, that's where the problems inevitably start.

Tip no. 6   Sell the value of prospecting internally.

This is probably one of the most often overlooked aspects of prospecting. In all the activity and hype of planning and implementation, salespeople may neglect to explain the value of prospecting to both the non-salespeople in their organisation and their own personal network. The reception staff, warehouse workers, administration team and their own sphere of influence outside the organisation get left out of the loop completely. In my observation, few salespeople bother to sell prospecting internally. That is, many salespeople completely neglect to sell their own people on the value of prospecting—on the value of the activities and initiatives they and the company are undertaking to generate inquiry.

The first priority of any prospecting plan, especially if this critical sales element hasn't previously been embraced with anything like the diligence required, is to outline to everyone, even the office gofer, the link between successful sales and the need for continuous and systematic prospecting activities. They should be aware of what is being done, when and why. They should also be briefed on how to handle any subsequent inquiries and what to expect.

The second related initiative you might consider when it comes to selling the value of prospecting is putting incentives in place that reward the non-sales staff or other team members for their prospecting efforts—especially those that actually result in attracting prospects to the business. Too often, sales teams believe they are working in a vacuum when it comes to cooperation and coordination with the other departments, divisions or areas. I have asked many a sales secretary about the sales team's prospecting initiatives only to be told they don't know what's going on or being planned, other than what they hear in the office gossip. They aren't asked to be involved. The sales team are invariably the first to complain when they feel they are carrying the whole fate of the company on their shoulders and that no-one else seems to care or understand what they do, or want to help.

> *Tip no. 7   Adopt a prospecting attitude.*

In order for you to prospect effectively, you must first understand the rules of your own 'inner game', and then compete and win this challenge. To even compete in their internal mental game, most salespeople must first adopt the right attitude towards prospecting in order to allow them to develop a 'positive prospecting mentality'.

Part of achieving or acquiring this positive prospecting mentality includes *taking the time* to do the following:

- *Get organised*. Ad-hoc, disorganised and inconsistent approaches to prospecting are likely to cause frustration and fatigue as you move from one prospecting activity to the next with little or no thought for the big picture, consideration of past and future prospecting activities, or idea of the results obtained.
- *Become systematic*. Starting with a clear understanding of your strategic prospecting goals, you need to work your way down the planning tree to your specific account or potential account objectives and the specific tactics you intend to employ to achieve these goals. Prospecting is a systematic sales element and, as such, it doesn't respond well to a hit-or-miss approach.
- *Find your own comfort level*. Find out what form of prospecting suits your natural abilities and strengths. Don't spend all your time doing things you cannot achieve or don't feel comfortable doing. Take the time to find out what works for you, your product and your particular situation.
- *Maximise your true potential*. As mentioned earlier, unless you can develop a true prospecting mentality, which can grow only from an acceptance of the importance of prospecting, you are unlikely to achieve anywhere near your true potential.

What stops us from prospecting?

It would seem—on the surface, at least—that the evidence in support of the importance of prospecting as a key element of the sales process is overwhelming! So why, in the face of this overwhelming evidence, don't we, as salespeople, prospect?

Over the years, I must have heard all of the reasons for not prospecting. Outlined below are some of the reasons most often given or suggested by salespeople I have interviewed or coached. I say 'suggested', because often the salespeople themselves aren't aware of the real reason they are articulating. Take a minute to review the following reasons and decide whether any of them apply to you.

Seven reasons for not prospecting

Reason no. 1   Fear of rejection and failure

More often than not, rather than the actual rejection or failure itself, it's the *fear* of rejection and the *fear* of failure that is the number one public enemy of salespeople. This, in my estimation, is the primary initiator responsible for well over half the barriers or roadblocks salespeople experience with prospecting.

This fear, rather than the rejection itself, festers and builds in the salesperson's mind, creating a major obstacle to sales success. I believe that if fear of rejection, fear of failure, or fear generally continues to stop you from prospecting, you'll almost certainly fail.

If you don't face your fears, stare them straight in the eyes, you will be average at best. That's right—*average*. However, it's more likely that you won't even reach this plateau. It's more probable that you will eventually leave the sales business altogether. In the end, it's your choice and yours alone. Make a decision. Learn to face your fears, feel the fear, experience the tension and do it anyway!

Reason no. 2   Low self-esteem

One of the direct linkages to self-esteem in selling is whether you see yourself as a value provider. Self-esteem is the key to building value and distinguishing yourself. If you don't feel good about yourself, about your product and what you do, you'll be unlikely to present a confident, professional attitude, the first step in building a strong professional relationship with your prospect. Self-esteem is a key not only to prospecting but to many other elements of the sales process. Work on your self-esteem continuously.

The deciding factor in dealing effectively with self-esteem is to *believe*. In fact, you need to believe in four things. You need to *believe* in:

1. the *value* of your product;
2. *you* personally, who can make the difference your prospect is looking for;
3. your *product*, which will improve your prospect's situation both personally and professionally; and
4. the *sales profession*, which is a worthy and honourable professional vocation.

Reason no. 3   Lack of knowledge

There are all sorts of issues that fall into this category of 'knowledge'-based reasons for not prospecting. It may be as straightforward as simply not understanding and accepting the importance of prospecting and, ultimately, the implications of not engaging in prospecting. Or perhaps it's as basic as not having, say, the computer-based skills to operate the prospecting software.

Perhaps, as I have found on some occasions, it's the perceived or real lack of knowledge which salespeople may have about their sales responsibilities, the product itself, the market they are operating in, or even their own management's expectations.

Lack of knowledge is a major factor in the development and maintenance of barriers to a successful prospecting mentality. However, I believe that once identified and accepted it's probably one of the easiest barriers to deal with.

Reason no. 4   Poor organisation

If you are guilty of 'just not seeming to be able to get organised', you're not alone. However, organisation is the framework on which a successful prospecting campaign is built. Organisation is, if you like, the structure on which you hang your various prospecting systems and strategies. Organisation and selling go hand in hand. They are inseparable twins in successful selling.

Reason no. 5   No time

This is an interesting one: 'I just don't have the time', or 'I know I should be prospecting, but I'm just so busy.' Remember, your ability to manage your own time is a key skill that will play a large part in your sales success.

Without time management skills, you will find it difficult to undertake any of the critical sales elements required to be a top performer, let alone find the time to undertake the prospecting sales element. Why? Well, sales professionals, because of the very nature of selling, need to achieve predetermined goals in a given timeframe, and thus time management is an essential skill.

Wasted sales time will cost you dearly. You will pay for wasted sales time in the currency that costs you most. You will pay by the loss of your:

■ energy;
■ motivation;
■ opportunities;
■ focus;
■ money; and
■ job (eventually).

So, get organised and make the time for prospecting. Don't accept any excuses—*accept only results*.

Reason no. 6   Not a priority

Usually this priority issue is directly linked to the importance you place on the prospecting sales element. If you don't view prospecting as an essential element in your sales success, you most certainly won't give it the priority it deserves, or needs, for you to place it firmly on the 'must-do' schedule of your daily sales activities.

Reason no. 7   Lack of motivation

We often hear someone say, 'I just don't feel like it', or 'I just don't want to.' Everyone accepts that there are activities we don't want to do, don't enjoy doing, don't look forward to doing. And motivation is a very personal issue, one driven by perception, personal values and goals. The majority of salespeople whom I find aren't motivated to prospect are generally not aware of two key aspects of prospecting: first, the direct link between their own sales success and prospecting; and second, their flexibility in being able to design and implement a method of prospecting that will comfortably fit their personality, sales style and behaviour.

You decide! Is it that you're not motivated to prospect or, to put it bluntly, you're not motivated to step outside your comfort zone, to do something different, perhaps to do *anything* different?

The simple fact of life in the complex sales environment that many salespeople have yet to grasp is that those salespeople who consistently spend their time engaging only in sales activities they want to do, or enjoy doing, are unlikely to be in a position to engage in the activities they want to do or enjoy doing in later life.

Five key positives of effective prospecting

Let's leave these negative reactions behind and look on the more positive side of prospecting. Which begs the question: what are the potential benefits of a good, healthy prospecting attitude?

Below are five key benefits that result from effective prospecting.

> *Prospecting positive no. 1   Sufficient quality prospects*

Effective prospecting ensures that you maintain a reservoir of potential quality prospects you can feed into your sales pipeline. Prospecting keeps you face to face with potential buyers, with opportunities and, ultimately, with successful sales.

> *Prospecting positive no. 2   Control*

Designing and implementing your own prospecting strategy allows you, to varying degrees, to decide who you will work with and when. It helps put you, the salesperson, in control of your own destiny rather than being at the beck and call of others. It allows you to determine the factors in your success, rather than accept those that are handed out or simply stumbled over in your often aimless rambling around your immediate sales environment.

> *Prospecting positive no. 3   Consistency*

Effective prospecting allows you to consistently earn an above-average income. It allows you to be proactive in getting face to face with those people who need and want what it is you have to sell. Prospecting consistently provides you with opportunities to demonstrate to suspects the value of what it is you bring to the table, if and when they are ready to buy.

> *Prospecting positive no. 4   Evening out of the slumps and bumps*

Selling, as any salesperson will tell you, can be a rollercoaster ride, with extreme highs and devastating lows. Prospecting allows you to reduce the incidence and severity of lows so that your results are more consistent. Prospecting helps you not only to raise the bar but to keep it in a higher position and reduce those bad or patchy periods that the average salesperson experiences, constantly complains about and usually blames on someone or something else.

Prospecting positive no. 5   Maintains awareness

Prospecting, by default, keeps you, your organisation and your product top of mind. It maintains awareness and keeps you in the forefront of your prospective customer's thinking. Your prospecting initiative often gets you thought of in the first instance. It's what gets you the invitation to the 'game'. Without it, you are just one of the spectators who wishes they had the chance to play.

Some final advice on prospecting

Perhaps now you find yourself in a position where you feel that you understand and accept the importance of prospecting, but you are having problems in getting the 'rubber on the road'. Some of the most common problems that I find salespeople experience with implementing prospecting strategies are outlined below. You might take the time to see whether any of these issues are causing you minor roadblocks once you have decided that *now* is the time to adopt a prospecting attitude.

Getting started problem no. 1   Too much planning

The tendency of most salespeople, when introduced to the critical importance of the prospecting sales element in the complex sales process, is to spend inordinate amounts of time researching and planning their prospecting, and as a result investing little or no time in 'doing'!

It's the age-old problem of 'paralysis caused by analysis'. Be aware of the problem. Guard against too much mental activity and too little physical activity. It's generally better to make educated guesses based on your research, then act, then review and revise your prospecting approach, than to try and design the 100% perfect, 'foolproof' approach before attempting to implement any prospecting strategy.

Getting started problem no. 2   Too many people

From experience, I would prefer salespeople to start prospecting with *too few*, rather than too many, prospects. Initially, it's far more effective to test your assumptions, implement your strategies and assess the outcomes of new prospecting initiatives prior to launching a full-scale assault of an untried and untested prospecting methodology or strategy.

Start small and let your prospecting grow.

Getting started problem no. 3   Not following up

The single biggest complaint I continually hear from prospects and customers alike is that the salesperson fails to follow up. Follow-up is, in my view, such an important issue in selling that you will recall I have nominated it as one of the 10 key sales elements in the 'anatomy of a sale' sales process, and have devoted a chapter to just this subject.

If you are going to implement a prospecting strategy, then part of that particular plan needs to involve a specific strategy for responding to, or following up on, all forms of inquiry, whether by telephone or face-to-face contact.

Getting started problem no. 4   Asking only for business

All too often, prospects feel that the only reason a salesperson communicates with them is to ask for business. And justifiably so! Very rarely do prospects feel that the contact has any real value or particular benefits for them: most prospects view the salesperson's prospecting initiatives as being based solely on the salesperson being after something or wanting something. The prospect thus often takes the rather cynical view that prospecting is very much a one-way street. Small wonder that prospects adopt the view that they won't hear from you unless you want something.

Be prepared to see prospecting as involving some give and take. Think of prospecting as a two-way street and one where you can start by giving—giving information, giving a *genuine* free service, giving a thank you. Remember, be prepared to invest in your prospecting activities *before* you expect a return on that investment. Demonstrate that you are interested in a sincere, personal relationship—not just a relationship that provides something you can get now.

Getting started problem no. 5   Infrequent contact

Infrequent contact is, in my opinion, the single biggest reason for not being able to effectively convert suspects into prospects. The cynical general public know from their experience of constant bombardment that they will probably never hear from the majority of salespeople who prospect by mail, telephone, Internet or facsimile, beyond the brief initial contact. A tremendous sales effort seems to go into these initial bursts of communication, with either no consistent, ongoing contact program or insufficient frequency to allow a relationship to grow and mature.

A contact once a year could be considered an insult and a joke. A contact once a quarter generally isn't good enough these days, where you are competing aggressively for the prospect's attention. To start to build a relationship you will need to make a minimum of seven to eight contacts each year with your prospect.

Getting started problem no. 6   Being negative

Don't be negative. It will affect how you are perceived by your prospects. Whether you are aware of it or not, whether you like it or not, whether you admit it or not, negative self-talk is one of the surest ways to feed the fear within, to elevate the force and frequency of your internal self-doubts.

What about qualifying?

You will note that I haven't said a word about 'qualifying' the prospect, other than to suggest in the early sections of this chapter that I didn't subscribe to the view that 'qualifying' was the process, in the prospecting element, for screening out all but your genuine prospects from entering your sales pipeline. Why?

You may recall that I suggested in Part 1 when we were discussing the differences between the traditional and value-based sales models that the qualifying process is usually nominated in the traditional sales process to be a major second step after building rapport. Qualifying is viewed in traditional selling as a step whereby the salesperson attempts to find out whether they are wasting their time with the potential buyer, and this sales step is usually carried out prior to spending any further time, real effort or costly resources on the buyer. Hence, in the traditional selling model, it appears before the 'presenting' and 'closing' steps.

What do the traditionalists really mean by the term 'qualifying'? It's been suggested by traditional salespeople that qualifying is the process of determining the responses to four major questions asked of your prospect. These four questions are:

1. *What* will the prospect buy?
2. *When* will the prospect buy?
3. *How* will the prospect buy?
4. *What* are the conditions under which the prospect will buy?

If this is a true snapshot of qualifying, then we might assume, using our value-based model of selling, that qualifying infiltrates all the sales elements, and more especially those of prospecting, needs, closing and negotiating. On this basis it would seem that the salesperson is continually qualifying the prospect right throughout the sales process, from the cradle to the grave. With this in mind, the term 'qualifying' is irrelevant as a fixed sequential step to be dealt with after building rapport.

Consider my definition earlier of a prospect. Consider the six key ingredients or criteria I suggested as being required for a potential customer (i.e. a suspect) to be considered a prospect. Don't they address, in prospect terms, some of the key issues that are often included in 'qualifying'?

Qualifying, to the traditional sales practitioner, is usually approached on the basis of a sales focus built around the number 1 fatal sales flaw, which you will recall is to be so completely focused on *what we, as salespeople, want to happen* as to lose sight of *what the prospect wants to happen.*

In my view, complex selling should be built on the foundation of *finding and delivering what the prospect wants to happen*. When this occurs, salespeople will automatically get what it is they want. Rather than adopting the traditional sales approach of viewing yourself doing something to the prospect, which ultimately leads to 'qualifying' the prospect in the very early stages of the sales process, perhaps you should consider qualifying *yourself*. Perhaps you should evaluate whether you are the right person for the prospect. I can assure you the prospect will be doing just that.

With this in mind, perhaps qualifying should be redefined as a process by the salesperson that can be best summarised by addressing the four separate areas of sales focus that the salesperson needs to adopt:

- *Focus 1*—Focus on what the *prospect wants to get out of the exchange*, not what you, the salesperson, will get out of it.
- *Focus 2*—Focus on what you, the salesperson, will *put into* the exchange, not what you will *get out* of the exchange.
- *Focus 3*—Focus on *demonstrating value*, and realise that to do this you must see yourself as a value provider.
- *Focus 4*—Focus on *what the prospect values* in order to be perceived as a value provider.

When it comes to qualifying, consider this. Rather than taking the view that qualifying is the process by which you, the salesperson, determine whether you are wasting your time, let's consider the completely opposite approach, outlined in the four areas of focus above. Let's accept the notion of 'qualifying' as a legitimate part of the sales process, *where you, the salesperson, demonstrate to your prospect's satisfaction why they won't be wasting their time by agreeing to talk to or meet you.*

Now, *there* is an approach to qualifying that I *can* accept.

chapter 14

Relationship—the foundation on which the sales process is advanced

T he quality of your relationship with the prospect can have a major bearing on the conduct of the sale. In fact, simply put, your ability to relate to your prospect is a critical sales skill.

On some occasions you will no doubt find it easy to build a relationship; it will seem so effortless, almost like falling off a log. So easy, you might be tempted to wonder what all the fuss is about and express disbelief at the notion that it requires anything even approaching a skill to carry it out effectively. At other times, you are sure to find it much more difficult. It will require a very distinct effort on your part and a fair degree of conscious adaptation of your natural behaviour to relate to the prospect.

Building a relationship may also require you to demonstrate a considerable degree of flexibility in accepting others' values or attitudes, especially in those situations where they are markedly different from yours. In extreme cases, you may well find it difficult to identify and share common ground with your prospect, and you may consider it wise to choose to 'sit this one out' or have someone else in your organisation deal with that particular prospect.

In this latter scenario, where you and the prospect seem to be on different wavelengths, the prospect is often labelled as a 'difficult' customer, a trouble-maker or worse. I often see, as a result of this person-to-person mismatch, salespeople rationalising their failure to connect with their prospect by indulging in all manner of creative excuses. I hear things like 'They just can't decide', 'They're just plain self-absorbed and seem to be all over the place', 'They just don't seem to want to share their thoughts', 'They continue to come across as cool, unconcerned and very guarded in their responses', 'They don't seem the slightest bit interested in interacting on a personal level', 'They only seem interested in getting answers to their questions', 'They seem to want to confront me every time we get together' and so on.

What is happening is that the salesperson and the prospect are operating on entirely different frequencies, hearing different things, interpreting messages entirely differently and, probably most importantly, operating from totally different behavioural and value perspectives. Here, there could be said to be little in the way of a shared or common relationship.

So, let's get down to basics. What is this critical sales element called relationship, and why is it so critical to your success in complex sales? Perhaps the best way to respond to this question is to begin by viewing the relationship element as comprising two primary objectives, as below.

Relationship

Where R = Your relationship objective with your prospect

$R =$

1. *Seek to establish, build and sustain a strong interpersonal relationship.*

   +

2. *Establish credibility and continually work at developing and maintaining a solid professional relationship.*

This first relationship objective, involving establishing, building and sustaining a strong interpersonal relationship, is best expanded on by using the analogy, as in the first part of this book, of a breakwater. As such, in seeking to meet this most basic person-to-person objective, you as a salesperson must appreciate two simple facts, as follows.

Fact 1:   *Without a good strong opening to the relationship and the ability to go on to establish and then develop a strong relationship element, you have built no 'breakwater' with which to resist the stormy seas that may from time to time seek to damage the tenuous interpersonal connection you have made to your prospect.*

The *interpersonal relationship* sales element is like the breakwater you see in almost any coastal town. Without this breakwater, when a storm hits, the boats sheltering at anchor in what were relatively calm waters will be blown about, tossed and turned. Some will break their moorings and end up on the beach or, worse, on the rocks.

Your interpersonal relationship with your prospect is the 'breakwater' to the problems and difficulties that will almost certainly arise in the complex sales process from time to time. Sure, the sea inside the breakwater might ebb and flow, rise and fall, but the damage to craft sheltered within is minor at worst. Without this strong, interpersonal relationship element in place, you will bear the full force of the problems that will arise during the sales process. These problems can lead to a weakening or a break in the connection forged between you and your prospect—a break that can be difficult or even impossible to repair.

> Fact 2:   *Unless you open well and work to develop and sustain a healthy interpersonal relationship element, your sale may go nowhere, or even run the risk of being hijacked by a competitor who, perhaps unknown to you, has built a superior prospect relationship.*

To explain this, let's extend the analogy of the breakwater by considering for a moment how the boats are anchored or tied up to the wharf. If you use a light line, then even the best breakwater protection in the world probably won't be able to stop the boat from moving on the swells to such an extent that the anchor ropes or mooring ropes eventually break. However, if you use heavier ropes, which is akin to your having a stronger interpersonal 'connection' with your prospect, the breakwater will do its job in modifying and reducing the extent of rough water that enters the harbour, and your strong 'connection' will hold the boat from breaking clear and floating free to be driven onto the rocks or, in the context of the sales, to be claimed by a competitor.

Establishing credibility and developing and maintaining a solid *professional relationship* was, you will recall, our stated second primary objective in the relationship element of the sales process. The tendency in most sales texts and with the majority of sales training is to refer to this establishment of credibility and professional relationship by using the word 'trust'. They talk about a prospect not buying unless 'trust' is in place. I feel that this isn't only an incorrect supposition—it's also possibly both misleading and dangerous. I believe that buyers don't necessarily need to really 'trust' the salespeople they deal with. I have come to this view for a number of reasons, one of which is that when this subject comes up and the question of 'trust' surfaces in sales training sessions, what follows is generally a very lively discussion. Some of the participants state categorically that as buyers they don't need, expect or look for trust in the buying–selling relationship. There is also a proportion who feel that trust *is* important. However, even they may have difficulty in reaching a consensus as to just *how* important trust is in the sales process.

Do you find this notion hard to believe? It's relatively easy to confirm— just ask a group of your colleagues or friends to explain what role trust plays in their own buying decision. You should find that some will say they need to feel that trust is in place before they buy, and that others won't be so sure. They will debate the meaning of 'trust', and then may or may not agree on its role in selling. Others will qualify their views, suggesting that trust *may* be important, depending on a number of conditions. However, a significant proportion just won't accept the premise that trust is an essential ingredient in the buying process for them.

The fact is that it appears that not all buyers are necessarily looking for trust. Some tell me they are *never* going to trust anything a salesperson says. Some buyers tell me they don't need it and are not looking for it, either consciously or subconsciously. In fact, by endeavouring to target this elusive 'trust' factor, salespeople often do considerable damage to the relationship.

What all buyers do seem to agree on when questioned is that they are looking for 'credibility'—the feeling that what you, the salesperson, say and do has some substance, that you yourself are of some substance, and that as an ethical professional salesperson you have the prospect's best interests in mind. Now, at the risk of confusing the issue, some buyers may eventually interpret this credibility in terms of the well-worn sales clichés of 'trust' and 'rapport'. They will even say to their peers, their family or their friends, when referring to a salesperson, something like, 'You should talk to Joe. You can trust him, I do!' And I'm sure they do. But equally importantly, some buyers will never use the word 'trust'. They might use words like 'competent', 'organised', 'knowledgeable', 'sincere', 'honest'. I, of course, cannot predict exactly what they might say, or how they might describe the salesperson. What I do know beyond any doubt is that some prospects simply don't or won't trust salespeople, so please cease to use trust as a prerequisite common denominator in the salesperson–prospect sales relationship.

Furthermore, as I mentioned above, I do know that while most customers agree they are not necessarily looking for trust in the relationship, they do all agree they are looking for credibility. All customers seem to agree that they need the salesperson to be credible. Is that putting words in their mouths? Perhaps it is. If it is, it certainly is unintentional. The fact is that trust, the old-fashioned byword of selling, doesn't cut it in this new millennium, and for that matter I doubt whether it ever did apply in the 1990s.

Foundations of the relationship element

What are the foundations, then, of the all-important relationship element in the complex sales process? I believe there are four major foundations on which your relationship should be founded.

Take a minute and quickly review the following four foundations that I believe you need to address in setting the scene for a well-crafted interpersonal and professional relationship with your prospect.

> Foundation no. 1   Building interpersonal and professional selling relationships involves recognising that your prospects are people, first and foremost.

Realise and accept that people have a natural tendency to operate from their own perspective. Realise and accept that all people operate from their own needs and wants, pursuing their own dreams.

> Foundation no. 2   Relationships are built on recognising that 'all people are motivated'. However, understand that they are motivated to do things for their particular reasons and not yours.

What this probably all boils down to is that whatever *you* think of trust and however you view the sales relationship is generally irrelevant. You need to uncover and tune into the prospect's motivators and find out how *they* wish to interpret the trust factor and how *they* want the relationship built.

> Foundation no. 3   Building a relationship requires that a 'connection' be made with your prospect. This invariably means that a number of major interpersonal issues must be addressed and a whole host of lesser, but nonetheless important, business issues factored in.

The major issue in building a strong relationship with your prospect is to establish and maintain what some refer to as 'rapport'. I prefer to refer to rapport as making a connection with the prospect, or simply 'connecting'. When it comes to those secondary issues, it's also important to be able to show empathy and clearly demonstrate that you view the selling process as a partnership.

The lesser but nonetheless critical inputs required to reinforce the relationship include simple, basic, normal behaviour, such as being considerate, courteous and thoughtful. Less obvious, but nonetheless still important, are such issues as demonstrating attention to detail and doing what you say you can and will do. Then there are the even more basic considerations, such as being on time, saying thank you, waiting until the prospect is ready, or waiting for the right time to do or ask for something, leaving some things that could easily be said but are best left unsaid, asking permission, spelling the prospect's name correctly and using their correct title. The list goes on. These small things often add up to a major impact, especially if you neglect them.

Foundation no. 4   Understand and appreciate that the relationship element is the very foundation of the sales process.

In fact, the relationship is the medium in which the other seven sales elements that directly require the prospect's input (needs, follow-up, barriers, positioning, closing, negotiation and ASS (After Sales Service)) are suspended.

If you go back to Chapter 11, where I first proposed the 'anatomy of a complex sale', comprising 10 separate sales elements arranged into five distinct phases, you will see what I mean. You'll see that the relationship element is indicated as a large shaded area in which these other seven key sales elements are floating. Think about it! Isn't your interpersonal and professional sales relationship intertwined with each of these other key sales elements? Wouldn't the type and quality of your relationship have a bearing on how you approached the other key sales elements with your prospect?

And isn't the reverse true? Don't each of these other elements affect the type and quality of the relationship to which they are inexorably linked? In fact, this key sales element, *relationship*, is inextricably linked to every element involved in the sales call.

In my view, the first place to start when it comes to sales consulting or sales training is to examine the relationship sales element in the context of the sales environment being considered. In particular, consider the relationship sales element in the context of both management's and the salesperson's perceptions of this key element. When you do so, investigate the relationship element by asking questions that help to clarify its place in the sales process, as well as the implementation and maintenance of this essential sales element.

Connecting with the prospect

Foundation no. 3 proposed the term 'connection'. What, then, is 'connecting' with the prospect and, perhaps more importantly, what exactly are the prerequisites?

The first prerequisite for connecting is to be interested in your prospects. They are people, after all, so there should be no shortage of material of interest. If you genuinely approach them with the objective of finding them interesting, you invariably will do just that. And in the process they will become interested in you, whether or not they overtly display this interest.

The second prerequisite for connecting is, if possible, to research your prospects. Learn something about them. Find out about their likes and dislikes, their interests, their hobbies, their successes, their fears. Learn what they think about certain subjects and the important issues of the day.

The third prerequisite is to approach connecting as a continuous process in which you represent no more than half of the latent potential. Understand that connecting isn't an event you participate in on your own—nor is it a result or a point in the process that you reach by yourself. Your connection with your prospect is a living, breathing interaction that is very dependent on both you and the prospect, and is in a constant state of flux.

Students of the 'trust' school of thought, however, talk about rapport, and discuss it as though it were a stage that should be attained, or at least attempted, just prior to qualifying and well before closing. These 'trust' pushers seem to view rapport as an event. It's spoken of in hushed tones, as something that should preferably be achieved by the salesperson and for the salesperson's advantage. Rapport is very much akin to the green lights in a motor race. Salespeople rev their engines and slip their clutches as they do what they have been told they must do prior to starting the race. They believe that rapport must be attempted and built and is represented by the lights turning from red to green, to signal the start of the great race. The objective of the race: being the first salesperson, to close on a 'Yes'. Next time you meet one of these true trust believers, ask them what they think rapport is and why they attempt to achieve it. You'll be amazed at the answers. In almost every case they will demonstrate that they are salesperson- and/or product-focused. They will talk about their product and about them doing something to the buyer. 'Partnership' and 'connection' with the prospect, and words of this ilk, will be conspicuous by their absence.

The fourth prerequisite is to understand that the true objective of connecting with the prospect is to use the connection to bridge to phase 2 of the sales process—identifying the prospect's needs. Without this connection, you have, in all probability, not earned the right to discuss your prospect's situation, wants or needs in any real detail. You haven't earned the right to ask the difficult questions; you don't have the necessary permits to allow you to dig for confidential, private and sometimes embarrassing information.

Without a strong connection to your prospect, you make it difficult to approach complex selling as a true partnership. Without it, you will be relegated to the ranks of the manipulator, the clever engineer, the user of tricky techniques and clever closes.

Five keys to connecting with your prospect

There are certainly far more than just five simple key statements or principles concerned with building and maintaining a strong, viable interpersonal and professional business connection with your prospect. You know many, if not most, of them from your own direct experiences and no doubt from the collective experiences of others who share their successes and perhaps even their failures with you.

However, it might be instructional to review the top five areas of focus that I see as the real keys to success in the critical process of establishing a connection with your prospect.

■ *Key no. 1—Tune out all external and internal interference.* This usually applies to everyone and everything except the person you are dealing with. Concentrate totally on the person in front of you. Understand that they are the most important person in your life at this particular minute.

■ *Key no. 2—Help the prospect to feel special.* Now, I didn't say *make* them feel special—I said *help* them to feel special. They generally know they are important, so *help* them feel special. Talk about the things that make them interesting, unique or special. They are, after all, unique, so it cannot be too hard to find out what makes them special.

■ *Key no. 3—Ask good questions.* Concentrate on designing and asking questions that show you have done your homework. Good questions are those that show you have a genuine desire to understand their situation. Good questions get them talking about themselves and their situation.

■ *Key no. 4—Reinforce your verbal interaction with non-verbal cues.* Use the appropriate body language to help open the door wide to good interpersonal communication. Don't underestimate the value, importance and critical role that non-verbal cues such as posture, expression, animation, eye contact and other such body language play in delivering your messages.

■ *Key no. 5—Find out how they feel and think.* Direct your questions towards uncovering how they think and feel about issues central to their lives and, in particular, to the sale. Remember, a partnership takes more than one person, so find out about your potential partners. They will in all likelihood tell you all you need to know, including how to influence them and how to position your selling proposal, if you establish, build and maintain a strong connection.

Opening the relationship

Be prepared to ask yourself a simple question at the beginning, before you embark on what you believe will be a fruitful sales journey for both you and the prospect. The question you need to ask yourself is, 'How do I really view the relationship element in the sales process?'

I hear answers that tend to fall into one of only two types. In one instance, I hear a response like 'I'm committed to understanding just where this prospect is coming from.' 'I'm committed to finding out more about this unique individual, what they think and how they feel about issues central to the sales process and exactly what it is they want and need.' On the other hand, I hear responses that tend to indicate a view that might be summarised as follows: 'I'm simply interested in establishing who I am, why I am here, what I know about their situation, and telling them what they want and need and how I can provide it!'

In the case of the first answer, the salesperson's total focus will be on the prospect. In the second, the salesperson's focus will be on—you guessed it—the salesperson. The lesson here is that you, as a salesperson, need to choose carefully where you shine your spotlight. Do you want to illuminate the prospect or yourself?

To take this line of thought a little further, it's not hard to imagine that the first viewpoint, that of a prospect focus, will almost automatically lead you to establishing and building a strong relationship and identifying the prospect's needs and what I call 'positioning' your unique feature benefit ideas.

I find from my own observations in the field that the second viewpoint above invariably leads to your establishing little or no meaningful connection with the prospect and inevitably leads to what I call 'product dump', where the salesperson assumes the prospect's needs and does little but dump copious features and advantages on the prospect.

The two very different types of responses above represent two different roads available for you to travel. The first road represents a value-based approach to selling, and requires the salesperson to invest substantial time, effort and personal control in the opening stages of the relationship and subsequently throughout the sale as the process unfolds. The other road is based on the traditional sales model, and acknowledges the prospect as part of an audience which the salesperson is committed to telling, persuading, cajoling and lecturing as to why they should do what the salesperson thinks is important.

As a salesperson, it's your choice. Think carefully about it. While not impossible, it's difficult to reverse course once you have embarked on the traditional 'tell' mode of selling. Be very aware of your opening signals to your prospect about how you intend to conduct your sales approach.

More on product dumping

Before we embark on investigating—one suggested structure for the opening to the relationship element itself—it's worthwhile to spend a little time outlining why, in my view, so many salespeople seem to become derailed or disoriented during the opening phase of this relationship element; why it is they revert to taking the line of least resistance (or is it the line of least persistence?) and consequently revert to dumping product on their prospect.

First and foremost among the reasons why salespeople seem to revert to product-dump mode is that they appear to prefer to stay in their comfort zone, where they feel secure and where their actions are usually based on a host of previous experiences—where the outcomes are generally known and, to some extent, are predictable. They believe there is far less risk in sticking unerringly with product. For example, by pushing product at every opportunity, they may believe that any rejection of the product isn't a rejection of them personally. On the other hand, opening and building relationships, exploring needs and positioning, can all be viewed as high-risk, unpredictable person-to-person activities, where the product cannot be used as a shield or an excuse. Here the risk is perceived as high that the failure to sell will be taken as a personal and professional failing.

Second, old habits are hard to break. The salesperson undoubtedly formed the view at some early stage in their career, either directly or by observing other role models, that product dump is a good method to stimulate and surface product-based needs, at the same time as bypassing objections. I believe the opposite is almost certainly true. My observations tend to indicate that product dumping generally bypasses identifying needs altogether; in fact, it contributes to stimulating and surfacing objections. However, once you do decide to change your modus operandi, once you experience the world of selling as 'product dump'-free, you will understand and appreciate just how much it has been holding you back in your professional sales career.

The third reason why salespeople consistently product dump is that often in the initial stages of the sales process the buyer demands, insists, invites or cajoles the salesperson to 'cut to the chase', 'get to the point', 'give me a solution', or 'tell me about your product'. Salespeople must resist the temptation to accommodate these requests, to tell their sales story there and then. This situation is generally more the result of a poor opening to the relationship sales element or of a less than competent execution of bridging to the next phase, identifying needs, than it is a real challenge from the prospect for you to talk about the product right now. The real danger in reverting to product too early is that you leave the opening phase of the relationship element far too early; also, you might be persuaded to skip the needs sales element almost entirely by acceding to your prospect's invitation to talk product. In my experience, the prospect's invitation to put your product on the table *now* is often a challenge, whereby the prospect is gearing up to bounce your product solution right back at you in the form of objections. With this in mind, I urge you to resist at all costs the temptation to allow the prospect to control the sales process. If not resisted, the sales process will spiral out of control and only end up in grief for you and confirmation in the prospect's mind that they were 'right all along' and you were 'wasting their time'.

Fourth, product dumping often results from those direct, confrontational, conflict-laced or emotionally charged sales situations that cause you to lose your way—to lose focus and then lose control. The attractive remedy, from your point of view, to these 'out of control situations' is to dump it all on the table as quickly as you can, answer any questions, then get the hell out of there, with an order if you possibly can. Here the urge to product dump is often overwhelming. You come prepared with a good plan, clear objectives and a definite conviction not to product dump, but circumstances seemingly beyond your control contrive and conspire to completely derail your planned approach.

We've all been in these difficult situations. Say you have been in the prospect's office 10 seconds and you hear the words, 'I'm in a hurry. I've got another meeting to get to, so tell me quickly what you've got for me today'. Or worse: 'You're the third salesperson I've had in here this morning. What makes you think that what you've got is any better than the first two?' My advice is to take a deep breath, pause, then stick to your game plan. Resist the urge to dump and run, which we know may feel good in the short term but is likely to do you major harm in the long term.

The fifth, and probably the second most often observed, reason why salespeople abandon working proactively on opening the relationship and revert to product dumping is because they believe they already know their prospect's situation and, hence, their needs. They cannot resist the temptation to lecture the buyer on their needs, and pontificate at length on how they can solve the prospect's problems. This is often displayed as an attitude of superiority, where salespeople respond to what they believe is an opportunity or invitation to tell all they know. This patronising attitude of 'I know what you need' is prompted by many causes. I have listed some of these causes below. See if you can identify some of the generators of the 'I know exactly what you need' syndrome that lead inevitably to premature product focus and, ultimately, product dumping.

What causes salespeople to think they know the prospect's situation better than the prospect does?

- *Cause no. 1—Salesperson's experience in the industry*. After so much experience in selling the particular product, you think you've 'seen it all', 'heard it all' and, probably worse still, 'know it all'—so why not, you think, share it with your prospect at the first available opportunity? Why not use product dumping as a convenient vehicle for confirming your expertise?
- *Cause no. 2—Cursory investigation of the prospect's situation*. You

spend just sufficient time collecting what you believe is sufficient, but is in reality often only cursory, information, to pigeonhole this particular prospect. Once that's done, all that is required is to go to the relevant box in your prepackaged menu of solutions and deliver the product answers in the form of product dump.

■ *Cause no. 3—A third party* told you what was needed and you took it on face value, or at least let it dictate the bulk of your sales strategy and actions.

■ *Cause no. 4—A raft of predetermined, planned questions* are floated to the prospect, and based on their responses you feel you know exactly what the prospect needs. What about unplanned questions, questions that are spontaneous and pop up in the course of the developing relationship?

If you adhere rigidly to your predetermined questioning agenda, apart from probably damaging any real relationship-building potential by appearing cold, blunt, self-centred, direct and inflexible, you will miss opportunities to gain valuable insight into how your prospect really thinks and feels. You will get only a small part of the story. So learn the art of going with the flow. See where your intuition, your natural curiosity, leads you. You can always go back to your script later when you have exhausted all the potential detours.

■ *Cause no. 5—Prior knowledge* of your prospect's organisation—among other things, their organisation's operations, plans, structures and current business practices and objectives—can lead you to believe you know exactly what is best for your prospect, in the context of their organisation's needs. In which case you might be tempted to believe the prospect is irrelevant and the organisation is omnipotent. Come on! The organisation is made up of people. People like your prospect. So don't sidestep the people in favour of the organisation.

■ *Cause no. 6—Non-specific needs and wants were mentioned.* Here the prospect mentions needs in a vague way or in no specific context and you immediately jump in, accepting and interpreting those needs as the prospect's real dominant needs and wants and unloading your impressive array of product knowledge on the unsuspecting prospect. The prospect says something like, 'We need a faster machine.' You can't believe your ears. This phase 2 stuff about identifying needs is easy! They actually tell you what their needs are with very little prompting. What a snack! You jump right in and respond with, 'Well, let me tell you about our copy speed. This machine . . .' and so you drone on.

Metaphorically speaking, you missed an important turn in the road somewhere and you find yourself happily hurtling down highway number one with cruise control on. At some stage you look back and find you have lost your prospect and are alone. You find out later that your prospect turned left at the last major crossroads and is on his way down highway number two, slowly coasting along, looking around for another salesperson to help solve his problem. You see, when he said 'faster', he was really talking about the time it takes for the machine to warm up before it's ready to take the first copy. The copy speed itself was, as it turns out, more than adequate.

'Dumb prospect', you think, when you eventually catch up with him somewhere way down highway number two. 'He really should have been clearer in what he was trying to say. After all, it really was the prospect's fault. Wasn't it?'

chapter 15

Needs

Your prospect's 'needs', one of the 10 key elements in the sales process, have two distinct sides to them, a bit like a coin.

Side one of the needs element revolves around the more widely understood phase 2 of the sales process of exploring and uncovering what I have called 'identifying needs', where the primary objective is to explore and uncover—that is, identify—the prospect's specific needs. This usually involves the following sales activities, although not in any specific or required order:

- questioning;
- listening;
- surfacing and dealing with perceptions;
- uncovering/developing the today state;
- formulating the tomorrow state;
- testing—getting feedback;
- determining the specific needs;
- establishing credibility;
- testing—perceptions/assumptions/understandings; and
- obtaining clearance to proceed to the next phase, 'meeting needs'.

The other side of the needs coin is more concerned with what you, the salesperson, and the prospect do with these needs, once uncovered. Here you might undertake the following sales activities, again in no particular or predetermined order:

- testing—assumptions/alternatives;
- introducing ideas;
- floating options;
- building and positioning your selling ideas;
- testing—needs; and
- recommending/suggesting/influencing.

This second side of the needs coin, while not strictly related to determining the prospect's needs, is the critical second part related to needs. While I said earlier that the first side of *needs* is all about *identifying* the prospect's needs, this second side is all about *meeting* the prospect's needs. It involves *positioning* your product in response to the prospect's needs.

It appears to me that most salespeople appreciate side one of the needs coin as a valuable, if not an essential, element and are prepared to accept this as the one and only *needs* element of selling. Few, it seems, recognise the importance of the second side of the needs coin. Few see the requirement to *position* product as a means of meeting needs identified in the previous phase.

Now, these two sides of the prospect's needs may be dealt with in the one sales call, and this is what can happen in less complex simple sales situations. The need can be relatively obvious. The prospect knows what the problem is, because it's relatively straightforward, *and* they know what they need to solve the problem. In other words, they are abundantly clear about their today state. For example, the print department is about to run out of a special report paper. They know all about what is needed—the tomorrow state. Based on previous usage, they know they need to place an order for a specific type of paper and how and when it is to be delivered. Consequently, both side one (identifying the need) and side two (meeting the need) can be accomplished in the same call.

But, as most salespeople involved in more complex sales are aware, both sides of the needs coin can involve a series of sales calls and sometimes many, many meetings over a long period of time, involving various levels and functions within the buying and selling organisations.

The golden rule to bear in mind when investigating your prospect's real needs is simply this: **if first you can accurately *identify* their real need, you can then usually provide a product to *meet* it!**

Needs hierarchy

Let's put things in perspective. All this talk about the prospect's today state (their current reality) and their tomorrow state (their results needed) can be a little confusing, especially if you have tended to operate from the traditional selling model, where every opportunity is engineered to tell, rather than ask, your prospect about your product. In this traditional sales model, you listen to your prospect only long enough either to find or manufacture an opportunity to dump product on them and then continue to alternate between dumping product and closing the prospect.

However, when it comes to being both prospect- and process-focused and working at the selling process by seeking to provide value, the prospect's needs look something like Figure 15.1. Let's call it the *needs pathway*.

Figure 15.1 *Needs pathway*

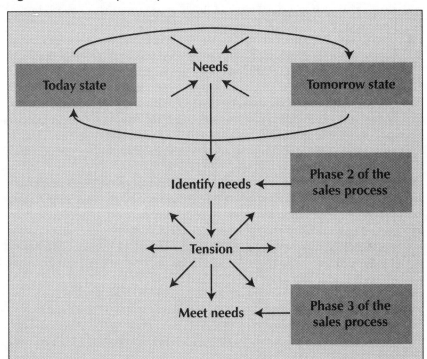

I suggested that if you can identify the needs, you will find that you are generally in a position to provide a product that will meet them. But let's be absolutely clear: you must identify them with the prospect first.

To identify and meet your prospect's real needs means that you must approach your prospect as a unique person. In doing so, you will be able to develop a real advantage over your competitors. This competitive advantage often boils down to simply how much more you understand about your prospect and their real situation.

Interestingly, by first focusing on identifying your prospect's real needs prior to any attempt at 'meeting' those needs a number of very real benefits accrue *to you, the salesperson*. They include the following.

Benefits of first focusing on identifying needs with the prospect

■ *Benefit no. 1*—Once identified, needs help you to convert your tendency to engage in generic product monologues (the ones you have been using to tell or convince prospects to agree with your proposition) into relevant, interesting, need-specific dialogues (stories constructed around benefits) that make eminently more sense to your prospect in what they usually see as their unique situation. We are going to call these stories constructed around benefits (or, as we referred to them earlier, feature benefit ideas) 'compelling sales stories'. But more on that later.

■ *Benefit no. 2*—Working on identifying needs helps you to hold back from dumping generic product information—that general 'how you can use this' type of information (i.e. advantages) that you might have a tendency to give at every presentation and which often means little to the prospect and their real situation. While salespeople are actively engaged in questioning, listening and testing, they come to appreciate that the buyer is indeed unique, which tends then to assist them in avoiding the folly of jumping to conclusions and telling, rather than selling, the prospect.

■ *Benefit no. 3*—In the process of exploring the needs sales element with your prospect and thereby working towards clearly identifying their needs, you can uncover the prospect's prejudices, perceptions and potential barriers to the sale, as well as become aware of hidden opportunities. When you engage in a dialogue and display a sincere interest in your prospect and their situation, you will be amazed at what they will tell you, if you just take the time to ask.

■ *Benefit no. 4*—A direct spin-off from sensitively and skilfully exploring the prospect's needs with them is that you will almost certainly get your prospect to 'buy in' to the process. Having done this, they will accept that they are an integral part of the sales process, rather than just an innocent bystander. As a result, they will appreciate that they are very much participants in the exercise to identify exactly what their today and tomorrow states are; as a consequence, the resulting gap (the prospect's specific needs) is honestly discussed and clearly recognised. They feel ownership of the process and the outcomes. It then becomes unlikely that the prospect will object to your product as positioned in the form of your compelling sales story, as they had a hand themselves in authoring these stories. They own them. They have even been known to consider the compelling sales story as being composed of their very own ideas and to work at defending them and convincing the salesperson and others in their own organisation of what has to be done.

How to identify needs

Some things in life are actually much more difficult in practice than they are in theory. Happily, identifying needs isn't generally one of these things. All it takes is for you first to adopt a sincere, personal interest in your prospect, and in the process explore with them, their organisation, their dreams, aspirations, current situation and desired outcomes, their barriers and opportunities. In other words, ask simple, concise and relevant questions, and adopt a genuine desire to learn about your prospect. And the good news is that you can undertake beforehand a relatively simple and painless investigation and prepare a number of these questions in advance.

The style, extent and form of the questions you ask are almost unlimited. This might grow out of a desire to find out answers to the following questions:

- What is the prospect's situation?
- What is the prospect's perspective of the situation?
- What is the prospect doing now? Why?
- What does the prospect want to do that they aren't doing now? Why?
- What are the prospect's perceived or stated wants and needs? What are their unstated or unrecognised needs?
- What barriers does the prospect face and what is their priority for each?
- Where do these barriers have their biggest impact?
- What are the prospect's buying criteria?
- What does the prospect like and dislike about . . .?
- What has the prospect already said 'No' or 'Yes' to?
- What is the prospect's decision-making process?
- Who are the competitors? What are your comparative strengths and weaknesses? (Where do I rank?)
- What are the prospect's specific timeframes/schedules?
- What would an ideal outcome contain?
- What can I present to build my credibility? What preliminary ideas do I have? What are the prospect's reactions likely to be?

By asking yourself these 'what questions', you can begin to design specific questions intended to provide you with a good sense of the prospect's current situation or today state, preferred or ideal future outcomes or tomorrow state, what some possible barriers and alternatives might be, and where you stand in the prospect's thinking.

Needs and the Nobel Prize

In 1953, it is said, Francis Crick burst through the doorway of the Eagle pub in Cambridge, England, and announced to those assembled at the bar that he and his colleague, James Watson, had 'found the secret of life'.

The secret he referred to was the shape of the now famous molecule called deoxyribonucleic acid, better known as DNA, which contains the entire genetic code that is inherited from one's parents. Watson and Crick had uncovered the double-helix (or twisted staircase, as it's sometimes called) form of the building blocks of life. For their work along with Maurice Wilkins, they received the Nobel Prize for medicine in 1962.

Why do I mention this fact? Because our sales element needs has much in common with DNA. In fact, we can use DNA as both an analogy and an acronym. An analogy because, like DNA, needs are also the most basic recognisable and individually distinguishable building blocks of a larger and more complex entity—in our case, the sales process. One applies to our inherited human characteristics, the other to our prospect's inherited needs characteristics. I say 'inherited' because, inevitably, the needs themselves arose or were inherited from past circumstances or actions.

In reality, they may be literally worlds apart, but if you take a minute to consider the significance of each, you will, I believe, come to the conclusion that they are each the basic building blocks on which a much bigger and more complex form is developed. Our human DNA makes up our genes, which in turn determine our human characteristics, and how we react and respond as we journey through our ageing process. On the other hand, our prospect's needs make up their true buying motivation, which in turn determines the required product characteristics and how our prospects might react and respond as they journey through the sales process.

I have spoken several times about the danger of not thoroughly exploring the prospect's needs and, as a result, of proceeding to 'sell' the customer on an incorrect 'assumed' need. I have also referred to these incorrect needs by such terms as 'non-specific' or 'general' needs.

You may recall that I gave an example of a hypothetical situation in Part 1, where a prospect requested a 'faster printer'. The salesperson took this to literally mean the prospect 'needed' a printer that produced more prints or pages per minute than their current one. In other words, the salesperson assumed, presumably because they saw no need to adequately explore and thereby correctly identify the prospect's needs, that the need for 'speed' was the real or specific defining need that would motivate the prospect in their buying process. However, what our salesperson subsequently found was that the prospect was in fact referring to the time it took for the printer to warm up and go through its internal self-checking modes. What they were referring to was really the time it took from sending a print instruction to the printer from their PC, to the printer being able to drop the finished article in the output paper tray.

Now, another prospect, stating the same need (i.e. a need for a 'faster' printer) might be delighted with this self-same printer. Why? Because they send instructions to the printer from the PC that contain hundreds of pages at a time. The warm-up period is then inconsequential. This other prospect is, like our intrepid but easily misled salesperson, concerned primarily with how long it will take to print a batch of 100 or so pages—not with the time taken to print one high-quality colour print a couple of times a day. What's more, because of its continued use, the printer rarely switches back to standby mode and thus the warm-up period is never an issue with this other prospect.

So what has all this to do with DNA?

First, as I suggested earlier, one side of the true needs element of the sales process involves 'identifying' the prospect's specific needs. Once identified, these needs, like the real DNA, are basic building blocks of a much larger and more complex thing. In the case of the real DNA they were, you will recall, the codes that largely determined the form of the human being containing these inherited characteristics.

Using our analogy, our needs, similar to the real DNA, were the basic building blocks of the complex sale. These needs also could be said to contain the codes that determine not the human form but the true buying motivation, and hence they will determine to a great extent the form of the salesperson's response to the sales process when dealing with these needs.

However, this is only the case when the needs, which the salesperson has translated from the dialogue with the prospect, are indeed their real or specific needs. Assumed or incorrect needs aren't the true DNA of the sales process. Assumed, non-specific needs are capable of derailing the sales process.

I suggest that, in order to highlight the critical objective of correctly reading the prospect's messages during the second phase of the sales process, we use the acronym DNA. This will serve to remind us first just how critical this phase is in determining the final outcome of the sales process.

Second, as an acronym, DNA as it applies to complex sales will now stand for *dominant needs analysis*. This describes in 'doing' language the major objective of this phase 2 of the sales process—that is, to analyse the prospect's current situation, their today state and their results needed, their tomorrow state, and to determine their 'dominant needs'. Their dominant needs, of course, are the expression we will now adopt to describe those 'specific' or 'real' needs I have often referred to, as distinct from the assumed or non-specific needs.

You as a professional salesperson need to analyse your prospects using a tailored DNA strategy and determine their dominant needs. Only when these dominant needs have been clearly identified by you and by your prospect, and are therefore understood and accepted, are you free to move on to the next phase, 'meeting needs'. Only when the dominant needs have been identified can you help your prospect move down your sales pipeline to the next phase in the journey to the outfall.

A final word on needs

While the sales process element 'needs' is the subject of this chapter, I recommend that you again review a number of chapters in Part 1. The needs element has been discussed in some detail earlier in those chapters dealing indirectly with needs, such as how buyers buy, features, advantages and benefits, and the philosophy of value-based selling as it differs from the more common traditional models that are salesperson- and product-focused. Why? Because these chapters have a great deal to say about the needs element, either directly or indirectly, in the context of the overall philosophy and approach required for value-based selling and a host of other considerations essential to understanding the relevance and importance of dominant needs.

When you move on to Part 3, and particularly the chapters dealing with questioning, you will again be addressing this critical sales element of needs. Only this time, you will consider the needs element from a sales skill viewpoint rather than discussing what it represents as a critical element in the sales process.

As a keen observer and researcher of sales behaviour, the interesting thing to me is that most salespeople acknowledge the important part played by the prospect's needs in the sales process. This is evidenced by a relatively simple exercise, where one can ask a group of experienced salespeople to come up with a simple, concise definition of 'selling'. Most salespeople will feature the word 'needs' or some derivative of it in their definition. What appears perverse is that in actual everyday selling situations, often lip service only is paid to needs, and many salespeople revert to their habitual pattern of 'product-dump mode'. The observable indications that support this view are simply that the second critical phase of the sales process, 'identifying needs', ceases to be fully explored or indeed explored *with* the prospect prior to attempts by salespeople to meet those needs—needs that, as a result, are not the prospect's dominant needs but are shallower, non-specific, assumed needs.

In other words, there appears to me to be a fairly large divergence between what salespeople know should be done when it comes to dealing with the needs element and what they actually do when engaged in sales calls.

chapter 16

Positioning—winning the challenge for their hearts and minds

We discussed in Chapter 15 the importance of needs, and suggested that needs had two *parts* or *sides*—in fact, we referred to needs as consisting of two sides of the same coin. Side one of the needs coin was the exploring and uncovering of needs, or what I referred to as the *identification of needs* phase of the sale. Side two, related to *meeting those needs* by positioning your product to effectively address those needs.

In order to successfully undertake phase 3 meeting needs, of the anatomy of a sale model, you need to position yourself, your organisation and your product as being totally aligned with these needs. This in turn suggests that you must have a very clear picture of your prospect's real needs in the first instance. And so must your prospect. Further, these respective pictures must match, or 'align', to use the term introduced earlier.

So you can see that I propose that positioning, while a separate and quite distinct element in the sales process, is inextricably linked to the needs element of the sales process. To put it perhaps more succinctly, I propose that you cannot effectively position your product without first thoroughly identifying those needs. Why? Because without clearly identified needs with which to link your selling propositions to the prospect's perceptions of their today and tomorrow states, you aren't selling, you are telling.

Now, before we go any further, it's important to appreciate that when you position your product with your prospect you aren't really doing something with the product. What you are in fact doing is working with the prospect to create selling ideas or propositions that will address their needs. In so doing, you are appealing to the heart and mind of your prospect. So when it comes to positioning, you must understand that, rather than doing something with the product, you are doing something with the prospect. You look for these ideas and propositions not inside the product, not even inside your own mind. You must look inside the prospect's mind if you are to work with them to effectively create these selling ideas and positions. You must, in other words, concentrate on the perceptions of your prospect and *not* on the reality of the product itself.

Positioning is *not* about presenting physical products or about ready-made sales solutions to a prospect's problems or, worse, to the salesperson's problems.

In a nutshell, we might simply describe or define positioning in terms of creating an outcome where the product will occupy a space or window in the prospect's thinking. Obviously a positive one at that. So what is positioning?

> Positioning = An organised and systematic strategy for working with the prospect to place the product in a positive window in the prospect's mind.

And the compelling sales story is the ladder used to climb up to this window in the prospect's mind. The compelling sales story is nothing more complicated than the delivery vehicle, made up of steps or rungs that allow you to position your product. And the various steps or rungs are the chapter of your story, each focused on a specific feature benefit idea which is created by both of you and accepted by the prospect.

Features and benefits revisited

This subject just had to come up again because features and benefits are your stock in trade. They are the means of avoiding giving a boring generic sales 'presentation' to your prospect and instead pursuing a sales 'positioning' strategy in partnership with your prospect.

I don't intend to duplicate those issues raised earlier in Part 1 when I took some time to explain features, advantages and benefits. So now might be a good time for you to turn to Chapters 9 and 10 and to quickly review those sections.

Given what we understand about this animal called 'advantages', it's extremely unlikely that they will play any direct part in the sales process as we address the positioning element. When it comes to the positioning element of the sales process, we are really interested only in features and benefits. To summarise what we have discovered so far about features and benefits, let's review two important discoveries we made earlier relating to a fundamentally necessary view of features and benefits.

■ *Discovery no. 1—Features are what the salesperson's organisation **puts into** the product.* They tend to be the characteristics of the product and can be used to differentiate your product from other similar competing products.

■ *Discovery no. 2—Benefits are what the prospect will **get out** of the product.* They can't exist without a prospect and they respond to the prospect's dominant needs.

With features and benefits in mind, I suggested that what each actually achieves in the sales process is as follows.

Features	= *Provide the credibility to reinforce what you say about a particular product.*
	= *Provide the cold, hard, indisputable facts that support the selling propositions and ideas, in the form of feature benefit ideas, that combine to create the compelling sales story.*

On the other hand . . .

Benefits	= *Provide the saleability and desirability and, most of all, confirm the suitability of the product.*
	= *Provide the translation in the communication process and make the story a 'good fit' for the prospect's perspective of the situation.*

And positioning?

Positioning	= *Actually provides the momentum that moves the sales process forward.*
	= *Creates a unique, compelling sales story, in the form of a storyline centred around the prospect's perceptions and made up of feature benefit ideas by addressing the prospect's identified dominant needs and appealing to the reasoning and emotion inherent in the prospect's buying process when meeting those needs.*

Positioning, then, is the sales element that allows you to work with your prospect to create a compelling sales story. Positioning is the primary sales element that responds to Phase 3, 'meeting needs of the sales process'.

Keys to positioning

With this notion of positioning in mind, it would be timely to discuss what I see as the five keys to effectively positioning your product, yourself and your organisation:

■ *Positioning key no. 1*—You must first adequately explore, with the prospect, the implications of the prospect's today and tomorrow states and their perception of the tension created by the gap between the two.
■ *Positioning key no. 2*—You must have a clear idea of the prospect's dominant needs as they develop from no. 1 above, and these needs must be accepted and shared by the prospect. That is, these dominant needs must align with the prospect's version of reality.
■ *Positioning key no. 3*—You must be able to strategically marshal feature benefit ideas to directly address those needs in the form of various parts or chapters of your compelling sales story.
■ *Positioning key no. 4*—Be prepared to hold back on delivering your feature benefit ideas long enough so that you can position them effectively in the form of a gradually unfolding compelling sales story.
■ *Positioning key no. 5*—Test your strategy by creating your compelling sales story a chapter at a time and factor in the prospect's feedback. Be prepared to rework your story if required.

Why position?

By effectively positioning your product, organisation and yourself in a positive window of your prospect's mind, you will find that there are a number of clear positives that arise that simply aren't apparent with the more traditional presenting approach to *telling your sales story*. They include:

■ *Positioning positive no. 1*—The prospect can directly translate the various feature benefit ideas into outcomes they can visualise, understand, want and feel they need and simply *must* have.
■ *Positioning positive no. 2*—Positioning gives the salesperson the opportunity to reshape and tailor their product knowledge, thereby encouraging them to discover and propose new benefits after talking to the prospect. Positioning allows the salesperson to selectively mould the product features in such a way that the product can be viewed as a direct response to a prospect's identified dominant needs.
■ *Positioning positive no. 3*—The potential for barriers to the sale emerging at the last minute will be reduced simply because you have created a compelling sales story, told from the prospect's point of view by taking the time to involve the prospect in the process. The simple fact is that as the complexity of the sales process increases, the

prospect has a tendency to resist 'solutions' that are presented too soon by a salesperson, and to resist stories told without their input.

Some words of wisdom on positioning

When it comes time to position your product in the heart and mind of your prospect, bear in mind the following:

■ Don't present any feature benefit ideas without having the necessary background information and reasoning to support them if and when required.
■ Don't attempt to position without first doing your homework and then checking your conclusions, assumptions, and even what you believe to be the facts, with your prospect.
■ Prioritise your feature benefit ideas based on your prospect knowledge and then combine these ideas in a variety of forms in order to author with the prospect the various chapters of your compelling sales story.
■ Don't be fixed on one best way or idea—stay flexible. Keep your eyes and ears open. Be prepared to revise, refine and rewrite various chapters of your story as you and the prospect work to create it.
■ Be confident and committed to your compelling sales story and tie the underpinning feature benefit ideas back to the clearly 'identified' and accepted dominant needs of the prospect.

Competitors

This chapter on positioning wouldn't be complete without focusing briefly on the touchy subject of competitors. We know that intelligence on your competitors is important. While it shouldn't dictate your whole sales strategy, it most certainly should be an issue you address with your prospect and factor into your positioning strategies.

You will recall that in Part 1 we discussed how prospects buy and I suggested a model of the buying process when considering this process from their perspective. You will recall that the vast majority of salespeople rarely consider the sales process from the prospect's perspective. Consider for a moment the key intervention points in phase 2, the evaluation process of the prospect's buying process outlined earlier. Here the prospect is evaluating you, your organisation and your product, and will in all likelihood consider their other options at this point. So, in this evaluation phase of buying, it's critical that you are aware of the other realistic options or alternatives available to your prospect out there in the marketplace and respond accordingly.

Some commonsense tactics to considering competitors are highlighted over the page:

> *Competitor tactic no. 1   Ask questions.*

Some examples of relevant questions designed to help you might include:

- 'Who else are you talking to about . . .?'
- 'What do you like/dislike about other . . .?'
- 'Why did you select them?'
- 'Where in the sales process are you at with these other vendors?'
- 'What conclusion have you reached with . . .?'

But be careful. Ask these types of questions *without increasing your competitors' status or stature and without damaging yours.*

> *Competitor tactic no. 2   Use competitive information to position against competitors.*

However, don't ever appear to denigrate them or their product. To do so is considered unprofessional and it could seriously damage your efforts to build a relationship with your prospect—especially if the competitor on whom you are commenting unfavourably enjoys an equal or better relationship with the prospect than you do.

> *Competitor tactic no. 3   Create opportunities to have your prospect rather than you make comparisons.*

You can achieve this by:

- knowing your competitors and their products;
- testing/checking your assumptions and knowledge about your competitor's offerings; and
- using questions with your prospect that indirectly address your competitor's known weaknesses.

> *Competitor tactic no. 4   Clearly position yourself, your organisation and your product as unique.*

Create a compelling sales story that sheds a distinctly different light on your prospect from your competitor's offering. Use positioning ideas such as: 'Unlike other . . ., the approach we have taken is . . .', or 'In our user surveys, we have found that most users of . . . would prefer to . . . rather than . . .'

Paint mental pictures

There is an old saying that suggests you should 'sell the sizzle, not the steak!'. Positioning involves building a compelling sales story, using your feature benefit ideas, which after all are nothing more than a collection of propositions in the form of strategic questions and/or statements. And remember, a story is nothing more than a comprehensive and ordered series of mental pictures and emotions created by these strategic questions and statements. This story creation approach is a useful method of viewing the positioning sales element as a means of presenting the sales interaction as being far less cold and detached for the prospect.

Some simple examples of language that might be appropriate in helping you to paint mental pictures for your prospect as you develop your feature benefit ideas are set out below. There are literally thousands more you could use.

Paint mental pictures

Old idea	New mental pictures and emotions
Pay	Invest, investment contribution
Deal	Opportunity for substantial savings, preview sale, spectacular offer
Sign	Agree/confirm/authorise/OK
Buy	Own, enjoy, take delivery, use
Negotiate	Agree, discuss, finalise
Enjoyable	Pure delight, sensational, fun, fantastic
Exciting	Astonishing, fascinating, sensational, sizzling, unbelievable
Simple	Foolproof, automatic, effortless, instant
Tested	Craftsmanship, certified, endorsed, proven
Guarantee	Trusted, assured, satisfaction, protection
Special	Unique, one of a kind, labour of love, incomparable
Improved	Refined, better than ever, reworked
Data	Insights, hard facts, foundational elements
Money	Opportunities, profits, fortune
Savings	Bargains, cut costs, rock-bottom prices
New	Advanced, latest technology, pioneering, future-oriented

How to do it

We have talked in general terms about positioning—what it is and isn't, why we do it, and what it achieves. Now might be a good time to talk about some of those more important positive actions you should consider when you are positioning your product, your organisation and yourself in the heart and mind of the prospect. Let's look briefly at the 10 major must-dos to position effectively.

1. *Look at the prospect.* Look at them when you speak. Demonstrate that you are interested in them and their situation.
2. *Get the prospect involved.* Ask them questions, get them to touch, handle or use the product. Actively work to involve them in the process.
3. *Appeal to their logic and emotions.* Don't completely found your story in one or the other, logic or emotion. Structure your story, and the component feature benefit ideas so that each is appealed to. Don't, for instance, assume that, as the prospect prefers a logical, structured approach to the sales process, they have no place for emotion.
4. *Control the demonstration/environment.* In inviting the prospect to view or use the product, or in setting the scene for your story, don't hesitate to control what is to happen. If necessary or appropriate, ask permission. Don't hand over control as you hand over the product or feature benefit ideas.
5. *Talk only about benefits that address the prospect's 'dominant needs'.* Be specific. Address the prospect's dominant needs. Don't ramble, waffle or lapse into stories that don't centre on your prospect.
6. *Pay attention to body language and personal space.* Tell your story with your audience in mind. In telling the story, don't lose track of the non-verbal feedback from your prospect or ignore their preferred method of participating in the process.
7. *Get them to visualise or experience the benefits/results:* Use a variety of initiatives, such as words/actions, success stories and questions to help the prospect to 'feel' the benefits embodied in your feature benefit ideas. Mix up your delivery to accommodate their preferred approach.
8. *Be enthusiastic.* Give the prospect the clear message that you believe in what you have to offer. Sometimes enthusiasm alone can separate you from your competitors.
9. *Don't overdo it—KISS (Keep it Simple Silly).* Know when to stop talking and start listening. Keep your message simple and deliver it in bite-size chunks, waiting for the prospect to digest the previous bite before proceeding.
10. *Do what it takes to facilitate their decision to buy.* Find out how the prospect buys and write your story in that form. Remove the road-blocks with them as your story unfolds.

Finally, a word on how to act as you position. Remember, the objective of positioning is to make an impact on the heart and mind of your prospect. To do this, wherever possible let the prospect visualise or feel the positive outcomes associated with their vision of their potential tomorrow state.

There are many ways to do this, but a basic rule is that, when you are discussing a feature of the product, *look at and even point to that feature*. Consider encouraging the prospect to touch or feel the feature and even to use the product as a means of demonstrating that feature. However, when you are talking about and positioning the various feature benefit ideas with the prospect, *look directly at them*.

Motivation

In Part 1 of this book, I said a little about motivation and the role it plays in causing prospects to move into action and make a positive buying decision. The feature benefit ideas that form the basis for each chapter of the compelling sales story are the means by which the prospect is motivated to act. In fact, I suggested earlier in my definition that positioning provides the momentum that keeps the sale moving forward.

These feature benefit ideas, as outlined earlier, are built from analysing the dominant needs of the prospect using questions, statements and ideas to promote the benefits of your product, organisation and yourself. The benefits are targeted at your prospect's identified dominant needs. While these needs are viewed as unique to your prospect, it would be helpful perhaps if we could group needs into what might loosely be called collectively various 'selling points'.

The list of potential buying motivators or 'selling points' is almost endless, and even seasoned professional salespeople are occasionally surprised when they come across a new interpretation or slant on an old motivation. Perhaps these selling points are close to those initial 'wants' or non-specific needs often expressed by your prospect.

Take a minute to look through the collection of potential selling points I have listed on the following page. As broad categories, have they applied to some of your buyers' expressed wants? Have they applied to you in the past in your role as a buyer?

Some of them will look strange, even nonsensical or illogical. Remember, the list doesn't have to make sense to *you*. It only needs to appear logical to the prospect. Just because one or a number of them are unlikely to motivate you to action doesn't mean they aren't therefore legitimate motivators in the mind of the prospect. And anyway, what does logic have to do with some buying decisions? But it is your role and responsibility as a salesperson to get behind these broad potential selling points or potential wants of the prospect and find out exactly how each can be distilled into a clearly identifiable dominant need.

The basis of all dominant needs

Potential selling points

- Tested
- Rarity
- Reliability
- Safety
- Pleasure
- Luxury
- Leadership
- Convenience
- Strength
- Silent operation
- Stability
- Workmanship
- Sanitary or cleanliness
- Self-esteem
- Speed
- Effectiveness
- Consistency
- Individualism
- Fashion
- Popularity

- Parental instinct
- Tendency to 'go along'
- Ease of operation
- Appearance
- Profit
- Performance
- Efficiency
- Durability
- Price
- Cost
- Service
- Quality
- Security
- Status
- Labour-saving
- Curiosity
- Investment
- Money-saving
- Pain-avoiding

Position yourself

So far I have tended to restrict the major focus of the discussions on the positioning of your product on the heart and mind of your prospect. But what about you? Consider that you might have an opportunity to position not only your sales propositions but also yourself and your organisation.

When you consider this, I'm sure that you will conclude as I do that there is absolutely no reason why you can't make yourself and your organisation, as well as the product, the focus of any positioning exercise with the prospect. How you appear and behave will have a major bearing on the prospect's perceptions of you (and consequently your organisation), and will be the major determining factor in how you position yourself in the eyes of the prospect. So think carefully about what you are trying to achieve as far as establishing your own image.

So what choices do we have? The good news is, many. The bad news is, you probably consider that you have *too* many choices. It may help if you think of your ultimate objective in terms of positioning yourself as being defined by four major options or categories. I touched on them briefly in

Table 2.1 of Chapter 2, when I proposed a simple four-quadrant sales model.

Perhaps an analogy will best serve to illustrate those four categories. Think of the Olympics for a minute. In any final of any event there are winners—the gold medallists who ultimately stand on the highest step of the tiered podium and receive the most attention. There are the silver medallists who also share centre stage, albeit at a slightly lower level and usually with less attention and adoration. Then there are the bronze medallists, at a slightly lower level again, still close to centre stage but clearly with two higher levels above. Then there is the fourth level—the rest of the competitors, who didn't place in the event but who no doubt gave their very best. These unplaced competitors did well just to get into the finals and perhaps even turned in a personal best. They were congratulated and commiserated with, but rarely do they demand or command the same media or public spotlight as the three medallists on the podium.

Who does everyone that competed strive to be? The gold medallist, of course! Who does everyone seek out for interviews, advice, comment and endorsements? Again, the gold medallist! This doesn't mean that those who didn't win gold are lesser human beings. It most certainly doesn't indicate that at some future time they cannot or won't win. It does mean, however, that for the time being at least, the accolade of champion goes to someone else and will remain in place for a fixed period of time. In the case of the Olympics, the gold medallist remains as Olympic Champion for a term of four years.

Let's now translate the Olympics analogy into the sales environment. Starting from the lowest common denominator level and working up towards the apex, see if the four levels identified below, to which you might as a salesperson aspire, make sense to you.

You will recall that in Part 1, when discussing the philosophy of selling, I talked about the four approaches to selling. The style I counselled you to pursue was that of a consultant. It might be worthwhile turning back to that section now, and reviewing it in the context of the above description of how you might potentially wish to pursue strategies to position yourself in the hearts and minds of your prospects.

What is your objective when it comes to positioning *yourself* with your prospect? You do have choices! You can stay in your comfort zone and battle it out at the competitor level to make the finals, or you can aim for a medal and get on the podium—perhaps not finishing in gold medal position at your first try, but certainly establishing your presence and providing your prospect with clear indications of your intentions and how you wish to be considered.

Remember, your ability to get onto the podium and work your way to the gold medal consultancy level is entirely dependent on your ability to position yourself as someone who can *deliver value* to the relationship.

Level no. 4 Competitor level (unplaced finalist)	*At this level you are perceived by the prospect as a supplier of product who they may or may not ask to come and talk to them. There is probably no one thing in the mind of the prospect that clearly differentiates you and your product from your marketplace. You could be viewed as just another listing in the telephone book. Loyalty doesn't enter the equation, and if you wish to move up to the next level of the salesperson–prospect relationship, your focus on positioning should be on customer service. This effectively means focusing on one or more of the following four initiatives: product differentiation, delivery, cost or convenience.*

Level no. 3 Commodity level (bronze medal)	*Here you are judged solely on your projected image or reputation based on past performances, and are considered as a candidate for inclusion in a list of potential preferred suppliers, but you are not assured of making the prospect's short list. When dealing with you, the prospect sees only the product and the organisation you represent. So here you are judged primarily by the product and you are seen as representing the product. As a result, you are not considered as separate from it. You could be considered by the prospect as almost irrelevant to the sale. They focus on your product as a solution to their problems. However, there are no definite guarantees that you or your product will be considered next time.*

Level no. 2 Competency level (silver medal)	*Here you and your product have established some credibility and a measure of reputation based on past performances and, as a result, you, your organisation and your product are considered reliable, competent and credible. The prospect views you and your product as a package and, while contacting you directly, might well speak to someone else in your organisation if you weren't available. Your past performances and solid references mean that you will probably be shortlisted to solve the prospect's problems. Or you have a wild card and will definitely make the prospect's short list, but once there you will enjoy no special privileges or attention.*

Level no. 1 Consultancy level (gold medal)	*Here the traditional sales model has become completely irrelevant and you, not your organisation or your product, are viewed as the valuable asset, as a partner who receives preferential treatment and the status to match. You are for the first time considered as separate from your product and even your organisation and the prospect sees that it is you, not your product or organisation, that provides what they need. You are 'top of mind' and often get the first call when the prospect has a problem. At this level, the prospect looks to you for advice and guidance and is usually prepared to pay for both.*

chapter 17

Follow-up—the potential competitive edge

Follow-up is an important element right throughout the sales process. Unlike some other elements which tend to play more of a critical role in the beginning, middle or even the end phases of the sales process, follow-up is a sales element that is required throughout every part of the process. Think of it this way: follow-up is a thread that weaves through the whole process and helps to bind the often delicate fabric of the sales process together.

So where and when should you bring this all-pervasive follow-up element into play? The answer is, quite simply, everywhere, anywhere and at any time! However, some areas of the sales process are more critical than others when it comes to the importance of follow-up. Set out below are four key areas where you should carefully plan and monitor your follow-up activities.

Follow-up: Four key areas

1. *During the sales process generally.*
2. *During the prospect's evaluation buying phase.*
3. *After the prospect says 'Yes'.*
4. *After the sale is concluded.*

Let's look at these a little closer.

1. Follow-up during the sales process

You may see this as self-evident, and you may well be right. However, as evidenced from my own experience as both a buyer and a trainer debriefing mystery shopper surveys and the like, the overwhelming response by prospects to this issue of follow-up is a mixture of disbelief, disappointment, frustration and contempt that nobody bothered to follow them up.

In one instance, my organisation undertook to telephone 12 motor vehicle dealerships in order to pose as a customer inquiring about purchasing a specific model of car. Of the relatively small proportion of salespeople (only three) who asked for and took my contact details, not one ever followed up by calling me back. So, yes, the need to follow up during the sales process is perhaps obvious, but the reality is that few salespeople do so on a consistent, planned basis.

Let's step for a minute into the head of your prospect and pose the question: 'In the prospect's mind's eye, what will follow-up do for you, the salesperson, during the sales process?'

■ The most immediate return on your investment of time is that in all probability your consistent follow-up will set you apart from the vast majority of other salespeople the prospect deals with, including your direct competitors.

■ Consistent follow-up helps to build credibility and establish competence, both of which are essential ingredients in developing a healthy professional relationship.

■ Follow-up helps to build and maintain urgency and momentum. It keeps the process rolling on and can't help but to inject a note of inevitability, enthusiasm, optimism and professionalism into the developing relationship.

2. Follow-up during the evaluation buying phase

Again, it could be argued that this is covered by the above section, but my experience indicates that this particular area of follow-up demands special attention. It's during this middle phase of the prospect's buying process that your selling proposition is most at risk, both from forces within the prospect's buying organisation and from your competition. Here you need to keep close to your prospect. You need to understand what is happening during this evaluation buying phase.

Changing a prospect's buying decision once it is made is like turning a large ocean liner: it takes time, persistence and considerable effort, and may result in too little movement too late. So, stay close to your prospects, find out what is happening and when, find out what other options they are considering, find out who else is involved in the decision, what glitches have occurred, and if there is anything else they need. The key objective during this follow-up phase is to uncover threats and barriers to your proposition and react by repositioning your proposition if needed. And to do it *before* the final decision is made.

3. Follow-up after the prospect says 'Yes'

It's not unusual to observe salespeople relax, breathe a sigh of relief and even take their eyes right off the ball when they hear the prospect agree to their sales proposition. This is only natural. After all, the hard yards you have put in, your persistence and total customer focus, have finally paid off. You believe you can afford to relax a little now.

The reality is exactly the opposite. If you mistakenly believe that you have reached the summit of this particular mountain and spend a little time relaxing, congratulating yourself and posing for the cameras, you have made a major error. It's tempting to think the whole thing is over. It most certainly isn't. I read a statistic that suggested that, on one particular mountain, more climbers have been injured or killed descending after having reached the summit than actually trying to get to the top in the first instance. Now this may not have the same outcome in all cases, but you clearly need to be even more vigilant, even more careful, after the prospect has said 'Yes'; you are tired, and your judgement may be impaired after breathing the rarefied air of success.

You need to keep up the follow-up after you hear the 'Yes'. Don't assume that the work is done. Now is the time when all sorts of strange and wonderful things can happen. Buyer's remorse can rear its ugly head, the buyer's internal politics can come into play, misunderstandings by users can surface and so on. Don't confuse reaching the summit with climbing the mountain. You still need to get down in one piece, so now you must concentrate even harder on keeping the sale from slipping over a precipice.

4. Follow-up after the sale is concluded

'Why bother? They bought, didn't they? And we delivered on time?', some might think. Well yes, they did buy, but there are two matters that are worth considering. These are customer satisfaction and the next order.

Customer satisfaction is important to you if you are genuinely concerned about your customer's needs. You need to check to see whether from your client's or customer's point of view the product is performing to expectations. You need to confirm things like:

- Was it delivered on time?
- Was it installed correctly?
- Was it what was expected?
- Is it operating up to standard?
- Are there any problems?

You must be proactive. One thing I have noticed is that customers often don't know exactly what to expect when it comes to the operational performance of the product they have purchased. They may not see any potential problems that will be evident to you *if* you follow up after the sale is concluded. You don't even need to speak to your customer directly. Consider leaving a message with their assistant or secretary that you were simply touching base, knowing they were extremely busy, and for any problems or concerns whatsoever leave your contact telephone numbers, perhaps even your home number. You might even leave a message that you will visit their operation (giving the date and time) to 'look in and make sure everything is alright'.

If you really want to impress your customer, schedule a site inspection and ask for feedback from the users of the product. Just make sure you keep your customers in the loop and they are aware of what you are doing and approve of it.

The other reason to provide solid after-sales follow-up is that you want to continue the professional relationship through to *the next order*. You need to keep reminding customers you are there in the wings until they need to talk to you next time, and the only way to do that is by regular follow-ups. They don't all need to be person-to-person, as long as your name pops up regularly and the customer perceives you as genuinely concerned about their situation.

One other key strategic reason for follow-up is that you can expand your knowledge of your customers' operations by observing their systems, procedures and potential problem issues ahead of times. You can then use this knowledge by being proactive and making recommendations and suggestions *before* a problem or situation develops, rather than *after*.

More about follow-up

The more complex the sale, the more important the follow-up element during the sales process. The same can be said of those relatively simple sales with a longer sales cycle. Follow-up can make or break the sale. If managed well, follow-up can give you the competitive edge you need to put you over the finish line ahead of the chasing pack. I know salespeople who use follow-up as a distinct competitive advantage as part of their strategy to win the sale.

In sales where the prospect has your competitors breathing heavily down their neck, follow-up allows you to stay close to your prospect. It allows you an edge that many of your competitors either don't acknowledge or simply don't understand.

Areas that require specific follow-up strategies

There are several 'hot spots' in the sales process that will demand specific follow-up strategies if you are to capitalise on the opportunities or overcome the barriers some of these can represent. These hot spots represent *red flags*, and you must recognise and respond to them.

When you hear 'We'll get back to you!'

When you hear this or something like it, you need to carefully consider your follow-up strategy. You need to uncover the reasons—the real reasons—for your prospect saying this. On hearing this, you should delve deeper and find out what your prospect is thinking and feeling. You need to find out why they said they needed 'time to think about it', to 'get back to you'. It may appear difficult to get to the bottom of this at the time. If so, you need to persevere patiently, to tread softly and follow up the prospect, clearly demonstrating a desire to understand their situation.

Where there is more than one decision maker

Here the internal decision-making process can be driven by the culture and politics of the organisation. In this case, the buying or decision-making process isn't clear or can even be consciously and intentionally obscured, and the roles, responsibilities, authorities and organisational relationships of the players, your prospects, may not be what they first appear. Here follow-up plays a major role by creating multi-level contacts that help to anchor the sale, and stop it being broken free by these unseen negative forces and set adrift to float aimlessly or, worse, ending up on the rocks and sinking without a trace.

Follow up when you say you will

This almost goes without saying, and there isn't a lot to be said other than to suggest that your competence and reliability—that is, your reputation and that of your organisation—are on the line when you say you will do something. Your great job of opening the sale and exploring customer needs can be completely overturned by not delivering on even the simplest promises you have made to your prospect during the heat of the moment.

I know that it's tempting when you are busy or otherwise focused to find excuses for not delivering *what* was promised *when* it was promised. You can, as many salespeople do, rationalise this by saying things like 'Well, it was only a day late', or 'It's late in the day, they won't be able to do anything with it if I deliver it now. I'll get it to them first thing tomorrow.'

It's just not good enough. Sure, problems happen and you believe your prospect will understand. So if it looks as if you can't deliver what you promised and on the day or at the time you promised it, contact your prospect immediately, tell them the situation and your suggested action, and then ask them for their thoughts. What you don't know is what promises or schedules your prospect has agreed to or made on the basis of your promises. Don't jeopardise your relationship with your prospect by making them look bad because you couldn't or wouldn't deliver.

Follow up after your competitors have made contact

Some salespeople are tempted to ignore their competitors or even to pretend they don't exist. This is very evident when, knowing their competitors have met or presented to the prospect, the salesperson prefers to completely ignore this contact or, worse still, retreat to their office and wait for the prospect to contact them. If there was ever a time to be proactive in attempting to take some measure of control, to look and sound as if you welcome competition and embrace the opportunity to prove you are the chosen one or the right one—the one who can best address your prospect's needs—now is that time.

You need to follow up, to get feedback, to test and ask questions. Who knows? This follow-up, hot on the heels of your competitor's offering, may be all that is required to draw the sale naturally to the resolution phase, to initiate the close or simply receive the order.

So having accepted follow-up as a necessary and constructive element in the sales process, where do we go on this subject? It seems to me that what I should now do is provide some positive guidance as to how best to go about providing follow-up. With this in mind, set out below are 10 simple statements that should go some way to helping develop sales strategies for following up your prospects. I have called them the 10 golden rules of follow-up.

Ten golden rules of follow-up

1. *Don't smother the buyer.* If you suffocate them with attention, you most certainly will kill off any chance of a sale. Be pleasantly persistent and relentless, not openly obnoxious and aggressive.
2. *Find reasons to stay in touch with your prospect.* Be creative. Invent reasons to keep up a dialogue with them. There is no limit to the ambit of these reasons. Follow up to make sure they received something you sent them, to make or confirm meetings, to ask them what they thought. Follow up to congratulate them or to tell them about a new development. Follow up to wish them luck, a happy birthday or just to say thank you. If you take the time, you will have no problem coming up with 20 or more reasons to initiate follow-up with your prospect during your particular sales process.
3. *Introduce your team.* If you are working in a team, even if it involves only you and your assistant, brief your team on the sale and take an opportunity to introduce them, preferably in person, to the prospect. This is a great aid to the follow-up phase, as anyone in your team, once introduced, can assist in follow-up, leaving you to orchestrate and manage the process, and deal with the more critical day-to-day issues, while dealing with other prospects. It also means that should your prospect need to speak to you urgently and you are unavailable,

they are more likely to discuss their particular issue with someone on your team whom they have met beforehand.

4. *Use a system.* It's generally impossible to predict in any detail the course of any one sales call, let alone the outcome of a future potential sales opportunity. However, don't use this as an excuse to avoid planning follow-up at the outset. And to do this you need a contact system—a system that allows you to schedule follow-up calls both at the outset and to revise this schedule as the sales process unfolds. The system should keep track of each contact you have with the prospect, whether it be person-to-person, by telephone, letter, email or whatever. It should schedule the next follow-up call, with the objective of that future follow-up call clearly stated.

There are, as you know, myriad ways to systematise your follow-up contact. You can use a manual diary system, card index system or computerised sales follow-up system. My view is that, with the proliferation of computers, especially laptops, and the availability of a large number of relatively inexpensive sales contact systems, there is absolutely no excuse for not taking advantage of the flexibility and sophistication of a computerised contact system.

5. *Tell your prospect.* Tell them that from time to time you will be checking in with them, following up as it were, to make sure that what was to be done was actually done or perhaps simply checking to see what the prospect thinks or feels about something. You may even feel inclined to ask them for permission to follow up—something like, 'From time to time, I will be contacting you to . . . Is that OK with you?' I have never heard of a situation where the prospect refused this request.

6. *Introduce yourself to your prospect's support team.* This allows you to follow up with the prospect without necessarily talking to them directly. This also has the advantage of allowing you to get additional views and a wider range of feedback. So, prepare not only your own team, but also your prospect's buying team, for a follow-up regimen.

7. *If in doubt, take the initiative and follow up.* What's the risk? The worst that can happen is the prospect won't take your call. So take the view that if you're not sure, if something concerns you, follow up.

8. *Use follow-up as a means of collecting valuable information.* Take the opportunity to follow up to gain additional information and meet others who are influential in the buying process, and add the information to your database.

9. *Make a commitment to be proactive right at the outset.* Decide right up front that you are going to stick closely to your prospect. Start that way and be consistent right throughout the process. Meet and exceed your prospect's communication expectations from the very beginning.

10. *Understand that follow-up is linked to closing.* I find that poor closing is often linked to poor follow-up. The inability of many salespeople to comprehend problems experienced when dealing with the closing element of the sales process, whether closing on a commitment to further action, asking for an opinion or obtaining commitment, is a primary indicator of a poor follow-up regimen. Throughout the sales process it would appear that if salespeople don't appreciate that closing is a process to be worked through *with the buyer*, then they almost certainly will fail to see the importance of follow-up with prospects. They won't view follow-up as a critical two-way interface that is woven throughout the whole sales process.

chapter 18

Barriers—learn to like and live with them

F irst of all, let's be absolutely clear about how you should view genuine barriers to the sale raised by the prospect, whether you choose the terms 'objections', 'obstacles' or 'problems' to describe them. They should be regarded as 'good, healthy life signs' in most instances. I believe that *obstacles*, *objections* and *problems* expressed during the sales process are potentially healthy because of the following.

- *They indicate that your prospect is listening to and evaluating your selling proposition.* Obviously, if you encounter bona fide objections, or the prospect shares with you their perceptions of what they see as genuine barriers to the sale, they are more than likely seriously considering your proposal. This is definitely good news.
- *They provide an excellent opportunity to demonstrate not only your enthusiasm and professionalism, but also your commitment, knowledge, expertise, experience and skill.* If addressed properly, these objections can assist you to establish your sincere personal and professional interest in your prospect and enhance your credibility in a way that is infinitely more difficult, if not impossible, to do if these objections are not voiced by the prospect.
- *They should be expected.* If you were in the prospect's shoes, wouldn't you probably have some concerns in a buying process that involved anything other than a relatively minor decision? Wouldn't you have some issues you needed addressed or clarified before you made a buying decision? In fact, I would go as far as to suggest that you should become concerned if your prospect *doesn't* at some stage raise their concerns. If they don't, it doesn't necessarily mean they don't have any. Quite the contrary! They will have them, it's just that you haven't drawn them out. And think about this: if you haven't surfaced these objections, obstacles and problems, you deal with them effectively.

Just remember that genuine objections, obstacles, barriers, or whatever you want to call them, are almost inevitable and a healthy 'life sign' for the sale. Don't accept the absence of these barriers as a positive indication that all is going well. It almost certainly won't be. So, why do prospects raise objections?

Why prospects come up with barriers

The reasons are many and varied. Again, assuming at this stage that we are dealing only with genuine objections, the most common nine reasons that prospects object might include the following.

1. *A 'connection' hasn't been established.* Here the prospect may well be attempting to slow down the buying process by objecting and throwing up roadblocks to the sale. They are not comfortable with the salesperson and/or the sales process, and objections are their way of diverting attention back to themselves and their needs.
2. *They are different.* Prospects have different needs and wants. They have different priorities. These differences, which are often not acknowledged or effectively addressed by salespeople, make the sales process stressful and impersonal for the prospect. This environment spawns problems and obstacles.
3. *They are difficult.* This is the most widely used excuse or rationalisation by salespeople to explain why they were unable to meet their sales objectives. They say things like, 'The prospect just couldn't make a decision', or 'They didn't seem to believe me', or 'They are just too difficult to deal with.' Now, I'm sure that there are some truly difficult prospects, and they will do or say things that may make it difficult, if not impossible, for salespeople to do their job effectively; *but*, the majority of these so-called difficult buyers are in my view simply different. It's often the salesperson's inability to adapt and be flexible that is the cause of problems. After all, the prospect sees no need to change their preferred buying style to meet the salesperson's preferred sales methods or ingrained sales habits.
4. *They are deliberately testing the salesperson.* The prospect might test the salesperson to see whether they have the conviction of their beliefs. Perhaps they are testing to see whether the salesperson can be counted on to perform when a sticky or tricky situation develops in the after-sales phase. Who knows what the reason for testing the salesperson will be? However, many objections are little more than mini character tests to see how the salesperson will react and so reveal more of the salesperson's true motivations and character. Price objections are a classic example of this.
5. *They are a natural reaction to the salesperson's selling style.* We have all seen many situations where the prospect has reacted negatively in various ways and to various degrees to a salesperson and their natural selling style. Unless this is addressed carefully and quickly, it will almost

certainly spell the end of the relationship, both interpersonal and professional.

6. *Self-protection.* Here the prospect raises objections usually right away, to protect themselves from becoming too involved with the salesperson. They believe that if at the very outset they can maintain a safe distance from the salesperson, it will be more difficult to be manipulated or fall under their sales spell.

7. *Caution and the need to avoid making a mistake.* This is a major factor in many prospects' decision-making process. As you would expect, this buying factor or attitude is bound to raise objections. Why? Simply because if they aren't raised, the prospect believes they aren't doing their job in considering the issues effectively, and as a result they will make a mistake.

8. *The prospect believes that objections and concerns are simply their part of the sales process.* The prospect sometimes sees it as their role in the sales process to erect roadblocks, and then go about enthusiastically carrying out this role. This isn't unlike the 'due diligence' that is carried out prior to organisations merging or being acquired. The prospect may feel that their responsibility in the sales process is to be the objective 'anchor of reality' and that the salesperson expects them to ask questions, disagree and ponder the issues.

9. *The salesperson generated the barrier.* Salespeople need to tread carefully and be wary of provoking objections. The ways sales-people provoke or generate objections are many and varied. Listed below are some common ways in which salespeople actually become the fundamental cause of the objection or barrier to the sale:

   - They answer questions with more generic product information instead of asking questions and seeking to understand and learn about the prospect.
   - They swamp the prospect with data in the mistaken belief that this is meeting the prospect's needs, instead of asking questions and tailoring a compelling sales story.
   - They ask irrelevant, unprofessional or 'dumb' questions, or make statements that indicate they haven't done their homework.
   - They assume that the prospect is like all their other buyers—they base their selling approach on a 'stereotyped' understanding of the prospect, their business and their problems and concerns, then jump to a solution based on these broad, unsubstantiated, totally incorrect and often irrelevant assumptions.
   - They deliver the sales story *poorly*. The positioning of the idea is so poorly implemented that the prospect is left with almost no option but to raise their legitimate concerns.
   - They push the sale too fast and beyond the buying phase currently being considered by the prospect. We talked earlier about the three buying phases and I mentioned a number of common problems, one

of which—involving the salesperson mistakenly moving on to the next phase before the prospect is ready to do so, especially by moving too quickly from the evaluation phase into the resolution phase—is sure to prompt objections.

■ They confuse advantages with benefits and assume that their carefully memorised and rehearsed catalogue of product advantages will meet the prospect's needs. These advantages, which are not really perceived by your prospect to relate to their particular situation, will be sure to cause them to object.

■ They fail to adequately position their product by carefully exploring the prospect's real needs. Here the today state must be clear to the prospect and their tomorrow state agreed. Unless the prospect fully appreciates their particular situation and has a clear understanding and appreciation of the ideas the salesperson is proposing, they see no urgency or need to change their current situation and will consequently object, often quite strenuously, to their sales proposition.

■ Their inability to negotiate an acceptable package or solution will almost guarantee objections at the last minute to their selling proposition.

■ They fail to fully explore the prospect's needs. This is linked directly, or could be the precursor, to a number of the reasons why salespeople generate prospects' problems raised earlier.

The fact is that we as salespeople have a great deal of influence on what our prospects will say and do. The common thread through all the above reasons (which is not intended as an exhaustive list) is simply that all prospects will operate from their own perspective. As a salesperson, don't expect to overlay your standards, your ideals, your values or your methods on the prospect.

Concentrate on extending yourself into the prospect's world and work to find out more about the prospect's perspective rather than focusing on attempting to justify your view of the world in the eyes of the prospect. Concentrate on two important actions—displaying empathy and asking questions. However, ask genuine fact- and feeling-focused questions—not leading questions designed to make your point, or delivered to show that you are clever and the prospect is naïve, or to allow you to switch to a safer track. When asking questions, have a genuine desire to learn from your prospect; don't lead or manipulate them.

We've talked about why objections are good and why prospects might object. Let's now look at what effect these objections have on those salespeople who don't see the positive side of objection and who don't appreciate or understand the prospect's reasons for raising objections.

Barriers and salespeople

Barriers to the sale have many and varied effects on salespeople who don't understand them, and don't appreciate them for what they are. The following are several typical reactions I have observed in salespeople as they struggle to deal with the fact that prospects have, and usually express, concerns and objections.

- *Gun-shy*. They approach the sale in an awkwardly tentative fashion with one foot still in the door ready to retreat. They talk too quickly, almost without pausing to draw breath, in an effort to establish very quickly and in some detail why the prospect shouldn't object to seeing them and listening to their story. They almost imagine objections and, as a result, often raise them themselves, leaving a negative impression with the prospect.
- *Frustrated*. The perceived lack of understanding and appreciation by the prospect of their own buying process leads the salesperson to feel a level of frustration, which then often manifests itself in either more aggressive or more passive sales behaviour.
- *Product-focused*. In response to objections raised by the prospect, the salesperson mistakenly believes that they need to dump more product information on their prospect. This is really an attempt to deflect the objections by swamping the prospect with a host of new information in the form of generic answers, or perhaps by comparing the prospect's situation directly with past experiences with other buyers.
- *Salesperson-focused*. The salesperson becomes defensive, mistakenly believing the objection is directed at them personally. As a result, they succumb to the temptation to dump even more product in an effort to divert attention from themselves or to avoid arguing openly with the prospect.
- *Confused*. This is perhaps potentially the most dangerous reaction to barriers to the sale by the salesperson. Why? Because unless the reality of barriers is understood, salespeople will never be able to deal effectively with their own emotions and consequently will continue to flounder when barriers are erected. So, why confused? Because many salespeople fail to appreciate that, like themselves, their prospects have an innate belief system, which has a major impact on the prospect's 'personal reality'.

With this in mind, you might consider that objections raised by the prospect are not the truth: they are simply statements rooted in their belief system. If you are having difficulty digesting this proposition, consider this. Prospects weren't born with objections to your product. These objections were learned or conditioned and, as such, you can help them to unlearn them.

Remember, the barriers to the sale can be dissolved, and to do so you don't have to:

■ change the world; or
■ change the product.

You only need to influence the belief system of your prospect.

One final word on beliefs: tread lightly until you are sure of what you are dealing with. Beliefs are powerful and highly emotional issues. People will go to great lengths to protect their deeply held beliefs: they will go to war, break the law and even be prepared to die. So don't treat your prospect's beliefs with anything even approaching contempt, disdain, derision or even indifference, or you may pay the price of a complete breakdown in your relationship.

Is the prospect for real?

So far we have discussed prospects' objections on the basis that they are realistic, bona fide and reasonable. But is this always the case? The answer from any salesperson with even a modicum of experience will be a resounding 'NO!'. So what drives these other types of, shall we say, 'non-genuine' objections? What is the root cause of these unrealistic or less than truthful expressions of concern and emotion from the prospect?

Generally I see problems and objections as falling into three basic categories:

1. *Genuine barriers*. Here the prospect genuinely has a real concern, objection, problem or barrier that needs to be addressed to allow the sale to progress.
2. *Non-genuine barriers*. Here the prospect is employing a smokescreen or diversion and usually does so consciously, so that the real objectives for discussing your product remain hidden. In this scenario, the prospect often has a hidden agenda and resists attempts to share the real situation. Unless the salesperson can flush out the real objections, if indeed there are any, and clearly establish the prospect's specific needs, they will be operating in the dark and more than likely wasting their time. The fact is that many barriers to a sale aren't genuine objections. They are smokescreens. Prospects use them because they have found them successful in the past in discouraging salespeople.
3. *Involuntary reaction barriers*. In this situation, prospects react often from their subconscious. They may react spontaneously or instinctively with an objection, which isn't a real objection or a valid concern in the long run. It may have its roots in a prior bad experience, in gossip, incorrect expectations or simply a misinterpretation of something said

by the salesperson. No matter what the reason, they should be approached carefully because, like any other apparently well-considered objection, these 'involuntary' objections are valid to the prospect. However, you will need to deal with this objection a little differently.

Counterproductive responses to objections

Before we move into positive strategies for dealing with objections, let's take a minute to look at some of the more adverse or negative responses by salespeople to their prospect's concerns and objections that I have observed over the years.

I must warn you that you may find some of your favourite ways of responding to objections in this list. This doesn't necessarily mean they are unworkable or ineffective, but rather that they are often perceived as manipulative or contrived by many informed and experienced decision makers, and may have the potential to do far more damage than good in the sales relationship.

What I do suggest is that you think carefully before using any of these, even those you feel have served you well previously.

- *Ignoring them.* This is a poor strategy to adopt when dealing with objections and is a realistic option in only one instance, which I will address in the next section. The prospect will usually be aware of and sensitive to any attempt to ignore a real concern. Ignoring the prospect's expressed concern is a sure way to drive a wedge into the relationship and can seriously jeopardise any good preceding work that has been done with the prospect.
- *The 'if' technique.* This is one of those attempts taught by many to engineer a quick close on the back of an objection or concern voiced by the prospect. Rather than putting the prospect's needs ahead of yours, you respond by suggesting a conditional response, such as: 'If I could demonstrate how you could . . . would you make a decision and buy one today?' If the roles were reversed, how would you respond? Would it really surprise you to learn that the prospect usually becomes defensive, aggressive or simply retreats as quickly as possible when faced with the obvious and blatant salesperson-focused approach to the sale?
- *Feel, felt, found formula.* This tried-and-true method has been a favourite among sales commentators and trainers for many years and still has a place in some instances. Those of you who know the response well will recall that this three-step approach is executed by, first, appearing to empathise with how the prospect feels ('I know how you feel'); then moving on to relating the prospect's concerns to others' experiences so that they perceive their concerns and feelings are very much like those experienced by others ('Others have felt exactly the

same way'); then administering the *coup de grace* by telling the prospect what others have found ('But what they found when . . . is that . . .').

Resist the temptation to jump to conclusions and compare your prospect's situation directly with others'. This defeats the earlier objective of treating the prospect as unique. You are sending mixed messages and sabotaging the prospect's perceptions of your competence and sincerity. In one instance I heard of recently, after the salesperson had used this technique the prospect looked him in the eye and said 'You are trying the feel, felt, found technique on me', and burst out laughing. Here the technique caused no real damage to the relationship, but this won't always be the case.

■ *Reflective questioning.* Using reflective questions such as 'So you think . . .' is fine if it is controlled, well-conceived and well-implemented. Usually this isn't the case. More often, it comes across as parroting. It comes across as laziness and an inability of the salesperson to shift gears and genuinely attempt to understand the situation from the prospect's perspective. There is rarely any real reason to overuse this technique and risk the relationship.

■ *Switching tracks.* Here I have used a railway analogy of 'switching tracks'. This is what the traditional train signalmen in the signalboxes used to do many years ago before computerisation and more sophisticated systems. Back then, to reroute a train, the signalmen would change signals, then with two hands throw the big lever that moved the tracks and diverted the trains left or right at a designated junction. In selling I often see salespeople do something similar. I see them verbally 'switching tracks' as they direct the conversation away from a problem area or a topic introduced by the prospect onto something else. It may go something like this. The prospect has suggested that they need 'something faster'. The salesperson responds, 'I can understand you needing something a bit quicker. Our basic models offer a range of preprogrammable speeds and are, you will find, generally superior to our competition. As such, we can offer you . . . and . . . I think you will agree that . . .' The salesperson has switched tracks. One minute the prospect is suggesting that speed is an issue and the next minute the salesperson has railroaded the discussion onto another track completely. Not only is it dumb, it offends the prospect's sense of a need for personal recognition as outlined in the first phase of the buying process proposed in Chapter 8. Imagine how you would feel in this situation.

■ *Product dumping.* This activity is bound to raise an objection. If you were a rational prospect, you might compare product dumping of all this perhaps relevant information to trying to rid yourself of mice with a shotgun. You might get the mice, although with all the collateral damage I don't know how you could possibly tell. And after all the noise died down and the smoke cleared and your ears stopped ringing, nobody would be sure what happened and which way the mice went.

■ *Contradicting the prospect*. Here there is some similarity with the feel, felt, found technique, except that the salesperson takes a more direct approach: they confront the prospect by suggesting that their view isn't correct and then kindly offer to point out the error of their ways. Nothing is surer to raise the stakes in the sales process to a dangerously overheated level than contradicting or arguing with the prospect. It shows little or no self-control by the salesperson and no recognition of the status of the prospect as an equal partner in the sales process.

■ *Making assumptions*. Here the salesperson interprets, or perhaps more accurately misinterprets, what the prospect is saying and jumps to incorrect conclusions. And if that wasn't bad enough, the salesperson often then compounds this error by heading off in completely the wrong direction. By the time they have stopped to draw breath, the prospect is nowhere in sight. We've all been guilty of this. The prospect mentions that 'size is critical' and off we go, talking at great length about the advances in 'miniaturisation' and 'battery technology', and how there are now much smaller sizes available. Then we find that the prospect is concerned that his last piece of equipment was 'too small'. The prospect mentions that they were always losing it and the buttons and screen were so small it was difficult to see and use. They apparently wanted something bigger!

Barrier dissolution—a new approach

So if most of our old techniques don't cut it anymore, is there a new and workable approach? Yes! But first you need to think about how you approach barriers to the sale. Forget, for a moment, about how you should respond. Instead, think about how you relate to the prospect and how they relate to you as you prepare to respond.

Ask yourself what is the best way of gaining and retaining cooperation from your prospect. How do you get them to act in partnership with you, to accept you, to help you build a bridge and ultimately to cross the bridge to your side? You know you will more than likely have to make numerous trips over to the other side to help, influence, reason with and resolve problems that your prospect sees in your proposal for the bridge-building project. When your prospect shows concern or fear, will you resolve this by telling them what to do, by changing the subject, by arguing, by telling them others have done it? It's unlikely.

The key both to building the bridge with your prospect's help and to influencing them to cross the chasm is to ask them questions. So let's look at a question-based barrier dissolution model for effectively dealing with prospect's genuine barriers, objections and concerns.

Barrier dissolution model

1. *Offer no resistance.*
2. *Identify what is causing the barrier to be erected. This is the first mission.*
3. *Decide whether the prospect is legitimate in their concerns or whether it's a ploy or smokescreen.*
4. *Seek to understand the real concerns of the prospect.*
5. *Recognise exactly how to reposition the product to effectively respond to the prospect's real concerns.*
6. *Reposition your product.*
7. *Test that what you propose is acceptable.*
8. *Close on the barrier and move on.*

Tactics for dealing with barriers to the sale

There is only one really effective strategy to employ during the barrier dissolution process, and I'm sure you have worked out what it is by now. *It revolves around asking questions.* You need to become accomplished at using the power of questions to unlock the barriers.

Let's spend a little time looking at how questions might be employed to achieve this objective—some ways in which you might respond to your prospect's concerns or objections by employing skilful questioning.

■ *Tactic no. 1—Ask the prospect to explain their barrier.* This often has the effect of diminishing or completely dissolving the concern—especially if it's an objection that has a purely emotive basis or one that is connected to popular public opinion or hearsay and gossip. When you ask prospects to 'Tell me more about . . .' or 'Could you please give me some more details . . .?', they often struggle to make sense of their own objection and will then dismiss it themselves.
■ *Tactic no. 2—Ask why the prospect thinks or says whatever it is that appears to constitute a barrier.* Ask 'Really! Why do you think that . . .? Could I ask, what is it that makes you say that?' This gets quickly to the nub of the matter and again forces the prospect to consider, in their own mind, the reason for or basis of the objection. Be careful to ask this question in a non-confronting manner.
■ *Tactic no. 3—Respond to the barrier with a simple question that relates directly to the objection.* The prospect says: 'It's too big!' Response: 'It's too big? What did you have in mind?' or 'Do I take it that you had something a little smaller in mind?'

- *Tactic no. 4—Use feedback on the barrier in the prospect's words but with different body language and intonation.* 'It's too big!' Response: 'It's too big?', with a slightly puzzled and surprised expression, then silence. The prospect will feel vaguely uncomfortable at providing so little definitive information and will often volunteer to fill the void by explaining their statement.
- *Tactic no. 5—Use other potential barriers as a background or platform to dig deeper to uncover what you perceive as the real concerns of your prospect.* 'One concern that was voiced when we first went to the market with this product was . . . What we found was . . . How does this issue relate to your particular situation . . .?'
- *Tactic no. 6—Test your understanding.* Ask for the prospect's opinion on some matter that you believe you have understood and listen carefully for their response: 'So, if I understand you correctly, you think this needs to be . . .?'
- *Tactic no. 7—Ask the prospect to repeat their stated barrier.* Respond to the prospect's stated concerns by simply asking them to repeat them: 'Would you mind repeating that, please?' Then smile as the concern is again stated and suggest something like, 'I love it when I hear buyers' concerns, especially that particular concern. Why? Because our company's best customers all seem to share that potential issue. Before I respond, can I ask a few questions to clarify . . .?'

Don't appear cocky, smart or patronising. If, as a professional, you feel confidence in your own professional abilities and those of your product, simply seek to communicate this to the prospect by demonstrating that barriers are expected from thoughtful, decisive prospects and you in turn look forward to the opportunity to respond to any that this particular prospect may have. Show confidence and the prospect often loses interest in the objection.

Depending on the quality of your relationship with your prospect, you might even say, in response to a concern, something like: 'I love hearing that. Can you say that again?', or 'You may not think so, but what you just said is music to my ears. Why? Because it . . .'

Principles of dealing with objections

The basic principles are:

- Use the barrier dissolution model to move aside the emotion and fear that often surrounds, clouds and sometimes completely obscures the real issues for both the prospect and the salesperson concerning the prospect's voiced barriers and perceptions.
- Understand that you are not really responsible for, nor in control of, what your prospect does in response to your best efforts. Their

behaviour is exactly that—*their* behaviour. Recognise it, accept it, and learn to deal effectively with it.

■ Remember, your behaviour is under your control. You must recognise and accept that your attitude to the sale, to your prospect and to yourself will almost certainly affect your sales behaviour, which includes your ability to deal effectively with your prospect's barriers to the sale.

■ Maintain at all times an enthusiastic, positive attitude, and keep your sense of humour armed and ready.

■ Separate yourself from the problems and emotions and concentrate on exploring the real underlying concerns and working with the prospect to manufacture a response to dissolve their real barriers.

■ Realise that as long as the prospect is expressing genuine objections and concerns, the sale is usually moving forward.

■ Understand that you can't go wrong asking intelligent questions in a diplomatic and sensitive manner. You will be surprised what your prospect will tell you if you just ask.

■ Never refer to the prospect's barriers as 'objections', 'problems' or the like. They are nothing more than *concerns*. In talking to your prospect, talk to them about their *concerns* or *fears*. Don't elevate them to the status of problems or objections when talking to the prospect about them.

Your second strategy for responding to barriers

Up until this point I have concentrated on one strategy for dealing with prospects' barriers. That was a strategy that was basically centred on waiting until the prospect voiced their concern, *then* swinging into action and responding to it.

There is another option—a second strategy, as it were. And it's one practised almost exclusively by truly value-based professional salespeople. This alternative strategy involves raising the potential barrier to the sale before the prospect does and dealing effectively with it. This strategy, then, is about *anticipation* and *disarming* the potential objection. This is a strategy adopted by all highly successful salespeople. Use statements such as 'If I were in your position, one of the issues might be . . .', or 'Quite frankly, if I were sitting where you are sitting, I would want to know about . . .'

Now, the objective here is not to surface barriers that don't exist, but to clearly demonstrate that you have the prospect's best interests at heart and to clearly confirm that you are prepared to tackle the hard issues in *partnership* with the prospect so that you can deliver to them a truly compelling sales story full of feature benefit ideas that apply to them and their situation.

One method of stepping outside your comfort zone and starting to use this second strategy for dealing with barriers to the sale is to try it.

I suggest you give some thought to this particular action plan:

- Think of three of your most often heard and most feared barriers to the sale.
- Select your most feared barrier.
- List a variety of potential appropriate responses to the barrier.
- Bring up the barrier to the sale first at your next appropriate opportunity in a sales call: 'If I were in your shoes, when it comes to considering . . . I might want . . .'

Try it! You might just find that it has a major positive impact on your relationship with that prospect.

chapter 19

Closing—begin with the end in mind

Arguably, the single most talked about element of selling, with the possible exception of prospecting, is closing. So, what do we understand by 'closing'?

The generally accepted understanding of the closing element in the sales process among experienced salespeople often suggests that, in practice, a number of standard memorised closes are relied on to bring the process to a head. The philosophy seems to be that these traditional closes are used to engineer or manipulate a 'Yes' from what these salespeople must view as a relatively naive or unsuspecting prospect. Anecdotal evidence from prospects suggests that many salespeople see themselves doing something *to* a prospect during closing.

The issue of the close has probably created more stress and generated more misunderstanding than any other single element of the sales process. Many promising salespeople believe they have failed to reach their potential because they are unable to become comfortable with the traditional closing models. These closing models affect the sales process by often introducing an adversarial approach, which focuses on using the closing element to extract or manufacture a commitment from the prospect when the seller is ready to finalise the sale.

This traditional closing approach generally fails in the complex sales process with today's buyers for a variety of reasons, predominantly centring on the overly simplistic and flawed view of the prospect held by the win/lose-oriented traditional salesperson. These traditional salespeople refuse to acknowledge that today's prospects are usually:

- more educated;
- more assertive;
- more cautious;
- more aware of their options;
- more aware of their rights;
- more cynical;
- more knowledgeable about the competition; and
- more conscious of a fast or manipulative close.

It's no surprise, I'm sure, to think of today's prospects as wanting quality products at competitive prices sold by competent salespeople whom they feel they can connect with. Why do I think so? Because that's what they tell me! Check it out for yourself. Ask the people you deal with. See what they say.

So, if today's prospects are wary of any closing that involves the more traditional 'stick it to them' approach, where the byword is 'Always be closing' or perhaps 'Close hard, close fast and close often', what is closing?

First, I suggest that you cease to view closing as the execution of a set of techniques *to use on your prospect*, but rather consider closing as the element that runs continuously in the background of the total selling process. If you can accomplish this, you will view closing as something *you work through together with the prospect*, starting right from the very first contact with them. I see the closing element of the sales process as essentially being all about *asking for and obtaining a decision from your prospect*—nothing more, and certainly nothing less.

Second, I suggest that you consider closing as containing three separate and quite distinct types of outcome. By default, this may mean there are three different forms the closing element may take:

- *Form 1—Advancing*. Closing on a specific commitment to progress or move the sale forward.
- *Form 2—Testing*. Closing on confirming a specific agreement or understanding on a particular issue.
- *Form 3—Asking*. Closing on a final positive buying decision or simply the old-fashioned 'asking for the order'.

Let's look at each of these in turn.

- *Advancing*. What is closing on a specific commitment to move the sale forward or progress the sale? Quite simply, it is asking the prospect to make a *decision in favour of a proposition to proceed to a next action step in the sales process*, when and only when you believe the prospect is ready, willing and able to agree. As you can see, I propose calling this type of closing 'advancing'. If you set an overall sales goal, sales strategies and sales objectives, then you will need to close the prospect on a series of commitments to move the sale forward. In the early stages of the sales processes, you may be seeking to move through a series of predetermined progressions, some of which involve minor and some major decisions in the move towards the final buying decision.
- *Testing*. What, then, is the second form of closing—closing on confirming a specific agreement or understanding on a particular issue? This form of closing I refer to as 'testing'. Testing is simply asking the prospect for an *opinion*, usually expressed in terms of asking

how they think and/or feel about an issue when, and only when, you believe you have effectively positioned your proposition and you believe the prospect is in a position to do so. In other words, testing is about asking for and obtaining specific feedback.

■ *Asking.* Finally, closing on a final buying decision. This form of closing outcome, which I refer to as 'asking', is simply asking the prospect for a buying decision *in favour of your compelling selling story when you believe the prospect is ready to decide and you believe they will buy.*

Once you look at traditional closing in terms of these three distinct forms of closing outcomes, it's doubtful that you will ever again view selling simply as a series of sales steps instigated by the salesperson with the aim of reaching a single closing outcome. You will never again view closing as working inexorably towards manoeuvring the prospect into a 'Yes' or pinning them down where no alternative exists other than to agree and buy from you.

Closing is, as I have said, a process. It begins when you are prospecting and when you set your call objectives. It continues through the sales calls as you determine the prospect's needs, deal with and then close on their stated and unstated barriers to the sale. It continues as you follow up, position your compelling sales story, or work towards demonstrating how your selling ideas address your prospect's needs.

Let's look at each type of closing in more detail.

Advancing—closing on a specific commitment to progress the sale

As mentioned earlier, in this form of closing the focus in on *checking the prospect's commitment* by asking them to make a relatively minor decision (not a buying decision) in favour of your proposition to move to the next logical stage to advance the sale. *This is done only when you believe the prospect is ready, willing and able to agree.* An example might be closing them on an agreement for the prospect to view a demonstration, or an agreement for the prospect to make a recommendation to others that something happen, such as a formal meeting with the purchasing department.

Below is a hypothetical discussion between a salesperson and a prospect in which the salesperson is progressing the sale by closing on a commitment to action and thereby moving the sale forward.

As it looks like this is a way to (reference to a customer need), I'd like to bring in Joe Smith, our specialist, to . . . and who can . . . What do you think? [Objective of call was to identify decision makers and influencers and progress the sale by setting up an appointment with the salesperson's specialist.]

Great!

Oh, that's terrific. I'm looking forward to coming in with Joe. I've worked with him for four years, and our customers find him to be . . . When next week would it be convenient to get together?

How about Tuesday?

Fine. 10.00 okay?

Yes.

Is there anyone else you'd like to have at that meeting? Tim. And his role? . . . How long has he . . .? Terrific. Just to be sure we use our time in the best way, what things do you want to be sure we cover? . . . Good. Anything else? . . . Okay. Thanks again for your consideration. See you Tuesday, June 29, at 10.00.

This advancing form of the close element is designed to advance the sale and to find out where you stand with the prospect. If you don't know where you stand, there is a greatly reduced chance of winning the business and little or no chance of knowing when to ask for the business.

There are a number of key milestones you should set before, during and after a sales call that should be tailored to each particular account. These advancements, as we will call them, are generally checkpoints that I have found to apply to most outside sales situations, *and* if considered will greatly improve the sales strike rate of salespeople. They are:

- *Advancement before the call.* Set two or three relatively simple priorities and design a number of potential closes that ask the prospect to agree to action to advance the sale to achieve these advancements.
- *Advancement during the call.* Aim to close the prospect on the first priority of your predetermined advancements, leaving yourself other advancement options.
- *Advancement after the call.* Re-evaluate your sales call objectives and set new strategic advancements, and design specific closes related to these advancements, planned for subsequent sales calls.

Remember, the whole focus of advancing is that you are positioning yourself as someone who is working towards helping the prospect to make the best decision given their circumstances, that is in their best interests and which they may not have been able to make without your assistance.

Testing—closing on confirming specific agreement

Testing is a form of closing characterised by simply closing the prospect on a question to determine what they think. The golden rule is, however, that you do this only when you believe you have effectively positioned your idea and only when you believe the prospect prepared to tell you what they think.

This part of closing is crucial to the effective interactive sales approach that is central to value-based selling. Test questions should be used throughout the sale to determine the prospect's feedback. Following are some examples of effective test questions:

- 'Are there any questions so far?'
- 'How does this sound . . .?'
- 'Is there anything you feel we have missed?'

This testing helps the salesperson to determine where they really stand in the prospect's mind, from the prospect's perspective. There is absolutely no need for you to guess where you stand or to assume anything. Thus, you avoid leaving a sales call not really knowing how it went. There is one simple rule to follow when it comes to this form of closing.

> *Test by asking for feedback and you will invariably get it.*

Testing will help you to build momentum and a solid platform from which to ask for agreement when closing on the final buying decision. It will also demonstrate to the prospect that they are truly involved in the whole process.

Finally, don't be afraid to test the prospect by answering their questions with a question. This helps to uncover their level of interest, priorities, needs and wants.

Asking—closing on a final buying decision

Because of the excessive emphasis placed by most sales managers, and hence salespeople, on asking for a buying decision, this form of closing becomes almost an unhealthy single point of focus *even before the sales call has begun*. This myopic view of closing has probably done more harm to buyer–seller relationships and caused more damage to the careers of a great number of potentially successful salespeople than most other causes combined. Salespeople who have suspected that there is a great deal more to selling than simply directing the focus of all major activity towards continually, almost single-mindedly, pursuing a 'yes' at the prospect's expense, have struggled to embrace the traditional notion of closing extolled as a virtue by many sales managers.

There is far more to closing than this single objective, and this form of closing should be considered only when the buyer is ready, not when the seller is ready. While it's certainly true that, in the vast majority of cases, without specifically asking for a buying decision there will be no sale, this doesn't elevate this form of closing to a pre-eminent position where all other forms of closing are of lesser importance or are even irrelevant.

While I certainly don't suggest that you don't ask at all, remember that asking for a buying decision should only come when you and the prospect have advanced together, tested the waters and options and reached a common path from which to make a decision.

Buying signals

Before we talk about those critical gestures, body language, expressions or words your prospect displays or uses that lead you to believe their mood is one of acceptance and they are ready to be closed on a final buying decision, I have some simple advice when it comes to closing or buying signals generally.

First, always be on the lookout for a whole spectrum of signals, verbal or non-verbal (body language), that indicate the prospect is ready to be asked for a buying decision. Remember, just because you aren't ready to close doesn't mean the prospect isn't ready to buy.

Second, use not only your eyes and ears but also your instincts. Read between the lines. What is the prospect really telling you when they say or do something? Don't accept their behaviour at face value. Ask yourself what is behind their actions, their questions, their statements. For example, when your prospect questions dimensions, or suggests that your product won't fit in the available space, couldn't that be construed as a signal that they are seriously considering buying the product? Far too many salespeople either misinterpret the buying signals or miss them completely.

Third, don't take for granted that you have closed the sale when the prospect leads you to believe that they are agreeing to buy. This is dangerous in the extreme. For example, learn to ask implementation questions. Learn to talk about what the prospect will do *after* they have taken delivery and are using the product.

Fourth, resist the habit to unclose: this is often called 'buying the product back'. Close on your last test questions *before* your big 'asking' close where you ask for the order. If you get a *yes* to your proposition to buy, *stop selling the product*. Some salespeople are so relieved, or perhaps don't even hear the *yes* in whatever form it comes, that they keep telling the prospect why their product is so good and you would swear that they had decided not to part with it after all.

Finally, don't assume anything when it comes to closing. You cannot say *yes* for the prospect, so don't assume things that will by default say *no* for them. Ask questions. Someone once suggested that if you can't get a definite *yes* to your closing question, get the next best thing—get *information*. Find out why. Why not? What needs to be done next?

So, what are some of the buying signals you should be on the lookout for? Obviously, this will largely depend on your prospect, your product and the sales situation. However, here are some generic buying signals I have found from my own experience and that of others that may indicate your prospect is ready for the 'asking' form of the close.

Ten buying signals

The prospect:

1. mentally places equipment in the right or designated location.
2. talks about issues that will arise from using the product;
3. mentally uses the product and discusses the future implications of doing so;
4. asks specific ownership-type questions—questions that indicate they have taken ownership/possession in their own mind;
5. discusses use of the product and dissolves barriers to the sale themselves, or in group situations they help others to dissolve their barriers to the sale;
6. makes notes and checks details, facts, sizes etc., or asks for final information to allow them to rationalise the sale with others;
7. becomes protective or possessive about the product in both action and word;
8. discusses the product as if the buying decision has already been made—for example, using questions that start with 'when' rather than 'if';
9. criticises small items associated with the purchase—finds minor issues that can be customised or tailored to suit their situation; and
10. asks implementation questions, such as payment terms, delivery arrangements, arrangement options, supply dates.

Closing—the last word

Finally, here are some general words of wisdom that I have found apply to the closing element generally. I have called them rules, and as you will see there are eight of them.

Rule 1   Where should you close? Wherever you can.

Rule 2   When should you close? Whenever the prospect's attitude is one of acceptance to you and your product.

Rule 3   Always test. Determine what your prospect really thinks and feels about you and your product.

Rule 4   Work towards gaining a series of advancements by 'advancing' on commitments to action before 'asking' for the order. This doesn't mean this cannot all happen in one call. It certainly can and does.

Rule 5   Ask your questions in a way that makes it easy for the prospect to say 'yes', but don't engineer or manipulate a 'yes'.

Rule 6   Establish by testing that the prospect believes the time to buy is now.

Rule 7   Before 'asking' for a buying decision, run a quick self-test. Ask:
- Does the product satisfy the prospect's needs?
- Have I effectively demonstrated the benefits?
- Has the prospect accepted those benefits?
- Have I dealt effectively with barriers to the sale?
- Am I selling to someone with the authority to buy? Now?

Rule 8   Accept that 'asking'—closing on a final buying decision by asking for the order—is easy if you:
- develop a strong interpersonal and professional relationship;
- stick to the basics;
- ask the right questions;
- understand the prospect's real needs;
- remain calm, patient and in control;
- prepare your strategy in advance;
- practise and are prepared to try something new;
- think of closing as a process that starts when you meet the prospect and continues into after-sales service;
- display confidence, enthusiasm and an understanding that sales are prospect-based, not salesperson-based, and are process-based, not product-based; and
- express a sincere desire to connect with and assist the prospect and gain the right to ask for their business.

chapter 20

Negotiation—reaching agreement on the finer points

N egotiation is often misunderstood in the context of selling. In this chapter I will propose a view of the role of negotiation in the sales process and a basic negotiation model, paying particular attention to when a salesperson should engage in the negotiation element of the sale and when to resist involvement.

This chapter, then, deals primarily with the various approaches salespeople may choose in dealing with this sales process element. Chapter 30, in Part 3, will move beyond this element and address some of the competencies or skill-based issues. It will provide basic practical guidelines which I and many others have found useful in undertaking negotiation and will alert you to a variety of tricks or traps set intentionally, or unintentionally, by buyers.

Very few salespeople seem to receive even the most rudimentary training in one of the most basic sales process elements—negotiation. Most salespeople evolve a negotiation style or approach based on their own sales style and life experiences. This method is usually rooted in the trial-and-error approach; as such, it can be very costly when it comes to negotiating complex sales.

Many salespeople see no difference between selling and negotiating. They see the two as essentially the same and may use phrases such as 'I'm negotiating the sale of a new . . .' to refer to the actual process of selling.

What is negotiation?

It would probably be instructive, before we move much further with this topic of negotiation, to take a minute to talk about what constitutes negotiation.

Negotiation, as it applies to the realm of selling, refers to a wide variety of transactions in which the terms of the exchange are initially quite fluid. These terms of exchange only evolve in the course of the various parties to the negotiation getting together to decide under what conditions or terms they will do business with one another.

There are probably as many definitions of negotiation as there are approaches and, for that matter, alleged experts and theories. Three definitions you might like to consider are:

1. Negotiation is the 'art of getting what you want by convincing others that they will benefit from association with you in business or personally'.
2. Negotiation is back-and-forth communication designed to reach an agreement when you and the other side have some interests that are shared and others that are opposed.
3. Negotiation is the process whereby two or more parties attempt to settle what each shall give and take, or perform and receive, in a transaction between them.

I offer the description below as one I have found to be simple, clear and, most of all, user-friendly. Note that I didn't say 'definition'. I am not attempting to define negotiation but to provide you with a useable description of this important element, which you will find present in most sales situations, although certainly not all.

Negotiation is the process that is embarked on when at least two parties, each of whom controls or is assumed to control resources desired by the others, communicate with the objective of agreeing on an arrangement for the exchange of some or all of those resources.

The important thing here is that you need to reach your own understanding as to what *you* believe constitutes negotiation, for without this understanding you will find it difficult to effectively approach, plan and implement complex negotiations. You need to be clear about how you view the negotiation process, what it is you are attempting to achieve and how you wish to achieve it. There are many and varied approaches to negotiation, and we will deal with two competing approaches a little later. Note that the above descriptions of negotiation all share the following points:

- There are *at least* two parties to the negotiation.
- All the parties involved in the negotiation must *share* some common *need*.
- In most, if not all, negotiations, there will be some *needs* that are not *shared*.

The crucial concept that salespeople must accept and understand is this: *negotiation, in our model, comes into play only when the prospect has found something they want.* In other words, negotiation only really comes into play as a complex sales element when you have effectively demonstrated value and when it only remains to decide the price, terms and/or conditions of the sale with the prospect.

The reason I have suggested that negotiation has a separate, but almost identical, place in the model to the *close* element is that, in some instances, all that is required is to write up the order and get a signature on the dotted line. However, on most occasions relating to the complex sale, the close element is often *just that*—the close of the true selling side of the sales process—and signals the beginning of the negotiation.

In fact, the move from *closing* after 'agreeing that the product meets their needs' to *negotiating* by 'agreeing to the terms' should be managed jsut as carefully as the transitions from other sales elements or phases need to be handled.

I suggest that you consider the model below as one possible four-step approach to moving from selling to negotiating:

1. Look (watch and listen) for 'buying signals'.
2. Confirm their 'agreement' to buy.
3. Acknowledge their 'agreement'.
4. Invite them to negotiate.

I cannot stress enough how crucial it is that you undertake these four simple steps before you commence negotiating. The four steps might go something like the following:

Step 1: Look for buying signals	*You have observed clear buying signals. The prospect is assuming ownership and is now asking questions about installation.*

You might move smoothly to the next step, confirming commitment to buy, by asking a question like the one below.

Step 2: Confirm their agreement to buy	*'Am I right in assuming that this is what you are looking for?'* *The prospect responds, 'Yes, well, depending on what it's going to cost, of course.'*

Step 3: Acknowledge their agreement	*'That's terrific. I really believe that your decision to select product X is one you will appreciate even more once we install the new machine and you get to see and experience the benefits first-hand.'*

> | *Step 4: Invite* | *'Now, if it's OK with you, I suggest that we* |
> | *them to negotiate* | *put this to bed and discuss the best way of* |
> | | *structuring this agreement to suit your needs.'* |

The golden rule is that you should enter the negotiation arena only when the prospect understands and accepts the value you bring to the table. Why? Because if you haven't established this value, I guarantee that you will end up 'bargaining', based almost exclusively on the issue of price. This potential for bargaining is also partly due to the widely accepted view of many salespeople and prospects that the 'buyer' is perceived to have more clout or leverage than the 'seller'. However, you can counteract this view, and more effectively balance this perceived 'power imbalance', by moving the actual balance point.

How do you do this? Easy—you 'effectively sell them on what you have to offer', and if they really need it and want it you will have moved the balance point to a more even one.

My experience suggests that the single most common cause of breakdown in a sales negotiation is simply that the prospect isn't 'sold' on your compelling sales story *before* you deal with the negotiation element. You will always find that you will negotiate for better terms if you have effectively 'sold' the product first, rather than doing what most salespeople do—attempt to sell the product on the 'terms' themselves, then wonder why price becomes such a big issue.

You will see that in Step 3 of this transition I have suggested you acknowledge 'agreement', because one of the cornerstones of successful negotiation is building on agreement. In short, if a positive response isn't forthcoming from your prospect at Step 2, by their confirming their agreement to buy, return to earlier elements in the sale process. Without commitment from the prospect at this point of the sale, your negotiation is probably doomed. It may even be sensible to call a 'time out' to differentiate the move from 'selling' to 'negotiating' in your prospect's mind. I have seen this tactic bring impressive results in more complex sales.

So why negotiate?

We negotiate for a host of reasons. But when it comes right down to it, we view negotiation as a viable means of getting what we want or need and, at the same time, as a way of resolving potential or actual conflict. So, as a general rule, we negotiate when the following conditions exist:

- a conflict of interest exists, or has the potential to do so, and we desire to 'settle our differences'; and/or

■ out of self-interest when we believe that we can use our influence to engineer or design a 'better deal' that satisfies our interests; and/or
■ the alternative to a 'negotiated settlement'—that is, no agreement is perceived as worse; and/or
■ you are prepared to invest in some 'give and take' and have the authority to vary terms/conditions etc.

These are generally the top four compelling reasons, either singly or in partnership, that focus parties on the potential of negotiation as a viable means of resolving actual or potential conflict.

Which brings us to the next point. Negotiation is a process, and it is very much like the sales process in that it has a number of essential elements that appear in most negotiations. The process of negotiation involves the parties using their common interests, whether stated or unstated, as a foundation on which to build an agreement and reduce differences such that the form of the final agreement is acceptable to all the parties concerned.

You can see clearly from this viewpoint that the negotiation element necessarily involves a measure of both conflict and cooperation. You can, by extension, also accept that, of necessity, negotiation will then involve the following initiatives if we are to avoid deadlock:

■ revising expectations;
■ reducing demands;
■ demonstrating give and take;
■ proposing and suggesting;
■ conceding;
■ agreeing; and
■ allowing adequate time.

If all these initiatives are present, you have the ingredients, at least on paper, for a healthy negotiation. However, should one of these ingredients be missing, it has the potential to jeopardise the chances of success. The absence of two or more of these initiatives usually means that the odds of achieving a mutually satisfactory outcome are slim.

An example of a situation where one or more of these initiatives are missing is when one party to a 'negotiation' has, or is perceived to have, all the power. If this is the case, the word 'negotiation' is used only advisedly to describe the process. What really exists in this situation may well be 'unconditional surrender' by one party.

Now, this concept of power in negotiation is in itself an ephemeral one—one that has been written about copiously in the many books published on the subject of negotiation. I don't intend to address the issue of perceived power in negotiation here, except to say that there are many forms of negotiation 'power'. The general rule is: if *you* believe you have negotiation power, then you probably do; and if you *don't* believe you have negotiation power, then you probably don't. Power is very much about perception, and rarely has a basis in objective 'reality'!

Two other points are worth commenting on before we more on to discussing the negotiation process itself. First, contrary to the widely held belief that 'negotiators are born', we are in fact all negotiators. We negotiate every day, and some of us even negotiate most of the day—when we talk to our family, our friends, our acquaintances, when we negotiate holidays, chores, meeting places, lunch orders and our children's home-work. On a professional basis, we negotiate with our colleagues about days off and duties. We negotiate with our boss about remuneration, holidays, responsibilities and sales outcomes. We all negotiate. However, many salespeople view only major formal negotiations carried out by senior personnel as being true negotiations.

When it comes to negotiating, we often just don't recognise we are doing it. We often think that to negotiate we need to do so in a controlled environment and adopt a formal, disciplined, no-nonsense approach to the proceedings. But this most emphatically is not so. Negotiating can be carried out when walking on the factory floor, standing in the office corridors, sitting at the boardroom table, or when face to face over a prospect's desk.

Second, it's been suggested that 'everything's negotiable'. I suggest that you review this premise if it's one that seems attractive to you. This second point is well worth discussing, because *not* everything is negotiable. For instance, try negotiating a reduction in a statutory charge—say, your local government residential rates—or the application fee for your new driver's licence.

This chapter on negotiation is only one chapter in a book focused on selling; as such, its objective is first to make it abundantly clear where negotiation 'fits' in the selling process. Second, in so doing I present what I view as an essential concept. This is that negotiation of the terms and conditions of the sale ideally proceeds only when the prospect is clear about and accepts the value that you, the salesperson, bring to the exchange. I believe that, contrary to what I observe in practice, the negotiation element of the sales process should never be used to 'sell' the product.

Having set the scene, it is now time to propose that there are two other issues that will provide you with a more complete view of the negotiation element and, ultimately, the processes and methodologies available to be adopted by you and the other parties to the negotiation. The first of these issues involves the *approach* taken to the negotiation; the second touches on the common *tactics* used in many negotiations. As I mentioned in the opening paragraphs to this chapter, I propose to leave the subject of tactics to the third part of this book, where I will deal with negotiating skills.

So, let's start now with the approach.

Two different approaches to negotiation

This concept of two opposite approaches to negotiating is critical to an understanding of where you and the other parties in the negotiation process are coming from.

Imagine for a minute that the negotiation process can be simplified into a single horizontal dimension, with all the different forms of negotiation approach represented by individual points on this line. Now imagine that the far left-hand side of this negotiation dimension involves a negotiation process with 100% competition and no cooperation, while the far right-hand side represents exactly the opposite—that is, 100% cooperation and no competition.

Let's give each position a name. Let's call the far left position 'bargaining' and the far right side 'partnering'. Note that, far from being hypothetical, these are both legitimate and widely used approaches to negotiating. Our negotiation dimension might look something like the model below.

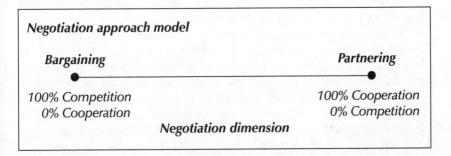

Negotiation approach model

Bargaining   *Partnering*

100% Competition   *100% Cooperation*
0% Cooperation   *0% Competition*
    Negotiation dimension

What has tended to happen is that the terms 'negotiating' and 'bargaining' have been used to describe different types of negotiation. We often hear of the term *bargaining* being used to describe the negotiation process that evolves as we attempt to agree on the terms and conditions of a purchase at the local markets or perhaps even when buying a car. The term *negotiation* we tend to reserve for the more complex and more structured processes that also tend to involve more time. For example, we negotiate when attempting to strike a deal with an employer concerning our terms of employment, or when we attempt to agree on the terms and conditions of a new office premises lease.

The point is that *they are both* very different and yet entirely legitimate forms of negotiation. However, it is, in my view, imperative that in a sales environment you understand and recognise the essential differences in approach, characterised by what I have termed the *partnering* and *bargaining* forms of negotiation. It is also important that you can demonstrate that you are flexible enough to adopt the appropriate approach, including, in a bargaining negotiating environment, moving the other parties towards a more partnering approach if this is more appropriate.

Bargaining vs partnering

The analogy that has been used in the past quite effectively to expand on the proposition that these are simply different approaches to the same thing—that is, negotiation—is that of a ball sport. Take, for instance, basketball and soccer: each of these very different sports is played by two opposing teams, each having their own half and each using a large round ball. However, the objectives and skills required to play these two ball games are vastly different. In soccer, only one player on each team, the goalkeeper, can touch the ball with their hands and then only in their penalty area. In basketball, their hands are *all* the players can use. In soccer the target or goal is on the ground; in basketball the target or basket is elevated. The point I am making is that while in the most basic sense they are both ball games, the objectives and approaches to each are radically different. The same can be said of the partnering and bargaining approaches to negotiation.

The next time you enter a negotiation, ask yourself, 'Am I ready to play basketball or have I come prepared to play soccer?' One isn't intrinsically 'better' or 'worse' than the other (the opinion of fanatical fans aside); they are just different. You could be good at both, but you usually have a preference and affinity for one. Negotiation is much the same. My experience suggests that most salespeople habitually tend towards one or other end of the negotiation continuum and often have difficulty recognising, understanding and implementing the other very different approach to negotiation. So let's talk a little more about these two almost opposing views of the negotiation element.

In the *bargaining* style of negotiation, the parties are generally of the view that the size of the 'pie', for which each is negotiating a share, is fixed and, as such, each is competing for the biggest slice. Here competition outweighs cooperation, often to the extent that each party may be attempting to gain the whole pie, leaving little or nothing for the other party. The essence of this approach is that the sum of the available pie up for grabs is fixed and that one party's gain is automatically the other party's loss. In the *partnering* style of negotiation (or, as it is often called, joint problem solving), there is *no* overriding view that the size of the pie, about which (not *for* which) the parties are negotiating, is fixed. The issue of 'bigger' only comes into play with the notion that all the parties are cooperating to increase the total sum of positive outcomes for everybody to share by adopting a win/win attitude grounded not in competition but in cooperation. In other words, in partnering, the parties are actually working to increase the size of the pie available.

Let's face it, in most sales situations the size of the pie isn't fixed at all. There are any number of possibilities, permutations, combinations and options available if, and only if, you work together to uncover or create them. So what determines where, on this negotiation continuum, your negotiation or part of any particular negotiation is to be grounded?

The issues that tend to dictate where on the negotiation continuum you are operating can be divided into internal and external factors. The *internal factors* category includes your skills and mental approach to the negotiation. By 'skills', I mean your interpersonal skills, conflict resolution skills, influencing skills and so on. Just as importantly, when it comes to the mental approach, what are the experiences, and ultimately the preferred approaches, habits and tendencies, of the individual parties involved? You can do little to change the skill levels of other parties during the negotiation, and little to change their habits or tendencies.

External factors, on the other hand, are external to the various parties and include such factors as the nature of the issues at stake, the relationship between the parties, the time available and the balance of power. Let's look now at a few of these external factors.

Issues at stake

The issues at stake often have a major impact on the approach to and, ultimately, the course of the negotiation. Are the issues shared, or are many of them important to only one of the parties? Are the issues simple or complex? Are they few in number, or are they many and varied and interconnected to each other?

Relationship between the parties

The relationship between the parties can be assessed in very simple terms. Is the relationship one based primarily on conflict or cooperation? Does the relationship include past shared experiences, or is it based on no prior shared experiences? Is the relationship rooted in trust or in antagonism? Is the true relationship between the parties independent or interdependent? Is the relationship expected to be ongoing, or is it a one-off encounter?

The relationship also involves the 'personality' aspect of the other parties. This aspect encompasses, as you might imagine such issues as the other parties' values, attitudes, feelings and beliefs and the allegedly more objective business issues such as 'needs'. These 'personality' and 'needs' aspects can be major determining factors in the relationship. For instance, personality will determine what is considered 'fair and reasonable', and needs will influence what might be called 'unreasonable' or 'worthless'.

It is probably not an overstatement to suggest that the relationship mix will probably have the greatest potential to shape the negotiation approach and, thus, affect the negotiation outcomes.

Time available

Time available for the negotiation will tend to affect not so much the initial approach, although it most certainly can do, as the conduct of the negotiation as time goes by. Partnering takes time, and the cooperative, creative approach cannot be rushed.

Balance of power

Power, as I have already mentioned, is very much a matter of perception. The boundaries between real and imagined power are often blurry. Power does tend to have a major effect on the approach to negotiation. For example, where power is perceived to be approximately equal, inconsistent or shared, according to the various issues under negotiation, then partnering can be, and is often, pursued. However, the tendency to bargain is often observed where one party believes, rightly or wrongly, that they have all or a major share of the power available.

Set out in Table 20.1 are some of the basic negotiating factors referred to above and an indication of which of these factors tend to dictate a more favourable attitude or disposition towards either the bargaining or the partnering ends of the negotiation continuum.

The interesting thing is that, despite the various factors above and the options available, research seems to indicate that as many as two-thirds

Table 20.1 *Comparison of various common negotiation factors*

Negotiating factor	More favourable to Bargaining	Partnering
1. Nature of interest and issues	Single issue, fixed sum, less complex	Multiple issues, increased sum, more complex
2. Relationship of parties	Independent gain, less formal, conflict > cooperation, win/lose	Interdependent joint effort, more formal, cooperation > conflict, win/win
3. Type of parties	Takers	Givers/takers
4. Time available	Less time	More time
5. Balance of power	Unilateral	Balanced
6. Creativity	Little or no creativity	More creativity required
7. Approach	Non-skilled	Skilled

of negotiators assume that their upcoming negotiations involve win/lose imperatives. That is, the partnering win/win approach (rather than the alternative bargaining win/lose approach) is naturally adopted by only about one-third of the parties. In other words, irrespective of the option presented, the habitual tendency or negotiation approach adopted by most negotiators—in fact, a little more than twice as many as their counterparts—was one involving competition to see who could come away with the greater share of the fixed pie. This should give you some idea of what to expect in most negotiation phases of the sales processes.

When it comes to negotiation, and in particular the two very opposite approaches I have described, it is worth remembering that there are not necessarily winners and losers. Many negotiations can, rather than pursue a win/lose approach, consider the more expansive and potentially more profitable win/win approach. Adopting and promoting a win/win philosophy will be conducive to creating an environment where each of the parties vigorously explores all available options; often, as a result, a host of unexpectedly attractive alternatives and creative solutions can be found for what often appear at first to be extremely complex sales negotiations, with little or no scope for creativity.

On the one hand, in bargaining, the apparent goals of each of the parties are at least initially irreconcilable. Or so it might well seem to the parties themselves, as well as any observers. Central to this conflict, or battle of wills, is an almost unassailable view that the resources to be shared are of limited quantity—that is, there is a fixed size of pie, as discussed earlier. Both parties usually then strive to win, where winning is measured by gaining more at the other party's expense.

Partnering, by stark contrast, is founded on the belief that the goals or objectives of each party aren't necessarily mutually exclusive—that one party's gain isn't necessarily the other party's loss. The fundamental picture of partnering is that by working together it is possible for each to achieve their goals. By working together, the sum total of their efforts is greater than the sum of their individual contributions. Let's look a little more closely at the respective strategies of each of the two competing styles or approaches to negotiation.

Bargaining strategies

When are they used?

We usually see bargaining strategies commonly adopted when both of the following two factors arise:

- *Factor 1*—The negotiation process is viewed as relatively simple and straightforward.
- *Factor 2*—Competition greatly outweighs cooperation.

In other words, the negotiation is one where there are relatively few issues involved, and the methodology adopted by one or both parties involves a competitive approach where the size of the outcome is viewed as fixed and the objective appears to be to take as many wins and score as many points as possible, usually at the other party's expense.

The first situation is a typical car sale scenario, where the basic issue is price and the bargaining end of the negotiation continuum is adopted by most parties in an attempt to pay, or receive, a sum of money as close as possible to each party's opening bid. The atmosphere is competitive, often aggressive, and can turn into a distasteful experience to those not experienced with this form of negotiation.

What is the process?

Two basic processes tend to determine the positions adopted by the respective parties:

- *Process 1*—The parties view the process as a means of exchanging resources to primarily *have their own needs met*.
- *Process 2*—*Supply and demand* have a major bearing on the terms offered and the quantum of the give-and-take engaged in.

No surprises here!

What is the overall strategy?

The general overall strategy adopted by bargaining-style negotiators involves all or some of these:

- *Strategy 1*— Find out what the other party *wants*.
- *Strategy 2*—Show them that you can *provide* it.
- *Strategy 3*—Demonstrate the *advantages* of your offer.
- *Strategy 4*—Focus on *influencing the other party to accept* your advantages as major benefits.
- *Strategy 5*—*Reduce the other party's opportunities* by differentiating what you have to offer to justify your terms.

What are the tactics?

Broadly speaking, the fundamental tactics employed, often unconsciously by those in the bargaining arena, involve many of the product-centred or salesperson-centred approaches to selling we discussed earlier in this book. These tactics usually involve one or more of the following:

- *Tactic 1*—Assess the value the other party will put on their various expectations—for example, their opening offer or entry point, negotiating range, target.
- *Tactic 2*—Manipulate the other party's perceptions of *your* position.
- *Tactic 3*—Influence the other party's perceptions of *their* own position.
- *Tactic 4*—Engineer the perception of opportunity, termination and delay costs.

Now, compare these strategies and tactics with those where we choose to adopt a more cooperative, joint problem-solving or partnering approach.

Partnering strategies

When are they used?

We see skilled negotiators pursuing a more partnering approach to negotiation when one or more of the following three factors are present:

- *Factor 1*—The issues involved in the negotiation are many and varied and may be complex.
- *Factor 2*—The implications of the outcome of the negotiation will have long-term effects on the ongoing relationship between the parties.
- *Factor 3*—The objective, right at the outset, is to grow the sum of potential positive outcomes to be shared by the parties by establishing a cooperative and creative problem-solving approach.

While this makes eminent sense and may seem obvious to all, a word of warning. This approach, no matter how determined and committed the parties are to it, requires considerable skill to prevent it sliding along the continuum towards the bargaining approach.

No matter how lofty your ideals, you need to be able to demonstrate the skills required to maintain this approach, and to do that you need to continually reinforce the following partnering processes.

What is the process?

The five primary processes that need to be consistently addressed for this form of negotiation include:

- *Process 1*—Demonstrate trust.
- *Process 2*—Reinforce a cooperative and creative interpersonal climate.
- *Process 3*—Be prepared to give and take.
- *Process 4*—Keep the *big picture* in mind.
- *Process 5*—Pursue interests rather than protecting positions.

The first four of these processes are relatively simple and, given that it's not my objective here to provide a full text on negotiation, will be left with no further comment. The fifth process, however, justifies further explanation.

Interests are different from positions, in that interests are the underlying concerns, needs, desires and fears *behind* a negotiator's position. Interests are what motivates the negotiator to take their particular negotiating position. Partnering requires an approach to negotiation where the problems are defined, and the other party's *real* interests, those often screened behind their stated positions, are explored. On this basis alone, the pie is expanded to include the other party's interests by generating as many feasible alternative solutions and options as possible. But the real key is understanding the other party's motivations and interests. If you can do that, you are a long way down the track to being able to negotiate creatively to satisfy the majority of all the parties' required outcomes.

The best negotiation story to demonstrate this is one that has long since passed into negotiation folklore. It's the story about two teenage sisters who were squabbling over who got possession of the last lemon in the fruit basket. The bickering went on and on until in desperation the girls' mother stepped in, took the piece of fruit, cut the lemon in half and thrust a piece into each girl's hands. A fair and equitable solution, one might think. But was it the best solution? In this case, absolutely not!

If the mother had taken the time to go beyond the similar demanding position taken by each sister, she might have discovered two very different yet compatible interests. One sister wanted only the juice and half the pulp to make lemonade. The other sister wanted only the rind and half the pulp with which to make a cake. Each could have got 100% of what she really needed, instead of half, if they both had taken the time to explore each other's interests rather than fight in an attempt to legitimise and defend their own position. In the end, neither ended up with what they really needed. Don't underestimate the power of exploring interests in helping to increase the size of the pie. Remember this story!

The rule that *must* be remembered when it comes to negotiation based on interests is that we really have no choice. There is no other feasible alternative. In order to settle our differences, we must look not at reinforcing and defending our positions but, rather, at exploring and resolving our interests.

What is the overall strategy?

The 'big picture' objectives pursued by those negotiators who follow the partnering approach to negotiation include:

- *Strategy 1*—Take the initiative in demonstrating and maintaining a cooperative approach.

- *Strategy 2*—Plan the negotiating agenda carefully:
  - look to start with issues that lend themselves more readily to a partnering approach; and
  - reserve the single, often larger issues, which may be prone to degenerating into a bargaining approach, until much later.
- *Strategy 3*—Present issues as problems to be solved together for the mutual benefit of each party.
- *Strategy 4*—Avoid raising or dealing with issues on an abstract level.

How can you achieve this? What specific tactics can you employ?

What are the tactics?

There are eight key tactics that apply equally to all partnering approaches to negotiation:

- *Tactic 1*—Demonstrate trust and a desire to cooperate by sharing information early in the negotiation.
- *Tactic 2*—Be prepared to put aside prejudices, precedents, routines and habits by constantly working to keep an open mind and exercising your imagination creatively.
- *Tactic 3*—Postpone voicing disagreement, engaging in interruption and restating your position until all reasonable discussion has been heard.
- *Tactic 4*—Explain your position *before* stating your negative response to the other party's proposal.
- *Tactic 5*—Build strong foundations on shared common ground before moving on to deal with the differences and problems.
- *Tactic 6*—When problems threaten to sidetrack the negotiations, backtrack and reaffirm the common ground.
- *Tactic 7*—Be prepared to demand a cooperative attitude.
- *Tactic 8*—Disapprove or object to tactics and facts rather than the other party's values or personal characteristics.

These eight partnering tactics are relatively straightforward, and there is probably no need for further comment other than a quick comment on the first tactic—sharing information.

Efficient information sharing using clear and open channels of communication is one of the most effective means of promoting good partnering practices in negotiation. This willingness to share information is radically different from the atmosphere which permeates the bargaining approach. Here the parties distrust each other, often openly, and actively work to conceal all critical information, releasing it only to manipulate the proceedings. In the bargaining approach to negotiation, the parties pursue information sharing only from the perspective of what competitive advantage they can gain from it.

Partnering involves sharing information about priorities, preferences and true interests so as to communicate your positions clearly and to gain a greater understanding and appreciation of the other party's needs.

This chapter outlined a philosophy of negotiation and two competing negotiation approaches. In the next part I will address how to recognise and combat the tricks and traps, both intentional and unintentional, set for the unwary negotiator by other parties.

PART 3

BRINGING THE PROCESS TO LIFE—
THE ESSENTIAL SALES SKILLS

chapter 21

Relating skills—building bridges with your prospect

W e all have natural relating skills. It's not a matter of ordering some from a shop or learning them from a book. Rather, it's about appreciating your natural assets and the natural preferences of your prospect, and learning to be more proactive in relating to your prospect.

When it comes to relating to your prospects and customers, you should understand that you already have most of the basic relating skills. To improve and grow in this area, you usually need only to:

- recognise those natural relating skills you do have and be aware of the times you use them; and
- use them according to what the situation calls for; or
- modify or adapt them to meet those situations that arise from time to time where your natural relating tendencies aren't necessarily what the situation calls for; and
- make building and maintaining a relationship an ongoing fundamental objective of each and every contact you have with your prospect; and
- understand that relating is never over. You are never 'there'. You don't reach a summit, where everything thereafter is downhill. You work at relating during every single contact, whether face-to-face, by email, letter or telephone.

Keep firmly in mind that the relationship you build with your prospect will likely be tested from time to time. You may not be the cause or, indeed, the instigator. It could be your competitor attempting to gain entry to the opportunities or to hijack the relationship, or it could simply be a sequence of events beyond anyone's control or ability to predict.

The strength of your relationship is the key not just to one sale or, for that matter, many sales. It's the key to how the prospect views your role. I talked in Chapter 16 about the four 'C' levels of service (Competitor, Commodity, Competency and Consultancy) as perceived by the prospect. With this in mind, consider that if you want to be seen as a 'consultant', someone at the very top level of the salesperson–prospect relationship, someone who is respected and called on first when it comes to investigating and helping provide answers to buyers' problems, then you need to first work on your relationship with your prospect. You must also continue to work towards the maintenance and development of that relationship as a first priority. Closing is no longer where selling is at. Complex sales require good, strong relationships—relationships that will survive the rigours and stresses imposed by complex, rapidly changing situations and the cut and thrust of the competitive business environment.

The ultimate example of the importance of building, maintaining and always working on an interpersonal relationship is the connection you have to your partner. If the relationship is taken for granted, if it isn't sustained, maintained and continually worked on, the inevitable stresses and strains of everyday life will soon cause it to show signs of wear and tear. Ultimately, a breakdown may result.

Good, strong professional and interpersonal relationships with your prospects and customers don't and cannot stop problems from arising. What strong relationships can do, however, is keep your connection with your prospect intact and healthy. It can allow it to survive major problems and obstacles that might otherwise destroy or irrevocably damage more fragile relationships. In fact, a strong relationship can take advantages of adversity and emerge from problems, challenges and major obstacles even stronger than previously.

Keys to relating

To sum up, when it comes to relating well with your prospect, there are a number of key considerations you might care to review. Until you get in the habit of checking these things almost subconsciously, you may wish to use them as a basic written checklist to be reviewed prior to commencing any face-to-face sales call.

This is not intended as an exhaustive checklist or schedule of all the essential elements, nor is it meant to be a sequence of steps. It is simply intended as a brief practical list of key issues that will affect your ability to develop and maintain a strong relationship, whether interpersonal, professional, or both.

Nine keys to effective relating

> *1. Establish common ground*

It is important, if not critical, to establish common links with your prospect. Here you are attempting to find areas of common interest, or at least areas where your prospect indicates interest and that they are comfortable discussing. If possible, look for and pursue areas where you also share an interest or know enough about to be able to contribute by promoting and expanding on the subject during discussions.

Remember, you're not likely to be the only one feeling a little unsettled, especially during the first meeting with your prospect. They are probably also feeling a degree of uncertainty about the course of the meeting and its outcome. If you can establish some common links with your prospect early in your relationship, preferably commencing in the very first call, you can build on these, expand into other areas and start smoothly to develop a successful professional and interpersonal relationship with them.

Once you know what your prospect's interests are, both inside and outside the work environment, you can further investigate and research these areas or, at the very least, take the time to pursue them when you come across them in your travels, reading or in talking to others. Shared interests allow you to network more effectively. Networking is, after all, about building a network of people primarily by meeting new people and relating to them based on your existing relationship with someone else. Networking is much easier, more fun and a lot more rewarding if you attempt to uncover areas of common interest or knowledge. Also, by investigating areas of common ground to further strengthen the relationship, you will be in a position to pass on information of interest that you come across, and names of people you meet, all of which may interest the prospect.

One small but nevertheless important point: don't assume that all your prospects will want to establish common ground before you get down to business. Some prospects will be far more inclined to pursue what they view as a non-business-oriented discussion after the business agenda is concluded. With others it will be relatively easy to begin to establish common interests and interpersonal links up front. Two things I know for certain:

1. You must establish, maintain and continue to expand these common links or areas of common ground if you wish to build a strong relationship.
2. The vast majority of prospects want this level of professional and interpersonal connection, regardless of how they might otherwise behave and appear.

If you are to establish a strong, healthy connection with your prospect, you *must* be prepared to explore common ground.

2. Do your homework

It has been suggested that the more you know about other people, the more sensitive you will be to them, their wants and their needs. This not only *sounds* like common sense but is exactly that. If you know little or even nothing about your prospect, it will be nearly impossible to stand on their side of the fence and understand how they perceive the world. Remember, you can't effectively influence other people without having a basic understanding of their version of the world as seen through their eyes. And to do this you need to undertake some research, ask questions, listen, observe and read. Even the most basic level of research provides you with invaluable information about how your prospects think, feel, value life, make decisions and so on. Doing your homework takes time, but it also *saves* time, and more importantly it can help to reinforce relationships that are under some pressure, whether the pressure be from the prospect's peers, their manager or the organisation's culture, or whether it is applied by your competitors or inadvertently by you.

There is no excuse for not doing your homework. This is one of the key issues that separates the professional salesperson from the average salesperson. Even at the most basic level, a simple telephone call to a colleague, to a fellow supplier, to the prospect's assistant, can yield surprising and often critical information.

3. Know, recognise and adapt

I covered this issue in a broader context in several earlier chapters. This strategy of knowing and understanding your own behavioural tendencies, recognising the natural preferences of others and then adapting by implementing strategies designed to meet others' needs by modifying your own behaviour is basic and as inescapable as any major truism in sales.

Knowing your own behaviour is akin to knowing exactly where you are starting from on a map. In fact, this analogy is a good one. Most people agree that to use a map (street directory, layout plan or whatever) to chart a route to a new destination, you must first start with one basic fact, and that is: 'Where am I now on this plan or map?' Knowing where you are in terms of appreciating your own behavioural tendencies is a foundational element when it comes to interpersonal relationships in any environment.

Next, 'skill' enters the equation—the skill that provides you with the ability to recognise and appreciate your prospect's behavioural preferences. These preferences could include how they make decisions, how they like to be presented to or how they prefer to relate to others, how and what type of objections and concerns they are likely to raise, what style of after-sales service they expect, and how they negotiate.

Recognition requires careful observation, a suspension of judgement, and a clear understanding that we cannot determine people's *intent* based solely on observations of their behaviours as interpreted by our version of reality. To do so is tantamount to our using our own values, behaviour and experiences to interpret how others think and feel and thereby *what they intend*, based solely on their external observable behaviour.

Adapting our behaviour is much more than simple mirroring or copying. It involves understanding and applying a behavioural model that is researched and validated. Only then can we carefully interpret others' behaviour in a validated framework and thereby appreciate how they might feel in any given circumstances.

Finally comes the information required to design a strategy to adapt. Invariably, when I ask groups of salespeople about adapting, they agree that yes, they are very conscious of adapting to the prospect's behaviour. They often describe in detail various strategies used to adapt in different circumstances. However, I see that these strategies may or may not be appropriate. Salespeople can indeed be great adaptors. But based on my own observations, I put forward two propositions:

■ *Adaptation proposition no. 1—Very few salespeople use any type of formal validated model on which to base their 'adaptation' strategy.* Most employ a combination of many inputs to decide on their adaptation strategy, such as gut feel, folklore, sales manager suggestion/instruction, company policy, peer group influence.
■ *Adaptation proposition no. 2—Very few salespeople adapt their natural sales style anywhere near to the extent they believe they do.* It appears that we humans are very much creatures of habit and, contrary to what we might be tempted to believe, we don't vary from our habitual ways of doing things nearly as much as we think we do. Why? The old comfort zone theory. When we move out of our comfort zone, we experience emotional pressure, stress and often fatigue. We, as an instinctive response, tend to return to our comfort zone at the earliest opportunity. But some of us have small comfort zones and others larger or more expansive ones: that is, some of us have natural flexibility or versatility when it comes to adapting and, as such, a greater range of movement inside our comfort zone, thereby permitting better adaptation prior to feeling stressed or pressured to resume our more natural, habitual behaviours.

Our ability to relate, to open the door for effective communication, to increase our awareness of others, to adapt our own external behaviours and to tune into our prospect's wavelength depends largely on three factors referred to above. To put it simply, our ability to adapt to meet other people's needs depends very much on our being able to:

- know *ourselves*;
- recognise and appreciate the tendencies and preferences of *others*; and
- adapt and adopt strategies for improved interpersonal connections.

---

4. Hone your skills

Treat each interaction with your prospect as an opportunity to learn, to improve, and to hone your skills.

Contrary to conventional wisdom, which stresses concentrating on overcoming your weaknesses, we suggest that you concentrate just as much on your strengths and your natural talents. Look for ways of using and capitalising on the natural talents and values you bring to your profession to a greater degree, as a way of improving those skills you require to effectively build relationships with others.

Make no mistake: skills can be learned: the bywords are knowledge, application, experimentation and practice. You cannot practise building relationships in a vacuum any more than you can improve these relationships in a vacuum. Look at the way you do things now and be prepared to apply what you have learned, to experiment, to take the initiative and try something a little different.

The interesting observation I would venture concerning skills is that each skill you have seems to affect all the other skills you possess. Therefore, if you improve in one particular skill, as well as having a positive, perhaps measurable, outcome for areas directly related to that skill, you will find that it will also influence positively a whole host of related, dependent and interdependent skills. A small improvement in one particular area can have a larger overall positive result in many other areas. For example, I have observed salespeople who have improved their questioning skills. This has, as a result, positively affected their ability to relate, to close, to identify needs, to negotiate. This almost inconsequential, you might think, sharpening of questioning skills ends up having a major impact on the sales process as a whole by affecting a range of associated skills. The message I would leave you with here is a simple one: don't underestimate the positive impact one particular skill improvement will have on other, often seemingly unrelated, areas of your sales process skills.

> ### 5. Check your attitude at the door

When it comes to attitude, there are two facets of this critical success factor that apply to the relationship element: your attitude to the *sales process* and your attitude to the *people* involved. I have spoken previously about both, but when it comes to your attitude to the sales process you need first to check that your attitude is one of being customer-sensitive or 'buyer-centred'. That is, you need to make sure your focus is not on yourself or your product, but firmly on your prospect. I spoke about this philosophy or paradigm of selling at length in the first part of this book. I believe that this is the only way to build value and the relationship in the eyes of the prospect.

With respect to your attitude to the people involved in the sales process, understand that relationships are built through tolerance and acceptance of the differences in others and that this can be achieved only through understanding your own attitudes and a measure of discipline in effectively examining and controlling your responses and behaviours. This comes from the basic premise that you are not dealing with products, organisations, or even outcomes and processes, but with people. Your attitude to other people must, by the very nature of the sales process, to a large degree determine your success in selling.

> ### 6. Use professionalism

The impression of many salespeople appears to be that pursuing a professional sales relationship is counterproductive or the very opposite of building and maintaining interpersonal relationships. They see interpersonal relationships as requiring them to exhibit a 'friendly, relaxed, people-oriented approach' and demeanour, whereas professionalism requires a 'task-focused, independent, results-oriented approach'. Other salespeople view the relationship-building sales element as paramount, something that should precede the business of the sale. Yet others view the relationship as something that tends to take place as an event. They consider the relationship not as a living, breathing, continuing and evolving process, but as something that happens very early as a means of preparing the prospect for what they, the salespeople, intend to do next.

A professional value-based selling approach acknowledges, and in fact demands, that the relationship element of the sales process surround and influence all other sales process elements involved in any salesperson–prospect interactions. It's the protective cocoon that surrounds and facilitates many elements in the sale process.

Part of this professionalism in your approach to the relationship is exhibited in how you go about implementing the various phases of the sales process. When it comes to relating to your prospect, professionalism demands that you display things such as the common courtesies, honesty, sincerity, an ethical approach and so on. Sales professionalism accepts that a phoney is easy to spot and argues persuasively against the view adopted by some salespeople that they need to pretend to be someone they are not.

---

7. Stay positive

The best way to stay positive is simply to concentrate on the positives. Don't dwell on the negatives. Don't immerse yourself in scepticism. Don't try and anticipate all likely outcomes. When it comes to relating, staying positive is a critical initiative in successfully establishing a strong sales relationship. Even the more conservative of buyers want to do business with positive, upbeat, forward-looking people. They want to deal with people who walk, talk and look like winners. And it's not possible to appear as a winner if you don't come across as positive. Now don't misunderstand: by positive I don't mean appearing to exhibit a complete disregard for reality, or thinking only on the bright side. Positive means considering the situation, assessing the pros and cons and, having made a decision on a course of action, moving forward in a definite manner.

One of the best ways of remaining positive during a sale, no matter what negative situations or setbacks occur, is to:

■ concentrate on what has been achieved so far;
■ reinforce the common ground and agreements reached;
■ rein in your subjective responses, keep a lid on your emotions and feelings;
■ keep a check on your own personal attitudes; and
■ understand that every setback has an associated opportunity.

Put simply, you need to decide whether you approach situations by seeing the difficulties in every opportunity or the opportunities in every difficulty.

■ Do you see a glass as being half-full or half-empty?
■ Do you concentrate on the ring of the doughnut or the hole in the middle?
■ Do you see the magnificent view through the window or the dirt on the glass?

You decide. It's your outlook, your life, your sale.

---

8. Observe the common courtesies

Even the most basic common courtesies can make or break relationships. Whether you ask permission to take notes or to take off your coat. Whether you take the trouble to remember your prospect's names and then use them in your discussions or in introducing them to others.

Consider the following questions:

- Do you sit down or wait for your prospect to do so first?
- Do you put your briefcase, folders, laptop computer or whatever on the floor or on the prospect's desk?
- Do you take other phone calls while with the prospect?
- Do you appear rushed, disorganised and dishevelled?
- Do you constantly control the conversation and interrupt, interject or ask questions you should know the answers to?
- Do you follow up? Do you do what you said you would do?
- Do you make a practice of being on time?
- Do you ask your prospect if it's convenient to talk if they are not expecting your call?

And so on.

This isn't intended as a manual on etiquette or manners, as most people are aware of the basic courtesies expected. It is nevertheless surprising how few salespeople demonstrate these basic courtesies when with the prospect. Next time a salesperson calls on you, check it out yourself.

If you are focused on your prospect, chances are that your focus on the normal human courtesies is much more natural. You may need to keep some specifics in mind, but if you are prospect-centred then consideration for the prospect will naturally lead to consideration of your actions. That is, common courtesy will be a natural extension of your selling approach. If, however, you have a tendency to focus on yourself or your product, inevitably your prospect will bear the brunt of an apparent lack of consideration in some areas—even if it's only their perceived lack of your consideration of them, their needs and feelings by you, the seller.

We all know what is expected. If not, talk to some of your colleagues and ask them what areas of common courtesy they concentrate on. Ask your friends and other customers what bad experiences they have had and file this away to make sure you don't follow suit.

Just be aware of and consider your prospect at all times and you cannot go far wrong.

---

9. Risk some risk

Yes, you read this right. Take a risk. Risk taking a risk. Nothing will change *if you don't change* and, in my experience, change is *always* accompanied by some element of risk. Don't be afraid to go out on a limb—after all, that's where they tell us all the good fruit is. In reality, you have no choice. Think about this: you can't avoid risk; it's not something you can simply decide to live without. If you really think about it, something is always at stake, something is always at risk. You can at best accept this and make a conscious decision about which risks to take and which ones to pass by, to say 'no' to. You cannot avoid risk by ignoring it, because doing nothing is in itself accepting a risk.

So, will you take these risks? Are you prepared to:

- risk believing in yourself, your skills, your dreams, your goals?
- risk acting on the assumption that what you say and do is important to other people?
- risk believing that you can make a difference?
- risk behaving as if you appreciate and accept that we achieve only as much as we are prepared to risk in the first instance?

Look the risk of failure in the face and accept that you won't settle for second best, for only a part of your true potential. Risk doing, saying, thinking, believing and feeling differently in order to build and maintain an exceptional interpersonal and professional sales relationship with your prospects. Consider that you only truly fail when you fail to deal with and accept risk as a normal part of your everyday activities. The only time you truly fail, then, is when you don't try.

Move out of your comfort zone and be prepared to experiment a little. Be prepared to take the first step in undertaking a lifelong journey of continuous personal development.

chapter 22

Presence skills—foundations of the relationship

P resence is all about you. In most respects, when it comes to establishing your presence with a prospect, your product doesn't even enter the equation. Presence is all about the skills you employ in projecting your image, in presenting your credentials as another person. It is a combination of many things. It involves, among other things, your personal style, your appearance and your attitude.

Your presence, contrary to what the word might suggest, is intangible. It's not concrete and it's not a simple matter of black-and-white principles or rules. Your presence, or lack of it, is felt in the mind of your prospect at both the conscious and subconscious levels. You could be said to have presence if, when you enter a room or situation, you immediately and positively affect the mood and behaviour of those present. You can set out to attempt to establish a definite perception of how you want the prospect to perceive you, but you must understand that they, not you, control how they will formulate these perceptions.

One simple test of your ability to generate or create presence is whether the prospect feels and thinks differently when you are around. In short, does your physical presence or 'being there' affect the prospect in positive and professional ways?

Traditionally, people who have been able to generate this feeling of presence, this almost palpable feeling in others, have been labelled 'charismatic' or 'influential'. Presence is a distinctly personal attribute, and its impact on the prospect can be very positive.

What makes up presence?

So, what might contribute towards determining your ability to create a real positive presence? I believe there is a whole mix of factors, some of which you will have little or no control over, but many of which you most certainly can control. These controllable factors include the following.

1. Speech

You most certainly can control your speech, although it usually takes considerable practice. The best method of receiving objective feedback usually involves recording yourself and then listening to yourself on tape or, even better, observing yourself on video. Speech involves a whole host of subfactors that combine to produce how you talk, which in turn does much to contribute to this intangible aura that is your presence.

Your tone, your intonation, your diction, your choice of words, your pace, your accent, loudness, all combine to make *you* sound like *you*. The question is, does the situation call for your natural speech pattern or does it call for you to change it? For example, does it call for you to speak faster or slower? Does it call for you to use more feeling or more fact-oriented language? Does it call for you to make more statements or ask more questions? Does it call for a more consistent, softer tone or a more expressive and louder tone? Does it call for an excited, enthusiastic tone or a more restrained and controlled one?

Word choice plays an important role in establishing and reinforcing presence. It could be as simple as the inappropriate use of jargon, abbreviations or nicknames, which can severely hamper your attempt to build and maintain a strong positive presence in the company of not only your prospects but also your peers and colleagues. Word choice and phrasing can, if not carefully considered, seriously erode the impact of what you say. For example, statements that start with phrases like 'I just wanted', 'You probably won't want', 'This may not' can reduce the impact of your comments and must be guarded against. They can have a surprisingly negative impact on your message and therefore your presence.

Not only the words you say but, as noted earlier, how you say them has a bearing on how your message is received *and* interpreted, which in turn goes towards establishing your presence. First, be aware of the pace of your speech. Is it appropriate? Is it under control? Learn to pause at strategic intervals. This pause can achieve a number of critical objectives. It lets you return to your normal breathing pattern. In fact, in many sales situations it's a good strategy to concentrate on slowing down your breathing and taking slow, deep, natural breaths. Second, pausing at the appropriate time allows or motivates the prospect to respond, to ask questions, to tell you what they think. Third, if you do have a tendency to talk quickly, and with even more pace as you become excited during the sales process, these conscious pauses help you to keep your feet on the ground and stop you from losing contact with the realities of the situation and your connection with your prospect. Finally, these pauses allow you to observe the prospect, read between the lines and plan your sales approach, rather than let it spiral out of control and find out too late that you have missed some vital signposts in the road that have left your prospect on a divergent path from yours. The fact is, it's extremely difficult to talk and to critically observe and evaluate at the same time. And in selling you need to focus more on observing, evaluating and adapting than you do on talking. So, plan pauses in your speech. The best way to do this is simply to ask a question and then hold your tongue.

Two other points worth mentioning that are often forgotten in the enthusiastic pursuit of sales results are: smile and modulate your voice. Smile, not only with your mouth but with your eyes, with your whole body. Show the prospect that this is after all not a matter of life and death. Modulate your voice to show your passion at appropriate times to clearly demonstrate your keen interest and desire.

By now you have probably got the message. Your speech in any given situation will have a considerable bearing on your ability to generate a presence in the company of others. So be aware of your own natural or habitual speech patterns and associated verbal tendencies, and be prepared to adapt them should you believe the situation calls for different verbal behaviours to effectively communicate.

2. Appearance

It will come as no surprise that your appearance has an impact on establishing your presence. However, I believe this is usually more likely to reinforce the prospect's overall impressions than to contribute in a major way to establishing a single overriding positive presence. Of course, it goes without saying that if you don't meet certain basic unspoken expectations when it comes to appearance, this will have a negative impact on your overall objective of establishing a distinct presence. Meeting or even exceeding these basic expectations goes towards reinforcing your credibility and background, and thereby allows you the opportunity to establish or develop your presence, rather than necessarily contributing to your positive presence in its own right.

Factors that go to establishing a credible appearance include personal grooming, dress sense, neatness, comparison with other people's appearances and so on. When it comes to appearance, it may pay you to consider a number of external factors in making a decision about your own appearance. First, it won't hurt to take a look at how the top performers in your own organisation, and in the industry generally, present themselves. Look at their clothes, their grooming. How would you describe their overall appearance? Second, do the same simple survey for your prospect/customer base. Then decide on an appropriate standard of presentation for yourself. However, remember that you are an individual, so don't be afraid to express this individuality. Find a way of expressing your own personal style without compromising any reasonable acceptable standards of appearance or making your prospect nervous or uncomfortable.

Three simple rules apply when it comes to appearance. First, don't outshine your product. Remember, the focus should be first on your prospect, second on your product and third on you. Don't present yourself as the star of the show. Don't make it difficult for your prospect to relax and concentrate on their needs and the creation of the compelling sales story.

Second, when in doubt about the appropriateness of your appearance, it's probably best to defer to the more conservative option. Don't be a pioneer until you have some understanding of the lay of the land and what you may be up against. So, when it comes to making decisions about your appearance, if in any real doubt, *don't*.

Third, understand that your appearance, while a critical factor in establishing your presence, isn't a substitute for being prepared. It doesn't take the place of good interpersonal skills, being truthful, doing what you say you can or will do, or hide sloppy or poor selling skills. Your appearance cannot and will not improve or cover up poorly conceived ideas, the inability to relate or a bad attitude.

What your appearance *can* do is help you to gain a winning edge. It can assist in creating a relationship with your prospect, whereby they are more conducive to you and your product. Presence can assist in reducing the impact of the various obstacles that might pop up during the sales process, but on no account should your appearance be leaned on as a deciding factor in your ability to sell.

3. Your unique strengths

In some ways, a major factor in creating a presence is not to underestimate or downplay your strengths. A great deal is said and written about working on overcoming your limitations and weaknesses, and in many respects this is a laudable objective when working at improving sales performance. However, when it comes to establishing 'you' as a positive force in the heart and mind of your prospect, I recommend that you concentrate on your natural talents and attributes. Don't be afraid or nervous about selling these as part of the intangible 'you'. If they are strengths, then consider them as valuable and unique assets that you can contribute to the relationship. One of the keys here is your 'uniqueness'. What better way of establishing your presence or separating yourself from others than by offering or exhibiting those strengths, behaviours, skills, experiences and values that make *you* unique?

The message is, don't underestimate the contributions you can make to any situation. Use your natural talents, display them, hone them, be proud of them.

4. The handshake

A great deal has also been said about the handshake. It does have some impact in the very early stages of a relationship and initially, like appearance, can go some way to reinforcing the prospect's immediate perceptions of you. Suggestions such as using a good firm handshake or shaking the hand of a woman only if she offers it probably make sense in the first-impressions phase, but in the overall scheme of things a handshake does little on its own to build the positive presence you are aiming for.

5. Eye contact

Eye contact is something that most salespeople pay little attention to. It's also something that has been proven to have a large bearing on your ability to establish presence. The best that can be said about eye contact is that if you are perceived to avoid eye contact when it's considered appropriate, you may unconsciously cause the prospect to feel unsettled, with the possibility of ensuing negative perceptions. These might include a lack of trust from their viewpoint and the potential for a perceived lack of sincerity from your viewpoint.

Don't be afraid to make direct eye contact with your prospect as you talk and listen during the communication process. Especially important, don't neglect to make strong eye contact with them during your initial introductions and handshake and during the subsequent greeting and goodbye phases of your face-to-face contacts with the prospect. At the same time, you must know when not to overdo it—when not to appear to stare, or worse, be perceived as initiating a contest with the prospect.

One point worth bearing in mind is that good eye contact generally means looking at your prospect, or looking into their eyes and maintaining this contact for a period of time. Glances into the prospect's face, even if frequent, are generally not considered to constitute healthy eye contact. In fact, they make you appear nervous, skittish and, as suggested above, perhaps reinforce a perception of insincerity and even unworthiness of the prospect's trust. If you are committed to establishing good eye contact, let your gaze settle naturally on the prospect first, then move your focus to their face and then perhaps to one eye. I have found that most salespeople indicate that it's easier to establish good, strong but not overpowering or provocative eye contact by focusing on one eye and holding that contact. While doing so, look at the eyes, notice their shape, their colour, their size. Salespeople tell me that this technique is helpful when it comes to establishing a comfortable measure of eye contact.

6. Body language

This is an extremely powerful generator of presence and has a great bearing on your ability to build and maintain a positive personal impact on the proceedings. But remember that body language is a two-way street, in that you need to carefully observe the body language of your prospect as well as manage your own body language. You have the ability to make your prospect feel more or less comfortable in your presence, so carefully consider and control those habitual behaviours you have—that in fact we all have—that could grate on or cause tension in your prospect. This tension is the natural enemy of presence, and serves to negate any positive gains you have made in establishing presence.

Control your distracting or negative habits. Observe the behaviour of your prospect. Respond with your prospect's preferred method of behaviour and expression. If they are more reserved, cautious, suspicious, then keep your distance. Don't touch them. Sit across a desk or table from them if possible. Don't put your briefcase, folder or computer on their desk. Move slowly, talk slowly, control your hand movements and facial expressions. Give them time to get comfortable. If you are dealing with a more outgoing, expressive, excitable prospect, it may be more appropriate to express some higher level of enthusiasm and excitement. In this case you may wish to talk faster, perhaps using more expansive hand movements and an animated expression. It may also then be appropriate to touch them on the shoulder or lower arm and to sit adjacent to them at a table or on a sofa.

In general, though, it is wise, no matter who you are dealing with, to concentrate on the following three body language cues if you wish to reinforce your presence:

- *Cue no. 1—Sit or stand erect.* Don't slouch. Look positive and eager without looking overly excited.
- *Cue no. 2—Commence by displaying a neutral body language*—one that is unlikely to cause any offence. Then observe and respond to the cues and clues you elicit from your prospect and slowly shift your body language in response.
- *Cue no. 3—Carefully control any annoying or distracting habits.* Videotape yourself. Watch what you do with your hands, with your expressions. Look at your stance and your sitting posture. Work towards eliminating any annoying or aggressive behaviours.

7. Attitude

What is attitude? Well, in the context of presence, it's a whole grouping of factors that indicate how you approach the interpersonal interaction. What many salespeople forget, or perhaps don't understand in the first instance, is that your attitude is clearly visible to your prospect. It permeates everything you do and say. You wear it like an intangible, but nevertheless palpable, zone of influence around you *all* the time. Your attitude is read and interpreted by your prospect as you enter the room, before you open your mouth or do or say anything of any real consequence.

I suggested in Chapter 1 that your attitudes to three things will ultimately have a great impact on your ability to exhibit and maintain your personal presence. Very simply, *your presence depends on your attitude to*:

- the business or profession you are engaged in;
- the people you meet and deal with; and
- yourself.

I think you will agree that these three areas of attitude will have a great bearing on how others perceive you. They combine to establish how you project yourself in the presence of others.

So, what specific factors might you wish to consider in undertaking a simple analysis of your attitude, especially as it relates to one or more of the above three areas? I think these attitude-related factors that go towards the previous three areas might include, in no particular order, the following.

Commitment. Are you committed to what you think, and do you display this commitment? Are your prospects clear that your commitment extends to helping them get what they need?

Problems. Your ability to face problems head-on and your willingness to effectively deal with them is a large component of the positive attitude you project. This is perceived as enthusiasm, goal orientation, positive drive and so on. Problems are everywhere. The question is: how do you respond to them and deal with them?

Self-reliance. This is often perceived by the prospect as your ability to draw on your own inner strengths and feelings to keep moving forward. It's the ability to think and act without needing to continually draw on the external environment for support. Indeed, it's generally most visible to others when you are called on to act in difficult situations, and where the sales environment is indifferent or negative towards you and your propositions and your choices of action, feelings and thought. Here your self-reliance will be tested.

Confidence. There is often only the finest of lines between displaying confidence and appearing self-absorbed—between appearing positive, optimistic and self-assured and being perceived as naive, cocky and egotistical. This is very much an individual personal attribute, and the extent to which you feel and display self-confidence is often dependent on the individual preferences of the other people involved, the situation itself, and the environment in which both the foregoing two factors are imbedded.

Don't be afraid to work to project a positive, self-assured attitude. In most, if not all, selling situations, a 'quietly confident' attitude is usually perceived as a 'plus' by your prospects. At times you need to assist in building confidence in those around you. Don't overdo it. If you are always viewed as running with the confidence factor on full, chances are you will be perceived as shallow, political and overly optimistic, and perhaps even as vain, unrealistic and manipulative. Learn to modulate the external expression of your self-confidence. After all, your prospects like to do business with winners. Learn to vary the intensity of the self-confidence flame according to the situation; however, don't let the flame burn too hot for too long or fall below a consistent simmer.

Responsibility. You need to understand that the only way you will succeed in selling and, in fact, in most endeavours is to take complete responsibility for your actions and the subsequent outcomes. That doesn't mean that, being only human after all, you don't sometimes succumb to feeling less than enthusiastic about the particular situation you find yourself in, or the particular outcome, or even to feeling sorry for yourself. Contrary to many books and the comments and observations of sales trainers and speakers, it's normal and completely natural, at times, to feel somewhat vulnerable and as a result be sorely tempted to shift blame onto someone or something else. It's much easier on your own self-image, on your self-respect, to assume that it's someone else's fault—to believe that the situation just wasn't fair, the rules were bent, your colleagues didn't help. The issue isn't that you allowed the complete denial of responsibility and negative self-talk to enter your head in the first place: after all, as I said, you are only human; the issue is that you let them stay there. The fact is, the longer you let them reside there, the harder it is to rid yourself of them. This shifting of responsibility for your actions, feelings, thoughts and success onto others is like allowing an unwelcome houseguest stay too long in your home. At first you don't feel comfortable and just wish they would leave of their own accord. As time goes on, you find their habits rubbing off on you, your behaviour changing, your attitudes and values being questioned. You need to show them the door before you become too complacent in allowing others to weaken your resolve to accept full and complete responsibility for yourself and your actions.

Continuous learning. Closely allied to the concept of self-responsibility is the issue of continuous, lifelong learning. I find that those who tread the path of assuming total responsibility for themselves also invariably embrace the undeniable truth that to grow, to improve, to be all that you can be, to reach even a fraction of your full potential, you need to imbue your thoughts, actions and interactions with a desire to learn. This manifests itself in a wide range of behaviours and perceived attitudes and values—not least of which are the clear, unadulterated goals centred on how you might improve your professional abilities and learn from others. It's this last point that is often interpreted by your prospects and customers as a sincere interest in learning about them and their situation.

It comes across as a genuine desire to understand more about them and their unique situation.

Proactivity. The ability to initiate, to start the ball rolling, to lead the way is displayed by those salespeople who are considered leaders in their fields, industries or organisations. They display a desire to start the race, to meet the challenges and to keep the momentum going. When problems arise, they understand that waiting for a solution to appear or for the problem to disappear aren't options. They understand that both of these outcomes are possible but only if you *make* them happen, only if you create the environment for opportunities to present themselves. It's the waiting part, the doing nothing but waiting, they dismiss as negative. Waiting itself is fine: patience is a laudable personal attribute. However, what they understand is that waiting and patience don't necessarily equate to inaction on their part. Rather, they view waiting and patience to be simply labels that describe that part of the process that occurs while a third party might be undertaking the next step. In the meantime, they are busy being proactive, stirring, looking for options, exploring avenues, considering alternatives. To the proactive salesperson, waiting and patience have nothing to do with sitting on your behind *until* something happens or someone else does something. That is simple laziness.

Curiosity. The single most noticeably lacking attitude in the vast majority of salespeople is genuine curiosity—the desire to find out more, to understand, to explore the 'why'! This lack of curiosity appears to stem from two major causes: an overreliance on product, and an ignorance of the fact that the sales process virtually balances on the knife edge of curiosity. The salesperson often ignores or completely misses the curiosity displayed by the prospect, and as a result gives a standard product-oriented presentation. They don't understand that their own natural 'curiosity' is the key to unlocking the real needs of their prospect. They fail to see that they and their prospect are on the same plank and curiosity is the fulcrum that balances the beam. They fail to appreciate that curiosity turns selling into a finely balanced process. Curiosity needs to be somewhere towards the middle of the plank if the sales situation is to be balanced. Salespeople need to display a degree of natural curiosity to move the balance point back towards their end of the scale. If they don't, they will find the curiosity balance point firmly up towards their prospect's end. As anyone who has had fun on a see-saw in their childhood will attest, with the fulcrum point firmly up towards the opposite end you as a salesperson will find yourself sitting with your backside in the mud and your prospect sitting uncomfortably high in the air, with their legs dangling in space and more than likely hanging on for dear life. Pretty soon they will find another playmate who knows how to use a see-saw.

The puzzling fact of life is that we as humans all have a fair degree of natural curiosity. However, whether it's a response to nerves, inadequate training, an overreliance on product or a lack of customer focus, this natural curiosity is often suppressed as we attempt to engineer a fast 'yes' from our prospect by attempting to fit any given sales situation into a predetermined script or system for selling. I am constantly asked by sales managers to train their people in 'advanced selling techniques', when in my opinion they simply need the basics explained or reinforced, and the major basic is the skill in asking good questions, driven by their natural curiosity.

Openness. This attribute is most apparent in salespeople when observing their response to objections and concerns expressed by the prospect and to other barriers experienced in the selling process. Those salespeople who have difficulty maintaining an open, eager attitude to interpersonal interactions are often perceived as being defensive and protective of their own views, products and, ultimately, what they would like to see happen as outcomes of the process. In short, they are perceived as being closed to the perspectives, ideas and situations of others, including their prospects.

It is virtually impossible to cross the void, stand on the prospect's side and look at the issues as they see them through their eyes, without accepting a measure of openness, a degree of acceptance that acknowledges or recognises that there is more than one point of view. In essence, openness is about appreciating that while a strong personal view is important, it's not necessarily in harmony with your prospect's view of the world. I'm not advocating that you as a salesperson maintain a flexible, even 'rubbery' viewpoint. Quite the opposite: I believe that you should and must hold strong personal values and beliefs. But be prepared to display a simple openness or willingness to explore others' views, especially as they relate to the selling issues at hand and to your objectives. Don't accept, as most salespeople do, the particular positions adopted by you and your prospect to be the only means of achieving a shared win/win outcome. Keep an open attitude and display a keen interest in exploring the other person's thoughts and feelings. The minute you close your mind to other possibilities, you narrow your options. If this closed and often negative attitude is allowed to remain unchecked, it ultimately results in a defensive, protectionist policy where the energy of both parties is directed towards validating their own respective positions. Pretty soon it's a matter of continuing a to-and-fro barrage aimed at winning at all costs, and having the 'opposition force' eat their words and admit their mistakes.

Avoid at all costs closing your mind to other views, possibilities and options, or you will see the sales process move from an open, interactive, influencing process to a single-minded, persuasive one and finally to a very defensive, personal 'take it or leave it' assault.

Drive. The final attitude we will consider is your drive. This is often described as the personal energy you bring to the sale and with which you infuse the process. It's often closely linked to other issues, such as your commitment, approach to problems, proactivity and confidence. However, your drive is usually your ability to proceed towards predetermined goals, and while it often manifests itself as a part of each of these other attitudes, it's very much one in its own right. It involves a range of elements such as vision, strategy, planning and willpower. It's all of these things and more, and it's none of these things.

Drive can best be described as an inner restlessness to move forward, to achieve, to do, to act and be acted on. Without drive, salespeople often lose their way; they lose purpose and focus. They lose sight of the 'why' of their actions. I suspect that it's impossible to have drive without having clearly defined goals. At the same time, it could be said that it's impossible to achieve those goals without drive. Essentially, drive and goals go hand in hand: they share a symbiotic relationship. The goals are the lights at the end of the tunnel, or perhaps the lights that are placed at varying stages throughout the tunnel. The drive is what keeps you selecting a new tunnel when you have reached the end of one tunnel and have the option of going on or stopping. Commitment, as discussed earlier, is what keeps you going forward when you are in the tunnel, but commitment tends to come into the picture once you have started to move, whereas drive is what starts you moving forward in the first instance.

Drive is what keeps you from succumbing to the fear of failure, to rejection, to uncertainty.

Presence and your success

When it comes right down to it, your ability to project a strong and distinct presence is a critical factor in your success in sales. Your very presence has the ability to modify your prospect's attitude and thinking. If you find this difficult to accept, you should think back to a situation where you experienced a change in the mood of a room of people when someone with significant presence entered the room.

If you can alter or influence your prospect's attitude and thinking and subsequently, via the selling process, provide them with the appropriate information, you will invariably influence their behaviour. So, when it comes to establishing your presence, consider the following self-evident truths.

Three truths about presence

1. Understand that most of the factors that go towards establishing your own presence are under your direct control.
2. Make sure your presence is working for you and not against you.
3. Understand that your presence is about you and how you want to be seen by others.
4. If you want to influence the thoughts and actions of others, you must work towards establishing a distinct and unique professional presence.

chapter 23

Listening skills—why we don't hear what was really said

S omeone once pointed out that the words *listen* and *silent* use exactly the same six letters. This was probably their way of suggesting, albeit in a very indirect way, that it might be productive for people who considered listening as an important behaviour to also consider talking a lot less.

Listening skills are one of the simplest and most productive skills to practise and implement in your everyday sales approach. (Note that I didn't say easiest!) When it comes to complex selling, listening provides a whole host of opportunities to learn about your prospect—to become genuinely interested in them and focus on them and their situation and needs.

However, many salespeople appear uncomfortable with silence and insecure when they themselves or their product aren't the centre of attention. To put it another way, most salespeople seem unable to maintain the focus on the prospect. Instead, they behave in such a way that they appear more comfortable when the focus comes to rest on them, their product or their organisation. Let's face it, when it comes to the four critical ingredients in the sale—the prospect, product, salesperson and sales organisation—the prospect is outnumbered 3:1.

Most salespeople appear to equate listening to losing control or see it as some kind of professional weakness. They feel uncomfortable, embarrassed or even bored when it comes to listening to their prospect for any sustained period. This, in my view, stems from a number of inappropriate perceptions of selling.

First, as briefly touched on above, many salespeople don't understand that listening is an important skill in the value-based sales process. They fail to comprehend that they should focus on the prospect or, knowing this, they fail to actually do it. They fail to appreciate that the best way to do this is to get the prospect talking and then listen to what they say!

Second, many salespeople don't consider listening a special skill. In fact, they often take the opposite view. They may feel that when they are listening and not talking, they are missing opportunities to tell, to convince, to persuade.

Third, salespeople view listening as the opposite of talking. They don't understand that listening is an active skill—a skill that needs to be consciously worked on. It doesn't just happen. They most certainly don't view listening *as the active act of collecting the audible and inaudible outputs from subjects and acknowledging, interpreting and responding to them.*

Fourth, most salespeople don't view listening as a basic requirement of value-based selling, the very foundation of this sales approach. They fail to recognise that you cannot effectively identify needs, position your feature benefit ideas, deal with barriers to the sale, negotiate etc., without actively listening. Listening isn't an optional activity. It's not something you as a salesperson pursue or embrace *if* you have time or *if* the prospect volunteers information. You need to understand and fully embrace the concept that you can 'listen' the prospect into buying. Listening is a proactive, positive, prospect-focused activity that directs *all* your attention on to what the prospect is saying and doing *and*, perhaps even more importantly, what the prospect is *not* saying or *not* doing.

Finally, most salespeople don't recognise the positive effect listening has on the relationship. It demonstrates respect, caring, and a desire to understand and help. Listening skills aren't an option if you wish to pursue a value-based sales approach. They are, and should be viewed as, basic core skills that go to the very heart of professional selling.

Salespeople need to accept that a good listener isn't someone who has run out of something to say. Rather, a good listener is someone who is well in control of the situation and is pursuing their objectives.

What does the prospect consider valuable?

So, how do skilled salespeople find out what the prospect wants and needs? How do they find out what the prospect would consider is valuable to them? They do so by using highly developed and proactive listening skills. Using the word LISTEN as a simple acronym, let's explore some of the key factors present in proactive listening. The acronym looks like this:

L = *Look* interested.
I = *Inquire* using questions.
S = *Stick* to the objective.
T = *Test* understanding continuously.
E = *Evaluate* the prospect's outputs.
N = *Negate* your own feelings.

Let's have a closer look at each of these six key factors.

Look interested

Give the impression that you are really interested in what the prospect has to say, what they think and how they feel. The best way to do that is to become genuinely interested in the prospect and their situation.

How do you focus your thoughts and actions on your prospect? Well, you could:

- *Look at your prospect.* Concentrate on what they say and how they say it. Look at their body language. Look them in the eyes.
- *Take notes.* Keep a record of key words and phrases they use. Note issues you may wish to explore later. Refer to your notes and use their expressions in the discussions.
- *Respond during listening.* Do this by making encouraging noises and gestures. Use simple words and phrases like 'really?', 'tell me more', 'uh-huh', 'is that right?' or look perplexed, raise your eyebrows, look serious or intense, or just laugh or smile in the appropriate places and ask questions.

All these simple behaviours telegraph to the prospect that what they have to say is important. In fact, it confirms to them that you believe that they themselves are important, and what they think and feel is important.

Inquire using questions

Put succinctly, to inquire could be as simple as just asking questions. Mind you, not just any questions—ask questions that are specifically designed to encourage the prospect to talk. Often grouped collectively and called 'open' questions, they cannot be answered with a simple 'yes' or 'no'. These questions often start with or include words such as 'what', 'when', 'where', 'how' and, on occasion, 'why'. (You need to phrase 'why'-type open questions very carefully so that you don't appear confrontational, judgemental or just plain difficult.)

The more open questions you tend to ask, the more likely you are to find out two things.

1. what you *want* to know; and/or
2. what you *need* to know

These two things are important in order to build the relationship and establish value in the heart and mind of your prospect.

Stick to the objective

Stay on target with your sales call objective. Remember, don't equate listening with handing over control. Quite the opposite: a major reason for listening is so that you can continue to maintain control and keep the spotlight firmly focused on your prospect. Carefully 'listen' the discussions back to the issues at hand by asking questions to keep the prospect on track. That's right: carefully listen the prospect towards the issues at hand.

Test understanding continuously

This refers to *your* understanding, not the prospect's. I'm not talking about testing whether the prospect got your message. I'm referring to feeding back to your prospect, at regular intervals, what you believe they have communicated to you. This is especially critical in areas where you have made certain assumptions about the prospect and their needs. All too often we hear only what we want to hear. So clarify those issues, feelings, thoughts and conclusions proffered by your prospect as often as necessary. This, when it comes to the more critical sales issues, translates to doing so 'as often as you can!'. Use simple phrases, such as:

- 'Am I correct in thinking that you . . .?'
- 'So, what you are suggesting is . . .?'
- 'If I understand the situation correctly, this means . . .?'

Far too many sales situations develop to a point where the salesperson's and the prospect's thinking diverge and they go off on completely different tracks. The prospect thinks one thing, the salesperson is thinking something entirely different. What is even worse is when you and your prospect agree on a course of action, and you are both agreeing to something which may be based on entirely different outcomes. This happens far more often in sales than you might think, and far more often than necessary. Even more frightening is the revelation that when this does occur, all that was necessary to avoid it occurring in the first instance was one or more simply phrased test questions designed to confirm that both of you had taken the same path.

So, get into the habit, when listening, of testing *your* understanding—rather than that you have been understood.

Evaluate the prospect's outputs

Consider carefully the prospect's whole message. Consider their words, body language and tone of voice. Consider what they have said and how they have said it. Also consider what *hasn't* been said. This last point can give you just as much or more information than what was actually said.

I refer to this style of proactive listening as 'three "i" listening'. This means 'listening with your *eyes* and your *intuition* and your *instinct*'. It's a lot like 'reading between the lines'. The word 'no', and for that matter just about any other word or phrase, can be interpreted in many ways.

You need to fully evaluate the message to uncover what was really meant or intended.

In addition to reading the prospect's real message by considering both the meaning of words and the tone in which they were said, are a host of other important factors such as what was said in terms of the accompanying body language and the pace of the delivery. If you are in any doubt about the consistency of the overall message from your prospect, if you feel their tone doesn't match their words or perhaps their body language blurs or even blatantly contradicts what they have said, you need to test what they really mean. You need to uncover what *hasn't been said*. One of the most effective means of doing this is by using the reflective form of question.

This consists of repeating back to your prospect what they have just said in the form of a question, with just the right amount of intonation to carry the genuine feeling of wanting to know more.

Use this questioning style sparingly. Don't use it to question everything your prospect says to you that you don't or won't accept. Use it only to get behind a statement expressed by your prospect that seems, on face value, inconsistent with aspects of their behaviour, whether their tone, intonation, pace or body language, or perhaps with your previous experiences with that prospect.

Negate your own attitudes and feelings

Now, I appreciate that your own feelings are a large part of who you are as a person and, as such, are an important ingredient in how you view the world and how you value others. However, learn to suspend judgement *while* you are listening to your prospect.

The fact is that the minute we start reacting to what the other person says, we stop listening with an open mind and start the judging process. The minute you lose control of your reaction to what others do and/or say, you have closed the door on the analytical and objective listening approach and have entered the arena of subjectivity and judgemental thoughts. If you maintain this approach, you will start drawing conclusions about what they had in mind—that is, their *intent*. You immediately commence labelling the prospect's actions with what you believe to be their real intent.

This is dangerous ground indeed. Unless you can really read minds, don't assume that you know what your prospect means, thinks, feels or really intends, based on cursory observations of their spoken words and body language.

If you find your mind reacting by making judgements *while* your prospect is talking, constantly remind yourself: 'This isn't about what *I* may or may not think or feel. This is really about *them* and what *they* think and how *they* feel.' Give your prospect your full attention and concentrate on understanding 'why'. *Why* they said what they said. *Why* they feel the way they feel. You will then be far less likely to react with emotions of your own, which will undoubtedly cloud or totally obscure your ability to listen to your prospect's real message.

If you can focus your attention completely on your prospect and on what they are saying, you will find, as countless other salespeople have, that your sales calls seem to go better. You will have less reason to interrupt, you will feel less defensive, appear more open and receptive, and learn more about your prospect's true feelings, needs and perceptions.

Poor listening skills

What causes poor listening skills? Few, if any, salespeople would disagree with the need to develop and continually demonstrate good listening skills. But very few of these same salespeople give much thought to the negative behaviours, or self-imposed barriers, that serve to keep them in the unnecessarily overpopulated area of poor listening in selling.

Let's have a brief look at the behaviours that obstruct many sales-people's pathway towards more effective listening.

'The lights are on but nobody is home' syndrome

This is usually the realm of the situational listener. These listeners act as if they are listening to person A but they are really tuned into person B or are somewhere else entirely in their own mind.

Your *willingness* to listen to your prospect has no bearing on this behaviour. You may be willing to listen but find your attention miles away or perhaps only a few metres away, listening in to someone else's conversation, activity or situation. While it's certainly true to suggest that if you aren't willing in the first instance, then you are only going through the motions anyway, willingness isn't nearly enough. You need to discipline yourself to carry out the actions of proactive listening—those actions you say you are willing to display and practise.

'Ships in the night' syndrome

I'm sure you have heard the phrase 'passing like ships in the night' used to describe a situation where people have come close to one another but each continues unseen, almost touching, but nevertheless missing connection with one another completely. So near, yet so far. Here the party or parties to the exchange are guilty of missing the real message completely. They are listening but not *actively* listening. They are intent on simply receiving all signals, not necessarily on discriminating between conflicting signals. They take things on face value, accepting first impressions. They see no value in pursuing the real meanings. They don't see that listening requires the listener to be proactive, to check, to test. They fail to realise that listening takes a disciplined personal effort.

'Now here's what I think' syndrome

What *you* think has a bearing on your ability to focus on what the other person is saying. Those salespeople who are overly concerned about what *they* think while listening to *others*, invariably engage in 'interrupting' others.

Usually, I find that the primary purpose of salespeople interrupting others is to impose their agenda on someone else. Interruption by one party, especially if continual, does little to engender an environment that is conducive to a healthy and comfortable exchange of information.

'No surprises there' syndrome

Here you hear more or less exactly what you thought you would hear. You hear what you expected to hear. If you believe you can predict the outcome of conversations, then most likely, as with any self-fulfilling prophecy, you won't be disappointed.

Rather than feeling extremely pleased and congratulating yourself on your ability to predict what your prospect says or means, perhaps you should use this 'gift' to more lucrative ends, such as picking the Powerball numbers or the winning horse in the next major national horse race.

'I'm too busy rehearsing my next speech' syndrome

The minute you start deciding on a response, planning or predetermining your next course of action, or rehearsing your response, you have stopped actively listening. You have in effect closed down your sensitive receptors, your inquisitive nature, your desire to learn why and to understand the prospect's situation and perceptions.

If you suspend judgement while listening, it's extremely unlikely that you will turn your mind to constructing your response, for the simple reason that, if you are suspending judgement, you are still focusing on understanding, not on being understood. Rehearsing your response or deciding on a subsequent course of action while listening means that you have decided that all the information is available and have shut down the active receiving side of your communication, while you concentrate on designing and practising a response to what you think you have already heard.

'How dare they say/think that?' syndrome

Whether this is what you say or think, the minute you entertain these types of self-talk you are headed down the path of defensiveness.

What I can say with considerable certainty is that your emotions tend to cloud and completely obscure the real messages being sent by your prospect. Ultimately, this leads to your adopting a primarily defensive strategy rather than one which encompasses an open desire to find out more, to learn and see the world through others' eyes. Once emotion is allowed to enter the realm of the communication process, I can guarantee that reason, understanding and the real needs of people will be lost in the interchange of statements that follows. This may escalate to insinuation, suggestion, insults and veiled threats, and ultimately to the 'digging in' of the various parties' respective 'positions' or views from which the 'opposition defensive line' is peppered with clever statements. Active listening is all but dead, and listening has switched to a survival mode, where the objective is to hear something that can be used *against* the stated interest of the other person.

'Waiting for a lull in the attack' syndrome

This is often observed in salespeople as they wait, not with the intention of listening and learning but rather with the intent to select the best opening to launch information they can use in their own defence or attack. Here they are listening simply in order to collect information that they can use in their own interest. They are selective in interpreting and retaining what they hear. The major purpose of listening is to collect sufficient 'ammunition' with which to launch an effective devastating offensive.

Interpretations have been made, decisions quickly arrived at, and now the single focus of the listener is to launch an often pre-emptive offensive, aimed primarily at bringing the perceived 'aggressor' into line with the listener's own attitudes and values.

chapter 24

Questioning skills I— what choices do you have?

Your ability to construct and deliver well-crafted questions, what might be labelled collectively as your *questioning skills*, will primarily affect two broad areas of your sales process. First, the skills will be a telling, if not *the* telling, factor in your ability to distinguish yourself from the competition. Second, your questioning skills will be a major force in your being able to differentiate your product from competing products or offers.

However, these are really overall sales-related outcomes, the 'big picture' of what your ability to demonstrate questioning skills has the potential to produce.

To be more specific about what initiatives can be achieved, from the client's perspective, by asking good questions, set out below are a number of key initiatives involved in questioning skills. If you accept these four key initiatives you will automatically understand and accept the major role good questioning plays in promoting the sale and influencing other elements critical to the sale.

So, let's have a closer look at the skill of questioning and the four key initiatives involved. Successful salespeople understand the following:

- *Key questioning initiative no. 1*—Prospects evaluate the level of your competence and judge your professionalism based on the quality and delivery of the questions you ask.
- *Key questioning initiative no. 2*—Good questions reinforce to both the prospect and salesperson the view that the prospect is unique, and assist in exploring the prospect's wants and understanding and identifying their real needs.
- *Key questioning initiative no. 3*—A full and detailed understanding of your prospects, their needs, wants, situation etc., must precede any attempt to sell.
- *Key questioning initiative no. 4*—Focusing on asking good questions and letting the prospect do most of the talking is the best strategy to adopt in certain phases of the sales process.

These four key questioning initiatives probably don't require additional explanation other than to suggest that most salespeople have a totally different concept, what one might view as a misconception, of the role and importance of questions in the sales process. It may prove instructive to review some of the misconceptions about questioning many salespeople exhibit.

Misconception no. 1—Salespeople believe they ask sufficient, good questions

Generally, salespeople don't ask anywhere near enough questions to effectively explore the prospect's needs.

How do I come to this conclusion? Simple observation. I ask salespeople a relatively straightforward question: 'Approximately what percentage of the time that you spend in your face-to-face sales calls do you spend asking questions?' Most people respond that they are asking questions at least 50% of the time they open their mouths to speak. However, my observations is that the vast majority of salespeople spend *less than 10%* of their talk time asking questions. But here comes the real problem: most of the questions asked are relatively shallow, exhibiting little in the way of effective strategies directed towards exploring the prospect's situation by varying the style or type of question. In other words, the questions are 'soft' and generally not what could be called 'good' questions.

And this isn't the worst of it. What I also see is that most salespeople, when faced with an opportunity to submit good questions and to dig deeper, blow it completely by concentrating on themselves and focusing on the 'I' factor.

Let's have a look at how salespeople jeopardise their success by letting the 'I' factor control their response to opportunities to ask good questions. Imagine, for instance, that the prospect says something like 'This new model you are promoting doesn't seem to be able to perform the key functions we require any better than our current model.' The salesperson completely misses a golden opportunity to find out more by responding in one or more of the following egocentric 'I' factor modes.

- *Mode 1—Interpreting.* 'Oh, so you don't see any real advantages in using this new model?' Now this isn't what the prospect said at all. All this serves to do is put the prospect on the defensive.
- *Mode 2—Ignoring.* 'Really, you don't think so? Here, let me explain (again!) how this new model really is the way of the future.' Here all the salesperson has succeeded in doing is alienating the prospect by ignoring their concern and carrying on as if they didn't say anything of any real consequence or, worse, as if the prospect was stupid.
- *Mode 3—Infuriating.* 'Well, does it really matter that it doesn't look like it's a major advance on the old model? After all, what is a major

advance if it works well and . . .' Well done. Why not simply insult your prospect and finish the job properly?

■ *Mode 4—Inferring.* 'Oh, so what you are saying is that you think this new model is much the same as the last one.' Please! Why turn a question into a major objection? Why restate or reword the prospect's questions and statements and send them back to them, rather than finding out *why* they think like that?

Misconception no. 2—Asking questions causes salespeople to lose control of the sales process

Nothing could be further from the truth. Good questioning reinforces control. Why? Simply because whoever asks the questions usually directs where the conversation goes, how long it stays in one particular area, when it moves on and where it moves to next.

Some areas of the conversation should be pursued—in which case, one should design and deliver questions that will dig deeper. Other areas will be left to explore later. Those salespeople who can construct and ask good questions will control the exchange. The key here is not to see 'control' as having negative connotations. Perhaps the word 'direct' has a wider acceptance. That's a decision you need to make. To me, 'control' isn't a manipulative descriptive term but a proactive descriptive term for one of the salesperson's key professional responsibilities.

When it comes to selling, the person who controls (or directs) the questioning controls the sales call. Now, I didn't say 'controls the sale'. Assuming you could control the sale even if you wanted to, is your prospect likely to let you do so? And is it in both your prospect long-term interests to do so? I doubt it.

Misconception no. 3—Questions create objections

Salespeople who consider good questions as dangerous either have something to hide or are uncomfortable with prospects who are capable of independent thought, who need to know or understand what it is you are offering or what it is they are buying and why. If salespeople are of the view that their questions will create objections, then they have a fairly negative view of objections in the first place, a fairly low opinion of the prospect in the second place, and in the third place the probability of some serious measure of doubt in themselves and their abilities.

If you are truly 'prospect-focused'—that is, if you truly embrace a value-based approach to sales—then you would, and indeed should, welcome objections. The simple fact is that good questioning doesn't create objections. It may surface them, it may clarify them, but it doesn't create them.

Misconception no. 4—Salespeople should know all the answers!

Many salespeople believe they should know absolutely everything about their product. In the real world, this is probably an unrealistic view except with the simplest products. What is worse, many of these salespeople extend this unrealistic view to include the notion that they should have the answer or solution to anything the prospect will need, and that accordingly there should be little or no need to ask questions.

This is a naive, if not totally unrealistic, picture of the sales process. These salespeople fail to accept or understand the following basic realities in today's selling environment:

1. Prospects are generally more aware of, more astute about and much more sensitive to the implications of their buying decisions.
2. The amount of information available to your prospects, about you, your organisation and your product, which is often available even *before* they get to see you face to face, is absolutely staggering.
3. The business environments and situations in which your products could be used may be continually changing, such that there may be almost no such thing as an accepted usual or normal use or situation in product usage scenarios.

The above are only three universal 'realities' that come to mind from my discussions with literally hundreds of salespeople. There are, no doubt, many others that conspire to make it almost impossible for anyone to have all the answers to all the questions, from all prospects, all the time.

Misconception no. 5—Good questions just happen

Thinking that includes such notions as 'I'll know what to ask when I get there' or 'I don't need to write my questions down, I'll remember them' implies that good questions just happen and that good planning has little or no bearing on the number, form, basis or potential success of the questions. These salespeople don't see the prospect as unique. They don't acknowledge that by spending a little time investigating the prospect's needs *prior to* meeting they will have the ability, based on the outcome of these investigations, to prepare a unique strategy for the sales call. Part of this unique strategy will involve designing a range of good questions—questions that begin to uncover the prospect's specific needs and wants based on hard evidence, observation and assumption directly connected to that particular prospect's situation. The simple truth is that the compelling sales story is *built with the prospect* using well-planned questions to identify the prospect's dominant needs and thereby propose a series of feature benefit ideas.

The above five misconceptions that many salespeople display could be likened to taking your car to your local garage or service centre for repairs. Would you expect the mechanic or service adviser just to listen to you and not ask any questions as you book your car in? Would you really expect them to take the view 'Don't tell me any more, leave it to me, I'll sort it all out'? Come on! If all your mechanic did was listen without asking any questions, you would feel uneasy, to say the least. You would expect them to ask some relevant, detailed questions about the problems you had described. Or would you expect them to have ready-made answers to all your questions or problems? Of course not. In fact, ready-made answers would be more likely to raise concern—hearing such glib responses, you would be far more likely to question their competence and intent.

Why ask questions? Thirteen positives that come from asking good questions

Good questions help the salesperson and the prospect work together to undertake a dominant needs analysis, and then, using the identified dominant needs to create a compelling sales story. This outcome is achieved in a number of ways. Some of them are relatively obvious, and could be said to have a direct consequence. Others are far less obvious but may be of no lesser importance. Consider below the positive influences on the sale that accrue from asking good questions.

Positive no. 1 *Helps the prospect feel important*

By asking well-constructed questions you cannot help but provide your prospect with a sense of self-importance. It sends a resounding 'I care about you and your situation' message to the prospect. They are made to feel a significant part of the sales process. This then assists in responding to the buying phase of 'recognition' as proposed in Part 1.

Positive no. 2 *Discovery surely follows*

Good questions allow you to elicit information, to uncover facts. Good questions allow you to replace assumptions with factual information, to clarify, check, and test for feelings, opinions and needs. Good questions help you to uncover perceptions and views on a range of issues central to the product and the prospect's situation.

Positive no. 3 *Assists in maintaining control*

By the nature of the form and delivery of your questions you can influence or directly control the direction, tone, pace and content of the sales call,

all of which are critical in maintaining effective professional control of the exchange. For example, questions allow you to postpone exploring specific issues until a more appropriate time and to smoothly divert to others. Good questions allow you to bring the discussion back on track if it should wander. Good questions stop you from responding too quickly; they allow you time to think, to digest the implications and to consider your responses.

Positive no. 4 Stops you from talking too much

The very action of asking well-constructed, relevant questions will be a major factor in improving your listening-to-talking ratio. By asking specific well-researched questions and listening to the responses, you automatically suspend the tendency to jump on the talking treadmill. Those salespeople who concentrate on asking questions in order to understand will talk much less than their colleagues who either ask few or no questions or ask loaded questions designed to elicit a specific predetermined response which they use as a springboard to launch their next product-centred offensive.

Positive no. 5 Makes the prospect think

By asking specific questions you can indirectly ask your prospect to re-examine their perceptions, beliefs, attitudes and conclusions relating to the sale. The act of asking for further information, or perhaps for a further explanation of a statement, if done in a careful and sensitive manner, can cause the prospect to review their own thinking. If, on re-examining them in the light of day, they cannot clearly explain their own thoughts and feelings to themselves in a rational, logical manner, how can they expect you to accept and understand them?

Also, believe it or not, asking questions can have the unexpected result of someone solving their own problems, or at least re-evaluating their importance, by being forced to examine their own views in the more logical, structured format of a considered response.

Positive no. 6 Defuses potential conflict

Good questions can help to avoid or defuse potential conflict situations. Instead of presenting an alternative view, or even engaging in open disagreement, a response based on good questioning asks the prospect to reconsider their stance on a particular issue without your needing to confirm or clearly nominate your opposition view. By asking and not telling, you leave the door open to explore opportunities.

Positive no. 7 Help the prospect to develop consequences

Without well-constructed questions the prospect often fails to understand and appreciate the full implications of their own situation. They may feel no urgency, or any real need to 'do something' to improve their current situation, their today state. In short, good questions often help the prospect to recognise and acknowledge the difference between their stated or implied 'wants' and their true dominant needs.

Positive no. 8 Persuades

After careful questioning of the feelings and conclusions offered by the prospect, they may be more inclined to question their stated views and consider your point of view.

By asking the prospect indirectly about the 'whys' of their decision, you can often influence their thinking to a far greater degree than the more usual tactic adopted by salespeople of giving reason after reason why the prospect's views are inappropriate or wrong. In fact, this latter tactic often forces the prospect onto the defensive. This is because a great number of the salesperson's prepared reasons, which centre on why the prospect should buy or agree, are simply not reasons that apply to the prospect. They may be perfectly well considered, but they are general reasons that may or may not apply to the prospect's specific situation.

Positive no. 9 Saves time and money

This one is pretty simple. By asking the right questions at the right time, in the right way, you can save both yourself *and* your prospect a lot of time and money.

By finding out what's important to them, how they think, what they think, how they decide, who else they are considering, and where you stand in their estimation, you can avoid many traps along the way and save both yourself and them a lot of wasted time, effort and money.

Positive no. 10 Provides an opportunity to deal with barriers in advance

Questions uncover any concerns and perceptions your prospect may have well in advance of any attempt to position your product by means of the compelling sales story you and the prospect will create. By asking your prospect how they feel about specific issues related to the sales situation and your particular product, you receive feedback that often alerts you to areas of concern that need to be further explored, avoided or dealt with at a more appropriate time.

The answers to your questions often uncover areas that will require specific strategies to be designed, often with the help and input of others. Advance notice of these potential barriers allows you time to consider how best to respond.

Positive no. 11 The idea becomes their idea

After you have asked well-designed questions about the prospect's situation and begun carefully to lay the groundwork to position your product, the prospect can begin to 'own' the solution well before you even begin to move towards discussing in any real detail what it is you are offering. This is one of the major motivators for prospects working with you on the creation of the compelling sales story.

Positive no. 12 Establishes a professional image

This issue was discussed early in this chapter so it doesn't bear repeating in any detail here, except perhaps to say that your prospect's perception of you as a competent, knowledgeable and ethical salesperson is critical to your success. This and other 'must haves' combine to build the professional image that you project in every dealing you have with your prospect. Part of your responsibility as a professional salesperson involves doing your homework and asking intelligent, applicable, probing questions that, as a byproduct, establish you as someone who can think and act like a valuable, experienced and knowledgeable professional consultant.

One customer I deal with on a regular basis once described to me the feeling associated with a 'consultant' asking good questions. He suggested that he felt safe and secure in the knowledge that he was the subject of something like a major medical examination. This client suggested that, at the beginning of the examination, he didn't know quite what to expect. As the examination unfolded he experienced a mixture of interest, concern, understanding and discomfort. However, when it was all over he felt relieved that absolutely nothing appeared to have been missed or overlooked. While some questions or procedures may have been unsettling, he now felt much more relaxed in what he perceived to be the development of a relatively intimate and sincere relationship with his 'specialist' medical consultant. (This is the effect you can also engender by 'examining' your prospect.) The other thing this particular client said that I found interesting was that now that he felt abundantly comfortable with the apparent 'professional' display by his doctor, he really had no particular desire or interest in going through it again with someone else.

Would this have parallels in the sales environment? I suspect it may well have. Your carefully designed questions, delivered with skill and appreciation for the prospect as a unique person, could enhance and develop your professional image while at the same time making it just that much more difficult for your competition to follow a similar path.

Positive no. 13 Uncovers the dominant need

This is, you might think, obvious. I agree. In fact, it's so obvious that most salespeople completely overlook this objective in the actual 'making' of the sales call.

Sure, when directly asked, they appear to readily confirm that questions 'uncover needs', or help them 'find out about the prospect's wants'. But what I often observe is the salesperson asking basic questions with the following unspoken and often unrealised objectives:

■ *Objective no. 1—Appear* interested, experienced and professional.
■ *Objective no. 2—Look for opportunities* and avenues to introduce the product as soon as possible.

Seldom do I observe salespeople taking control by asking well-researched questions. It's rare to see salespeople conduct their questioning by also being prepared to take interesting detours before returning to the main route of predetermined questions, or to make notes of what has been said, or not said, and of other areas to explore later. It's rare to see a salesperson who appears prepared to dig deeper and to find out what the prospect really thinks and feels—to find out what they need. If, on the other hand, salespeople are prepared to question, to dig deeper, along the way they uncover all manner of interesting facts and feelings, and a whole raft of information. All the while, they hold off dumping their product or prescribing a solution. They believe, as I have mentioned before, that as performed by a professional practitioner, *a good prospect examination must always precede determination of the prospect's symptoms and the subsequent diagnosis of the prospect's needs*.

Questioning is all about uncovering hard targets. In traditional selling, the salesperson *tells* the prospect what the targets are, then in effect says, 'Stand back and watch me hit this.' With value-based selling, the salesperson understands that the real targets can be uncovered only with the prospect's help, and the compelling sales story can be engineered and built only *with* your prospect's assistance. While it's up to you to deliver the package, its real target and what is included in the package that you will deliver can be built only with the prospect.

To sum up, consider the art of questioning prospects as a means of your listening while they talk themselves into needing you, your organisation and your product.

The when and where of questions

I spoke about the 'why'. You will recall the 13 positives or benefits of asking good questions, so now might be an appropriate time to answer two related questions that are often asked by salespeople. These are 'When should I ask questions?' and 'Is there anywhere in particular that it should be done?'

My own experience and observations are that the answers to these two questions depend very much on the situation you find yourself in. However, at the risk of oversimplifying the responses, I suggest that the answer to the *when* is *always* when you feel you need to know more, and the answer to the *where* is basically *anywhere*.

Now this needs to be tempered, as I said above, by the particular constraints and implications of the situation you find yourself in. For instance, it would be wise to carefully choose the time and place in which you are requesting sensitive or confidential information about the prospect's business. But I would rather that salespeople, at least initially, accept *always* and *anywhere* as reasonable responses to the *when* and *where* of questioning, then overlay their own experience and common sense rather than come up with a system of rules or procedures that are unrealistic and unworkable.

One word of warning. There is one definite exception that calls for a *never* response. And that is when asking for the order (the 'asking: closing on a final buying decision' form of the close element) or when stating the price, terms or conditions of purchase. *Never*, ask a question after this. Always wait for the prospect to respond to your statement before opening your mouth again. Asking a question before you have received a full response here is often suicidal. Resist the temptation at all costs.

So, why don't salespeople ask questions?

To be honest, I find this a difficult question to answer myself. Especially given what I believe to be an overwhelming body of evidence and reason that supports the acquisition of strong questioning skills as a clear goal for those who wish to develop their sales results beyond the mediocre.

From coaching sessions with underperforming salespeople—that is, salespeople who aren't achieving what both they and their management believe to be their true potential—I observe they *all* share the common negative behaviour of demonstrating poor questioning skills. From my discussion with these salespeople, it appears that there are four primary reasons why they don't use questions and are therefore unable to appreciate the skill involved and the positive effects of delivering good questions.

Why not no. 1—Lack of knowledge and/or skill

These salespeople don't understand the very broad range of potentially different types of questions available, or how to design and ask good questions.

My experience with coaching salespeople suggests that, rather than focusing on a long and detailed argument and explanation addressing this lack of questioning, they should just go out and 'ask questions'. At first, *any* relevant questions, just so that they get into the habit of asking questions. The skilful honing of their questioning skills can come later. They report back that the experience of just 'doing it' gets them over the hump of their initial, often fearful, concerns about 'how'?, 'when?' and 'what should I say?'. Having done this, they are in a far better position to receive the needed knowledge and training in questioning skills.

Why not no. 2—Don't realise that questioning is an important activity

Salespeople often don't ask good questions because they don't really see the point. They don't view the act of doing their homework and designing and delivering good questions as leading to anything concrete or positive. When I pursue this line of thought concerning questioning, they often tell me that, in their view, questions have only two primary purposes:

1. as a courtesy to inquire about the prospect; and
2. to uncover sufficient details to allow the salesperson the opportunity to move directly to discussing their product.

They don't understand that if they viewed the prospect as unique, they would see the need to dig deeper to understand the prospect's particular situation, wants and needs. They would then understand that they must uncover the real dominant needs, explore the prospect's today state, investigate their tomorrow state with them and explore the gap between the two. If they viewed the prospect as unique, they would understand that they build their feature benefit ideas and hence the compelling sales story with the prospect, by asking questions.

Why not no. 3—Don't value their time

This is a relatively simple 'why not' and has similarities to the previous one. Here, salespeople don't generally feel that their time is valuable. 'Why not no. 2' is predicated on the salesperson not feeling that what the prospect thinks and feels is valuable—that is, they don't value *the prospect's time*. In this case, they simply don't value *their own time*.

Any salesperson who values their own time, which describes *all* professional salespeople, will spend any face-to-face time with their prospect wisely. They will seek to obtain the best possible return, for both themselves and their prospect, on their expenditure of time, talent and resources. They will understand that, even from the prospect's perspective, time is a valuable ingredient and should be treated as such. As a result, they plan, do research, design agendas, confirm available time, set realistic timeframes and, most of all, they ask good questions when the opportunity to do so presents itself.

Why not no. 4—Fear

The fear of appearing unprofessional, of looking silly, of being rebuffed or of being too personal, are just some of the phobias that salespeople share with me when I broach the issue of questioning with them in coaching sessions.

Fear is a powerful thing. It is capable of stopping us in our tracks. It's capable of preventing us from doing the things we know *must* be done. As the saying goes, 'Feel the fear and go ahead and do it anyway.' And if fear is stopping you, ask yourself 'What are the consequences of not doing . . .?' Chances are that the consequences of not doing whatever it is you fear are worse than the outcomes that you fear so much and that often don't eventuate anyway.

Some classic 'don't dos' when it comes to asking questions

Questions are a very personal issue. What you feel comfortable with when it comes to the pace, delivery, subject matter, depth and order of questions, for instance, are all things you will treat differently from others, depending on your behaviour, attitudes, values, skills, experience and training.

As I mentioned previously when we discussed the when and where of questioning, there are probably very few hard-and-fast rules to be followed. However, in general terms, there are a number of 'don'ts' that apply to most of the situations you will find yourself in when it comes to questioning. These will, of course, need to be considered in the context of the particular situation or relationship in which you find yourself, but it's worth taking a minute to review these 12 basic 'don't dos' of questioning.

Don't do no. 1—Don't focus on the product

Observation of many salespeople engaged in sales calls indicates to me that when they switch their focus to the product (assuming they had it elsewhere to begin with), the good questions usually dry up. They cease being concerned with the prospect and begin to focus on justifying or rationalising their 'product solution'. This invariably leads to . . .

Don't do no. 2—Don't ask leading or dumb questions

Again, my experience in observing salespeople who achieve little except to potentially harm the relationship is that they ask leading questions or questions they should have known the answer to. Also in this category of 'not to be asked questions' are those that are confrontational, hostile or derogatory. Sound obvious? You would be surprised how often such questions creep into the exchange.

Don't do no. 3—Don't ask questions about your competitor's product

Asking the prospect for information about your competitor's product is a definite No! Now, before you reach for the phone to ring and abuse me, there are two caveats to this one:

1. Don't ask unless you already know the correct answer and have a specific strategic reason for asking.
2. This 'don't do' applies only to the competitor's product—not, for example, to their bid, proposition, offer, or how the prospect views such things.

Don't ask your prospect to provide you with intelligence on your competitors or their product. That's *your* job. It's part of your professional responsibility to know what else is out there that you will be competing against.

You may ask, however, a question directed to uncover the prospect's understanding about a particular facet of a competing product. Here you might say something like, 'Does that model provide you with the eight copies a minute you require?', knowing full well that it doesn't.

Don't do no. 4—Don't be afraid to ask

If you need to know something, don't be afraid to ask. Perhaps it's how the prospect will evaluate your offer. Perhaps it's how or when they will make a decision. Perhaps it's as simple as wanting to know what they think about the compelling sales story unfolded so far. The simple rule is: *ask!* Or, to put it in more instructive terms, as it applies to many salespeople *don't be afraid to ask!*

You may need to be diplomatic, especially if you are attempting to unearth sensitive or confidential information. However, as a general rule of thumb, if you need to know something you think only the prospect can tell you, don't be afraid to ask. My experience, and the experience of countless salespeople who report back to me on this issue, is that they are often surprised and amazed at what information they will be given if they just construct and deliver good questions covering those areas they feel they need to explore further. A related issue is one of exploring the prospect's thinking. Again, use common sense and tact and you will be surprised what the prospect is prepared to share with you.

Lastly, don't be afraid to ask questions that demonstrate that you have done your homework—questions that demonstrate your commitment to the prospect, such as: 'I noticed in your annual report that . . . Can you give me some background on . . .?'

Don't do no. 5—Don't focus solely on your questions so that you stop listening

I discussed this very issue from another viewpoint in Chapter 4. Basically, don't be so preoccupied with or intent on asking *your* questions that you fail to listen to the response. That is, don't focus so much on what *you* want that you feel you no longer need to hear what the prospect is saying. Doing this will invariably lead to the next 'don't do'.

Don't do no. 6—Don't rigidly follow your agenda

An outline or agenda, whether it is shared, tabled or simply used as your own personal 'route map', is only a guide. Learn to develop questions 'on the run'. Learn to detour, to explore side roads and issues that come up during discussion. Learn to note other areas that need exploring later in the discussions, perhaps associated with other specific issues or as stand-alone areas for further questioning—perhaps for preliminary research by you prior to exploration at a later, more appropriate time.

If you become preoccupied with following your original script, you will miss opportunities to explore associated areas that often have a large bearing on developing the compelling sales story and, ultimately, on the outcome of the sale. So, stay in control, use the route map you planned prior to the sales call, but stay flexible. You can always backtrack anytime and resume using the script—what I call the main road—at any time, if your trip down a side road leads to a dead end.

Don't do no. 7—Don't assume anything when you can ask a question

Don't assume you know something, and don't guess something if you can test it by asking a question—especially if the assumption, estimate or guess is likely to have a major bearing on the outcome of the sales call.

This is especially important when it comes to critical information you have that may even have been mentioned specifically in previous discussions. The golden rule here is not to assume that nothing has changed since last year, last month, last week or even yesterday. Don't get so locked into your agenda that you look back and find your prospect nowhere in sight. Check, don't assume.

Don't do no. 8—Don't lose focus on fully exploring their today state

Don't stop asking questions when you hear something that sounds like the 'problem'. When your prospect suggests, as a response to your questions, that they need or want a 'faster computer', what do they mean? Most salespeople, on hearing this, will immediately assume that the problem is the speed of the CPU, and start dumping product about their new, faster, state-of-the-art PC.

Think about this for a minute. The jumping-to-conclusions approach will be sure to cause the prospect some stress if what they were really talking about was the speed of the network software, or of their printer, and not the computer itself.

You need to focus on the prospect's today state. You must be prepared to go beyond your mental pictures of the prospect's words and continue to dig deeper, to help develop the consequences and implications of their remaining in this today state, as well as to explore the opportunities associated with their vision of a better tomorrow state.

Don't do no. 9—Don't ask more than one question at a time unless you have a specific reason to do so

Many salespeople are guilty of this. Just tune into any discussion between a buyer and a seller and you will hear examples of double- or triple-barrel questions—questions such as: 'When would you need it, in what quantities, and how much would you be prepared to pay for this initial order?' It's bad form. You can achieve exactly the same result by asking the questions separately. You will then have more opportunity to explore the response to each question in more depth. By asking the questions separately, you will be less likely to receive shorter answers and less likely to distract the prospect by having them grapple with two or more concepts at once. This 'don't do' becomes even more critical as the complexity of the questions increases.

The only exception to this 'don't do' rule is where you are purposely attempting to hedge. Here you are attempting to keep your options open and not paint yourself into a corner. For example, a strategic double-barrel question such as 'You seem to suggest that delivery might be an issue; would you prefer same-day delivery, or is the more usual overnight delivery service acceptable?' might be effective if you are attempting to find out more about the customer's dominant needs prior to committing yourself to a definite response.

Don't do no. 10—Don't ask questions for your prospect

If you have a genuine question, as suggested earlier, then ask it: be careful *how* you ask it, but don't be afraid to ask. However, don't engage in second-guessing your prospect by asking questions *for* them. Questions such as 'I know you will be interested in the new finance options available, won't you?' or, worse, 'You would be interested in our new range of colours, I'm sure. I think the red one might be your choice. What do you think?' can cause real problems in the relationship with the prospect that will affect the outcome of the sales process.

Don't do no. 11—Don't table your questions unless . . .

Tabling questions or asking questions in advance of their logical order are often excellent ways to introduce and explore the more complex issues involved that may well depend on the outcome of in-house discussions by the prospect and/or further research and thought before the issues are ready for open discussion. When tabling a question, don't do so without sufficient background information and explanation. Set out the reasons for asking the question to assist the prospect in understanding where you are coming from and where you're hoping to go.

When it comes to responding to questions from your prospect, don't table these questions or suggest that you will deal with them later unless you clearly have the prospect's permission to do so.

Don't do no. 12—Don't interrogate your prospect

As I have already suggested, asking your questions in the right way is as important as being prepared to ask them at all.

Even the most courteously framed and diplomatically delivered questions will seem like an interrogation if you don't break the questions up with comment, feedback, humour and anecdotes. Be very careful not to make the prospect feel as if they are being interrogated.

The golden rule

When it comes to asking questions, there appears to be one golden rule that applies to all questioning: *Once you have asked your question, shut up and listen to the prospect's response.*

Why? Well, when I ask salespeople that question, few of them understand why. Very few seem to really appreciate the consequences of continuing to talk after asking the prospect a question.

- Continuing to talk may be considered by the prospect to be rude.
- Continuing to talk may be construed as nervous and manipulative behaviour, which has the potential to damage the relationship.
- In the ensuing silence after a question is asked, the prospect may be thinking, and won't appreciate their opportunity to deliver a considered response being ignored or overridden by the salesperson.

When I ask salespeople why they feel the need to fill the silence, their answers boil down to a desire to 'rescue the prospect' from what they think might be a difficult situation for the prospect. Perhaps they feel that *they* have caused the difficult situation, and therefore feel some measure of guilt.

If 'Keep your mouth shut after you ask a question' is the golden rule, then perhaps the platinum rule is: *Don't interrupt.* If you continue to talk after you have asked a question, you are effectively jeopardising your chances of success. If not giving the prospect the opportunity to respond is like shooting yourself in the foot, then interrupting their prospect's response is tantamount to shooting yourself in both feet. And if, like many salespeople, you engage in both behaviours, you are in serious trouble, and no amount of well-researched, well-construed and well-delivered questioning will save you. So, think carefully before you fill the silence. If you continue to imbue the communication process with the sound of your own voice, how is the prospect going to be able to say 'Yes'?

chapter 25

Questioning skills II—question strategies for exploring the basic simple sale

I have presented in previous chapters what I hope are compelling arguments in support of the key role of questioning skills in the sales process. Those arguments include outlining the key questioning skills issues as understood by successful salespeople, as well as some of the misconceptions I hear all too often about questions, providing an overview of the specific benefits salespeople can obtain from asking good questions, and considering why salespeople just don't seem to ask questions. I have also outlined 12 major 'don't dos' when it comes to asking questions. Now might be an appropriate time to move on to delivery issues, such as how to construct and ask questions.

Question delivery

I have already mentioned the importance of *how* you deliver your questions. How you ask your question, and what you say, are just as important as asking the questions in the first place. And the more complex the sale, the more questions you may have to ask to explore the prospect's today and tomorrow states and develop the implications of the gap between the two.

So, let's look at a number of relatively simple strategies for delivering questions. I believe the best way to explore these questioning strategies is first to propose and then review a range of different styles or types of questions. To do this I propose to look at six different styles of questions that incorporate and go beyond the two basic types of questions, these being open and closed questions.

Delivery style no. 1—Pre-emptive questions

These are questions that start with phrases or words such as:

- 'Just to make absolutely sure we are on the right track, could I ask . . .?'
- 'So that I can brief our specialists accurately, I will need to know . . .'

■ 'For us to recommend the best solution for this particular situation, can you tell me . . .?'

Using these types of pre-emptive statements helps to soften the impact of what may be direct, personal, or very detailed or invasive questions. This is an especially applicable type of question when asking for information in sensitive and confidential areas.

The strategy here is to signal beforehand that a question is coming that is important and which the salesperson understands the prospect may find difficult or be reticent to answer. By employing this style of question, you provide a realistic reason for asking the questions and thereby soften their potential impact.

Delivery style no. 2—Give-and-take questions

Here you will volunteer information up front and in return ask for information from the prospect. What you are doing is in fact offering to swap information. But the key to this style of questioning is as follows:

■ *Key no. 1*—You have to take the risk and go first, and give your information prior to asking your question.
■ *Key no. 2*—Your information should be something the prospect doesn't already know or that isn't immediately obvious to them or to a casual observer.

By first volunteering information, then asking for information in return, you can often find out far more than if you asked a straight question. For example, consider the direct question 'How are you finding the current market?' compared to the same question framed as: 'What we are experiencing in the current market is . . . This seems to be supported by the experiences of a number of our more forward-looking customers. How are you finding the current market?'

Get the picture? It's pretty simple, really.

Delivery style no. 3—The more direct 'why' questions

There are situations where the best way to dig deeper in order to understand a prospect is to ask them *why*. The delivery of this style of question can vary. For example, it can be as direct as 'Why is that?', using the appropriate questioning body language and intonation so as not to present it as a direct personal challenge or affront. Compare this to the softer and potentially less confrontational 'May I ask why you . . .?' or 'That's interesting, please tell me more. Why do you . . .?'

When you need to clarify the prospect's thinking and penetrate the emotional and often very subjective baggage that may accompany your prospect's opinions, often dressed-up by the prospect as objective fact, the best way is often simply to ask *why*. This simple strategy is useful in helping to build direct, meaningful dialogues and avoids the trap of asking only planned questions. By questioning a response or statement made by your prospect, you are putting your agenda on hold.

Why questions are particularly useful for:

■ helping the prospect to clarify their own thinking;
■ clearly defining the prospect's dominant needs;
■ exploring the reasons behind the prospect's thinking;
■ helping to differentiate you from those competitors of yours who willingly accept the prospect's opinions and statements at face value; and
■ building your credibility by helping you to develop a professional image and relationship.

Why questions are probably the most important, and yet often most feared, style of questions from the salesperson's perspective. Many salespeople equate *why* questions with being too direct, too personal and too involved in matters that shouldn't and don't concern them.

Without *why* questions, you are employing only a part of your resources. You are working with one hand tied behind your back. Learn and practise the use of *why* in your dialogues with prospects.

Delivery style no. 4—One-word questions

The best strategy to adopt at times to attempt to get you closer to the prospect's real feelings, especially when subjective, non-specific words crop up in their opinions and statements, is to take a significant single word they have used and repeat it as a single-word question. Again, you must support this by using an appropriate sincere questioning expression and tone to convey your real objective—that is, your genuine desire to learn more, to understand.

The single-word question invites your prospect to elaborate, to explain without your needing to comment further, contradict or respond in any direct fashion that will lock you into a course of action or commit you to a view that will cause confrontation and conflict.

Words like 'impressed', 'concerned', 'disappointed', 'high', 'low', 'big', 'small' and so on are relative at best and vague at worst. So, if your customer uses words like this, rather than immediately retreating to defend your product, risking confrontation or appearing to lock into a fixed position in response, be prepared to use this one-word question strategy to get behind the prospect's thinking.

Delivery style no. 5—Each-way-bet questions

To some this may appear manipulative or unethical. This is the view of those salespeople who tend to see the world as largely composed of black-and-white issues with little or no room for grey areas. If asked with a genuine desire to learn more about the prospect, I don't believe this style of question is either unethical or manipulative. Still, it should be used sparingly.

Let's face it, while you may be very clear about your own values, morals, attitudes and behaviours, you usually don't know your prospect to this extent. Unless you can read minds, what I usually observe in salespeople–prospect interactions, at least as far as the prospect's values, morals, attitudes and behaviours are concerned, is that many salespeople apply their version of reality, right or wrong, in interpreting their prospect's actions and statements.

Professional salespeople know and understand that when it comes to other people there are, at least initially, lots of grey areas that influence the communication process, and it pays to find out more before they commit to a specific response, either positive or negative. Responses to their prospect's statements or questions with the each-way-bet style of question is one way of avoiding the need to respond without knowing all the facts, and without understanding what the prospect means or appreciating their views.

This strategy is particularly important when dealing with the hostile or aggressive prospect, who may be setting a trap or baiting you. It assists in establishing that you are not maintaining any fixed position unless you obtain more information. Examples of this each-way-bet style of questioning response might be:

- 'Well, that depends on . . . What exactly was your . . .?'; or
- 'Our usual mode of delivery is . . . However, we have found that some of our customers prefer . . . What do you have in mind?'; or
- 'Yes, we have certainly done that before. However, we have also done . . . and . . . What do you really need?' and so on.

The rules when employing this questioning strategy are fairly simple.

- *Use your own best judgement.* Decide whether you need to commit to a definite response or find out more about the prospect's thinking first by employing this style of question.
- *Use it to avoid ambush.* Consider using it whenever your prospect makes a statement about your product that you believe will be used against you later.
- *Use realistic examples and observations.* Be able to support or back up your statements or claims in response to this question by citing real-life examples if need be.

■ *Use a conservative approach*. Don't exaggerate. Stick to realistic options and alternatives and keep it simple.

Delivery style no. 6—The 360° question

Here the objective is to learn more about the prospect's situation by responding to their question with a question of your own. Again, some may think this unethical on the basis that the prospect's question deserves, maybe even demands, an answer. And so it does. But let's get real: what it demands is an answer that corresponds to the real question, not the assumed or, worse, the wrong interpretation of the prospect's question.

Those salespeople who insist on responding to every question with a clear, brief, direct answer are far more dangerous than those who hold off responding *until* they are clear that they understand the question and the feelings and facts behind the question.

The objective of these 360°-style questions is to seek to respond to the prospect's initial questions with a question that prompts them to provide further background information about their initial question. This may go something like:

■ 'That's an intriguing question. Before I attempt to answer it, tell me what prompted that question?'; or
■ 'Could I ask why you think that is a major issue?'; or
■ 'Is . . . important to you?'; or
■ 'There are a couple of answers to that question. Could you tell me more about . . .?'

This could be considered a derivative of the *why*-style question discussed earlier, which would be partly true. However, these types of questions are specifically used where you may hold, or even sense that you hold, an opposite or non-aligned view to that of the prospect on the issue being probed. It should also be considered where you sense that they are asking you a loaded question on which they already have a very fixed view. Such a situation can result in a damaging 'demand spiral', where you each adopt increasingly fixed positions and focus your energies on firing verbal salvos over the disputed territory, demanding that the other party see it your way. To avoid this situation, you need to ask the prospect to clarify, explain and describe their feelings. Usually, you will find that they are eager to do so. The *why* style of questioning could also be used, although that more direct form of questioning can tend to increase the tension levels in those situations and should be reserved for areas that require explanation of what the other party is really saying, rather than providing an opportunity for the prospect to get their past unhappy experiences and situations out of their system.

Exploration strategies

What you may have observed is that, to date, there have been no words of wisdom forthcoming on an overall strategy or framework for using questions to explore the sale from the prospect's perspective. I propose to address exactly that issue here.

I propose that, for the sake of establishing some rather broad parameters within which to formulate a basic questioning strategy, we consider three basic categories of selling environments, as follows:

1. basic simple sales;
2. sophisticated simple sales; and
3. complex sales.

Now, I acknowledge that many sales situations cannot conveniently be slotted into one of the three categories of sales described above. However, in this instance, this basic model serves a valid purpose. This is to recognise, in principle at least, that there are differing sales environments, and for the purposes of this and subsequent chapters on questioning strategies the proposed three broad categories provide a useful guide. With this in mind, I will now provide an outline of each of these three types of sale.

Basic simple sale

'Basic simple sale' describes a situation where the prospect is, as suggested earlier in this book, aware and clear about the implications of the gap between their today and tomorrow states and is aware of what is required to bridge the gap. This situation, by its very nature, usually demands minimal selling skills.

Consider the following situation. Recently, when rushing out of your office for a meeting, you found that you had inadvertently left your leather compendium and fountain pen in the conference room, where you were using it earlier that morning. You are very clear about your today state: you are now rushing to an important meeting without a pad and pen. You are also clear about what is needed—that is, your tomorrow state. You need an A4 lined pad, preferably with prepunched holes, and a basic writing implement, preferably with blue or black ink. You know that to bridge the gap, you need to borrow or buy the necessary items. You are aware of the implications of not doing so—that is, turning up at your next meeting with nothing to write on or write with. You elect to pursue the second alternative, so you stop in at a newsagency on your way to your meeting and inquire about pads and pens. After the sales assistant has asked a couple of basic user-oriented questions (size, number of pages etc.), you make a quick decision on a pad and move on to the pen display.

With a veritable multitude of pens back at the office, you have no need of anything expensive or ostentatious. It comes down to colour, type and cost. You leave the store with a new A4 lined pad and a black felt-tip fine-point pen of unknown origin.

The sales assistant required minimal sales skills. In reality, the sale centred around knowing her stock and asking very simple user-oriented or product-oriented questions. How many pages in the pad? What size? Colour? Thickness? The salesperson–prospect relationship was almost irrelevant in this simple sale. In fact, left to your own devices you could probably select the items yourself.

Sophisticated simple sale

Now imagine a second sales situation: you have decided to purchase a new pair of jeans. Your old ones just won't do any more, except for painting or gardening. You know that your today state is unacceptable and you clearly understand why. However, you have only a blurry vision of what your tomorrow state looks like. This blurry vision may seem reasonably clear until you walk into a shop and discover that you are completely ignorant of just how many styles, colours and fabrics in jeans are available these days. You are now feeling confused and just a little frustrated, and you are not sure what is required to move you from the current reality (the today state, which is clear and not in dispute) to the results needed (the vision of the tomorrow state, which is unclear and confusing). Here the salesperson needs to have a certain degree of selling skill, and while the relationship is important, it's unlikely to be critical. In this situation the experienced salesperson asks a mixture of basic open and closed questions with the objective of finding out what you really want and need.

Complex sale

Contrast the above situation with the third category of sales situation, the complex sale. You are considering upgrading your CAD software. You know that it's an expensive exercise—in terms of both direct purchase costs for upgrades to the software and hardware, and indirect costs, such as downtime while you install the new software and hardware, implement training programs for all relevant personnel, and contend with the inevitable errors resulting in decreased production as you and your team learn to use the new system.

Are you sure that your current software situation is all that bad? After all, plenty of other design and documentation practices appear to be operating effectively with far less sophisticated software. Do you know exactly what you need? There are, it appears, a host of software options out there. Some you know well and others you are vaguely aware of, and heaven knows how many you may be unaware of. As for exactly what is needed to close the gap between the vague notion and unsure acceptance of your today state and your even vaguer notion of the vision for your tomorrow state, well!

In a situation such as this, the prospect knows, or at least senses, that their current reality is unacceptable but they are unclear about the vision for their results needed and how best to bridge the gap between the two. They are unclear about the vision of their tomorrow state because they readily acknowledge that they don't yet understand all the realistic alternatives open to them. This situation is tailor-made for the professional salesperson who practises their craft with definite purpose and skill and who appreciates that the relationship with the prospect is a foundation element in the sales process. Such salespeople understand that they need to move beyond the very simple user-oriented and product-oriented questions (basic simple sale scenario). They appreciate that they must move beyond the various basic open and closed questions (sophisticated simple sale scenario). They understand that, as professional salespeople, they are consultants who are charged with, and readily accept, the responsibility of demonstrating and helping the prospect to obtain the best value available. To do this they work to understand, develop and deliver a range of much more specific questions. They know they must have a questioning strategy that goes beyond the hit-and-miss or generic approach adopted by many of their colleagues.

Let's take some time to review a specific questioning strategy that might apply to each of these three hypothetical types of sales situations: the basic simple sale, the sophisticated simple sale and those which are the primary focus of this book, the complex sale. In diagrammatic terms, Figure 25.1 shows the three types of sales exploration strategies we will discuss.

Remember that your customers buy a product to satisfy a need. In fact, you will recall that I have listed 'need' as one of the 10 major elements of the sales process. But what exactly is a need? I said earlier that a need is nothing more than the gap between where you are now and where you want to be at some stage in the future—between the today state and the tomorrow state.

I have also suggested that there are therefore two sides to a need:

1. a move *away from* a problem situation (i.e. pain)—the current reality or today state; and
2. a move *towards* a more desired outcome (i.e. pleasure)—the results-needed or tomorrow state.

The gap, or need, is the tension created when we consider the *pain* caused by dissatisfaction with the present situation and the *pleasure* felt with the vision of a more satisfying future. These aspects become more critical as the complexity of the sale increases and must be explored, identified and accepted by the prospect to a far greater degree as the complexity of the sale escalates.

Figure 25.1 *Exploration strategies*

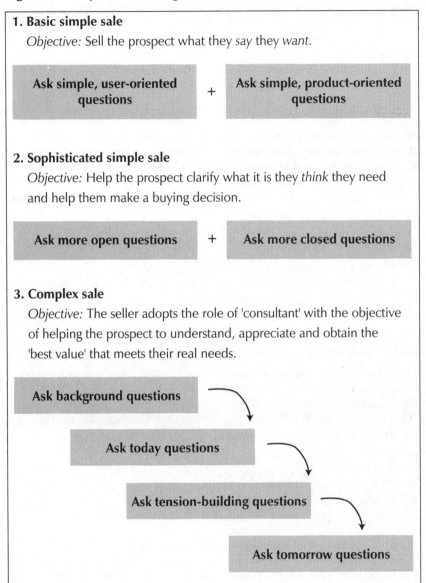

1. **Basic simple sale**
   Objective: Sell the prospect what they *say* they *want*.

   Ask simple, user-oriented questions + Ask simple, product-oriented questions

2. **Sophisticated simple sale**
   Objective: Help the prospect clarify what it is they *think* they need and help them make a buying decision.

   Ask more open questions + Ask more closed questions

3. **Complex sale**
   Objective: The seller adopts the role of 'consultant' with the objective of helping the prospect to understand, appreciate and obtain the 'best value' that meets their real needs.

   Ask background questions

   Ask today questions

   Ask tension-building questions

   Ask tomorrow questions

Exploration strategies for the basic simple sale

In the three hypothetical types of sales, the simplest of the trio, the 'basic simple sale', generally requires only the most basic level of questioning. I have termed this strategy for exploration 'user-oriented questions' and 'product-oriented questions'.

Three of the more common types of user-oriented and product-oriented questions include assumptive, either/or and 'yes' questions. In this basic simple sale, they assist in moving the prospect forward, towards a favourable decision. Let's look quickly at each of these common types of 'user-oriented' and 'product-oriented' questions.

Question type no. 1—Assumptive questions

These are questions like:

- 'When would it suit you to schedule training?'
- 'Who will be using it most of the time?'
- 'When, ideally, would you like to take delivery?'
- 'What features do you like best?'

These questions do two things important in simple sales: first, they build involvement by the prospect in the sale process; and second, they appear to talk past the decision to actually buy by assuming a positive outcome. They ask questions related to using and operating the product, or about the product characteristics required by assuming ownership.

Practise using these questions, as you will find them invaluable in helping prospects to override their own particular fear of giving a straight-out 'yes' to your buying proposition in the basic simple sales processes.

Question type no. 2—Either/or questions

These are similar to the assumptive questions above, in that you position the sale beyond the buying decision. But in this type of question it's not the situational outcome of the purchase, but the product itself, that is the focus, and the question is structured by providing choices to stimulate the prospect's thinking and thereby their response:

- 'Is this for business or pleasure?'
- 'Will this be installed in your local branch or at your main office?'
- 'Will you or your consultants be confirming the options you require?'
- 'Would you prefer the larger-capacity bins or will the standard one suffice?'

These questions allow you to check your assumptions and gather further information about the sale, yet retain control by limiting the response to a positive one that confirms their interest and intent to make a final buying decision. They can choose one of the options, or they could respond with one you haven't provided.

Question type no. 3—'Yes' questions

'Yes' questions, as the name suggests, are designed to encourage a positive response. Provided they are not manipulative, stupid or insensitive, they ca n be a legitimate and valuable way to question your prospect.

These questions might include:

- 'Based on our investigations, we believe that this is a very useful feature for your situation . . . Is that how you see it?'
- 'What about the . . .? That was very much what you suggested you needed, wasn't it?'
- 'For your type of use, you can probably see the value in this . . . can't you?'

These questions are designed to establish common ground and build value in the product. They also serve to move the buyer closer to a decision by confirming the positive aspects of the product and that these are directly related to the prospect's expressed dominant needs.

Some salespeople have suggested that other potential advantages of this type of question include helping to build confidence in the process with the prospect, by again getting the prospect into the habit of agreeing or saying 'yes' and having them confirm that their investment in the relationship so far has been worthwhile.

I suggest that even in the simplest of sales this form of question needs to be handled carefully. Some market segments have in the past relied far too heavily on this form of question in a manipulative and insensitive way.

One way to reduce the risk of appearing to manipulate a response with this 'yes' question is to reverse the order and use opinion in the form of a question, rather than a potentially direct confronting statement that either has to be agreed to or contradicted, leading to confrontation. Rather than ask the 'yes' question in this form:

- 'You can see how this product *is* perfect for your situation, can't you?'

you might consider

- 'Can you see how this product *might be* perfect for your situation?'

The three types of questions discussed above are very useful in advancing the simple sale, but can become increasingly irrelevant as the complexity of the sale increases. Why? Because the decision-making process in the simple sale is considerably less complex, the risks much reduced and the interpersonal relationship less critical, if at all.

These questions are more appropriate for demonstrating a customer service focus than a true sales focus. They are used more sparingly as the complexity of the sale increases. That is, as the needs of the prospect, or their tomorrow state, become less clear, as the decision-making process involves more people and/or takes more time, there is far less likelihood that these types of question will assist in identifying or meeting needs or building value or will contribute to establishing and developing a professional relationship.

chapter 26

Questioning skills III—question strategies for exploring the sophisticated simple sale

F | or the more sophisticated but still relatively simple sale, one where the prospect is perhaps clear about the shortcomings of their today state but unclear about the *exact* potential vision of a tomorrow state, a more sophisticated range of questions that go beyond simply focusing on customer service are required.

Here the focus should be firmly on exploring the prospect's real needs and clearly demonstrating value in the positioning of your product. The key is to appreciate, understand and be able to deliver an exploration strategy that includes a range of questions, crafted to explore the prospect's situation and position you, your organisation and your product.

These questions can be broadly divided into two basic categories: open and closed questions. I don't propose to amplify the distinction between these much-discussed two forms, other than to set out their basic characteristics, focus and a number of examples (see Table 26.1) simply to confirm the differences between the two forms.

It is my intention here, and in the next section, to focus primarily on open questions. With this in mind, let's look at a range of more sophisticated types of questions appropriate to identifying needs and assisting you in positioning your feature benefit ideas.

Question type no. 4—Decision-making process questions

These types of questions need to be delivered tactfully, otherwise you risk damaging the relationship. However, the risk is worth considering, as the answers to these types of questions provide invaluable information, especially early in the needs identification phase of the sale.

These questions focus, as you would expect, on the aspects of the sale concerned with the actual decision-making process of the prospect:

- 'How was the project budget set?'
- 'Who is likely to be involved in your evaluation and decision-making process?'

Table 26.1 Two major forms of questions

Open questions	Closed questions
Characteristics:	**Characteristics:**
■ Require an extended answer	■ Require only yes/no/brief statement of fact
■ Draw out more general information	■ Elicit more specific details
■ Promote an increasing dialogue between parties	■ Have potential to shift the direction of discussions
Focus:	**Focus:**
■ Uncover prospect's real needs and wants	■ Clarify points/issues
■ Learn what prospects do, think and feel, and how they view the situation	■ Force decision
■ Help establish a 'connection'	■ Verify information
■ Control/direct the sales process	■ Set the stage for a close
Examples:	**Examples:**
■ How do you . . .?	■ Do you still buy . . .?
■ How is it working?	■ When will you be needing . . .?
■ Who are your customers?	■ What are you using now?
■ What areas need improvement?	■ Who does your buying?
■ Tell me more about . . .?	■ When do you buy?
■ Oh! Why is that?	■ How long has it been since . . .?
■ Could you please explain . . .?	■ Have you heard about . . .?
■ What would you do if . . .?	■ Is it okay if . . .?

■ 'How will you make the final decision?'

Questions such as these are often seen by salespeople as prying into areas that are of little or no concern to them or the product itself, or are seen as inconsequential because the salespeople believe they have little or no control over them. This may, or may not, be true.

I believe that these types of questions (some of which can be more effective if framed in the closed question form) are critical to positioning your proposal. In fact, I believe it is difficult, if not impossible, to effectively design a compelling sales story without knowing the answer to a raft of these all-important decision-making types of questions.

Question type no. 5—Check questions

These are used primarily to find out or confirm how your prospect views you, your competitor, your organisation, your efforts to date and your product. The questions are especially useful in the initial stages of the needs identification phase of the sales process to establish where your prospect is before you go too far down the wrong track. They can throw up all sorts of issues or subjects that will require further exploration, usually at a later date. These questions include:

- 'Who are the other suppliers you are talking to?'
- 'How do you feel about . . .?'
- 'What do you think about . . .?'

You need to be careful not to appear to be denigrating the competition, no matter how inviting the opportunity may appear.

Few salespeople appreciate that by utilising information gained in your research you can design these questions well in advance to help your prospect draw comparisons and thereby help them to discover weaknesses in your competitors' propositions as well as in their own assumptions and perceptions.

Questions like 'From what you have suggested, it would appear that a quality assurance-focused manufacturing process is an important ingredient. With this in mind, tell me what level of importance does an independently certified system have in your overall criteria for assessing your needs?' can be asked in a more direct, closed form, such as: 'Is a certified quality assurance manufacturing process important to you?'

This question takes on a new dimension when, due to your intelligence-gathering efforts, you are aware of two things: one, your prospect is inclined to put weight on a quality assured supplier; and two, your major competitor hasn't achieved an independently audited quality assurance system.

Don't underestimate these seemingly basic information-gathering questions. They can be extremely strategic in positioning you, your organisation and your product.

Question type no. 6—Situation questions

Questions that yield valuable information concerning a prospect's situation, albeit through their eyes, are almost mandatory, unless, of course, you believe you can read your prospect's mind. These types of questions might include:

- 'How does your manufacturing facility . . .?'
- 'How does that work?'
- 'How many . . .?'
- 'What structure have you found that best . . .?'
- 'Under what circumstance are . . .?'

You need to be very careful, however. I see many salespeople who seem to get stuck in a rut when it comes to asking situation-type questions and they can come across to the prospect as boring and repetitious. You should be prepared to show that you have done your homework by combining those questions with a simple statement about your prospect's situation that shows you have taken the trouble to find out something about them first.

Question type no. 7—Personal questions

You might think there is no place in the selling process for personal questions. What if I were to suggest that they can provide very interesting and valuable insights into your prospect's personal values, attitudes and interests? They might also tell you why they might feel the way they do about a range of issues and subjects, such as:

- their personal interests or hidden personal agenda in the overall business context;
- past experiences and outcomes that will influence how they view you and your product this time;
- the politics involved, including possible alliances and potential opposition;
- the formal and informal interpersonal networks, both internal and external to the prospect and their organisation; and
- potential barriers to your ideas.

These questions include:

- 'Approximately how long have you . . .?'
- 'What do you plan to do when . . .?'
- 'How is your . . .?'

Note that all these questions include the words 'you' or 'your', or, for that matter, the prospect's name, and target the prospect's personal views and feelings.

Don't underestimate personal questions. When used politely, diplomatically, with sensitivity and genuine interest, you can open a window into your prospect's world.

One final point about personal questions. Be careful when it comes to potential non-work-related questions. Some prospects are less inclined to discuss apparently irrelevant questions until they have become comfortable with you. However, don't be intimidated or discouraged. Plan these questions in advance and, if in doubt, link them to the business at hand; be prepared to wait for the appropriate time, perhaps after the business issues have been dealt with, before pursuing them.

Question type no. 8—Big-picture questions

The focus here is to use your prospect's overview of their business and their long-term goals or vision, and encourage them to look into the future with you.

Sometimes it takes coaxing and a series of questions to help the prospect leave the present behind and begin to dream and verbalise their vision for themselves and their organisation. This also includes asking them to share their short- and long-term goals, strategies, tactics and motivations. These questions might include:

- 'What changes do you see in the next . . .?'
- 'What is your overall position on . . .?'
- 'What is your view on . . .?'
- 'How does this current development fit your . . .?'
- 'What was your main reason for . . .?'

Again, a word of caution. When asking big-picture questions, you must not only feel interested, you must also convey that genuine interest and curiosity. You will come unstuck if your prospect perceives your questions are founded on a critical, judgemental basis. You must be prepared to share your own thoughts and experiences with the prospect if you are to pursue this line of questioning.

If you can look *with* your prospect into *their* future, you have done something few of your competitors will or indeed can do. More importantly, you can then begin to create with the prospect a compelling sales story and clearly demonstrate how you can help them get there.

Question type no. 9—Spontaneous, unplanned questions

As a ballpark estimate, about 50% of all your questions should be spontaneous questions—questions that weren't planned prior to the sales call. Follow your instincts and put your planned agenda of questions to one side while you test your detour down this side track to see what information it yields and what secrets it offers up.

Experience tells me that you never know where these unplanned questions will lead and generally, unless your time is limited and you have other issues that must be dealt with, you should be inclined to ask these spontaneous-type questions and perhaps find yourself uncovering useful, pertinent information.

Of all the types of questions used in this sophisticated simple sale, this is usually the type ignored by salespeople who are too focused on either themselves or their product. These salespeople see no merit in following the side roads and back roads; they prefer sticking to the main road— one that is infinitely safer, although usually more crowded, well-travelled and far less interesting. Value-based salespeople make spontaneous questions an imperative; they use them to differentiate themselves and their product and build a compelling sales story that draws on the important but less obvious needs of their prospects.

Your approach to exploring the prospect's situation

It's one thing to understand the need to design exploration tactics around the different styles and *types* of questions available and promote their use; it's another issue altogether to be able to implement the exploration strategy.

Why? Because if your strategic exploration approach isn't appropriate, you will find it difficult to design and deliver the types of questions that you will need to ask in order to find out what your prospect really needs, wants and thinks.

I've talked about a number of issues in other areas of this book related to your approach to exploring the prospect's situation. However, it is worth reviewing again the critical components of a healthy approach to questioning. Consider the five strategic questioning tips below and think about how your approach compares on each of these five issues when it comes to asking questions.

Strategic questioning tips

- *Get your radar operational.* Don't accept what the prospect says on face value. Don't make assumptions. If in doubt, I look at the non-verbal clues and listen to the verbal ones.
- *Be a consultant, not a teacher.* Build your compelling sales story with your prospect. Don't lecture—ask. Be a partner, a consultant, not a teacher who dispenses information from a textbook using lecture mode.
- *Listen.* Don't focus your energies on pursuing your own agenda to the detriment of your prospect. Listen to what they say and, equally importantly, what they *don't* say.
- *Involve the prospect.* Involve your prospect in the questioning process. Work with them to build more powerful, more credible, more specifically targeted questions and therefore a far more influential approach to identifying their dominant needs.
- *Prepare your questions in advance, but focus on answers.* When you

are in the presence of your prospect, you need to have done your homework and to have prepared sufficiently in advance to be able to focus the majority of your energies on what your prospect says, rather than what you are going to say next.

I have set the scene and discussed the various types of questions that might be said to be appropriate to the first two categories of simple sale. Now it's time to explore the differences in questioning strategy required for success in the more complex sale.

chapter 27

Questioning skills IV—question strategies for exploring the more complex sale

W hen it comes to exploring needs for a more complex sale, there are, in addition to those types of questions already proposed, four primary types of questions. These are each focused on dealing with a particular aspect of the sales process I proposed in the more complex 'psychology of selling' model discussed earlier in Chapter 8.

The four types of questions are as follows:

1. background questions;
2. today questions;
3. tension-building questions; and
4. tomorrow questions.

I will review each of them, and then suggest a simple exploration model for the complex sale that proposes a framework for the inclusion of each of these four distinctly different types of questions.

So, let's look at these four different types of questions, then see how they work together in the exploration of needs in a more complex sale. Specifically, let's see how the strategy helps the prospect and salesperson move beyond wants to assumed needs, and how it enables them to work to further refine these assumed needs into true, specific dominant needs, which are then the hard targets for positioning.

Question type no. 10—Background questions

Background questions help to build the platform from which you launch your exploration of dominant needs in the complex sales model. These types of questions usually uncover or surface the prospect's 'wants'. It may be necessary to backtrack to this platform several times during the sales process before again focusing on the other types of questions to dig further and refine the prospect's true needs.

So what exactly are background questions? In a nutshell, background questions are simply questions that explore basic background information about the prospect. The sole objective of these types of questions is to provide the seller with basic, but nevertheless important or even critical, information about the prospect. This information could include basic facts about them and their organisation, as well as data on how they operate, their business structure, history and so on.

As I suggested, these questions aren't designed to uncover dominant needs but to build a solid platform of 'wants' on which to move to launch the next three types of questions. When it comes to asking these types of background questions, there are generally four simple rules you need to keep in mind:

- *Rule no. 1—Be economical.* Be disciplined. Make sure you know where you are heading. If you overdo these types of questions, pretty soon the prospect will begin to think they are being interrogated.
- *Rule no. 2—Focus.* Concentrate your questions on the areas you wish to explore in detail now. Don't take a scattergun approach. If the prospect can see where you are headed, they are far more likely to actively cooperate.
- *Rule no. 3—Do your homework first.* These questions are designed based on your first doing your homework, researching your prospect and their organisation. This is essentially the difference between background questions and the situation questions proposed for the sophisticated simple sale. Background questions can serve to demonstrate a measure of competence and professionalism on the salesperson's part.
- *Rule no. 4—Consider using a 'missing information' approach.* Rather than come straight out and ask a background question, ask the background question by inviting the prospect to fill in the missing information, or gaps.

This is the major difference between situation questions in the sophisticated simple sale and these background questions used in the more complex sale. The latter have a specific focus, and delivering the questions as an invitation to fill in the blanks is getting targeted on a particular issue. Even at this early stage of the questioning process with these types of questions, you are very much controlling the focus.

Background questions might include:

- 'From what we can see . . . how many packages do you actually buy on a monthly basis?'
- 'That certainly seems to argue against the general trend in this industry. Tell me more about . . .?'
- 'So you actually . . . That's somewhat surprising given . . . How do you see this developing in the future?'

■ 'Based on our calculations it would appear that . . . Is this close to the real situation, or have we missed something important?'

When it comes to planning background questions, always bear in mind that your focus should be either directly or indirectly related to the particular areas of concern, problems or difficulties your prospect is experiencing related to your broad area of 'consultancy'. I say 'directly or indirectly' because it's not unusual to find the skilled salesperson asking background questions that can appear immediately removed from the 'product'. However, the information revealed by the prospect in response is often directly related to the business at hand.

Also bear in mind that while the questions are related to the prospect's problems—that is, their today state—they *are not* designed to immediately explore these problems in great detail. Think of background questions as primarily being focused on collecting good, usable intelligence on the prospect and their business—intelligence you cannot get anywhere else. Don't judge or respond subjectively in any way to the prospect's answers. Focus on gathering information; suspend comment or judgement for the time being.

When designing these background questions, I suggest that you make a list of potential questions and then ask yourself two questions: 'Can I find this out any other way?', and 'What specific areas directly related to this do I need more background on?' Think of background questions as being limited, or rationed, in number. Keep the background questions for those areas that require responses from your prospect directly.

Remember that background questions are those questions that are required to permit you to build a solid foundation or platform for asking more detailed questions. Background questions provide you with information—the raw material—that is essential in allowing you to effectively and efficiently explore your prospect's needs.

Question type no. 11—Today questions

Today questions are those designed to help penetrate and explore the prospect's current unsatisfactory situation, their concerns, priorities, problems and difficulties that surfaced in response to background questions—what I termed early in this book their 'current realities'. The objective of these questions is to uncover the prospect's perception of *their* current reality, *their* concerns, feelings etc. These questions centre on taking the prospect's expressed 'wants' and, by exploring their dissatisfaction with the present, prompting them to offer more detailed statements of needs, which by and large will still require further exploration. Hence, I refer to these today questions as assisting in uncovering 'assumed needs' by having *the prospect* directly or indirectly, thinking about and further defining their problems.

Designing these questions requires you to undertake two simple initiatives:

- *Initiative no. 1*—Do your homework in advance, either by researching the issues yourself or by utilising information gained from asking background questions.
- *Initiative no. 2*—Plan these questions carefully, taking account of the prospect's responses to background questions.

These questions might include:

- 'What areas do you feel need improvement?'
- 'What is working as far as . . .?'
- 'How important is it that . . .?'
- 'How have you found . . .?'
- 'When do you experience . . .?'
- 'What circumstances are likely to . . .?'
- 'In which areas do you want to see an improvement?'

The best way to design these questions is to research your prospect's situation by employing background questions and, with this detailed information, consider your product. In particular, consider how it is linked to your prospect's problem business processes. Work hard to uncover a number of ways your product could positively affect potential or actual problems for your prospect. With these in mind, convert the ways of solving potential problems into questions designed to elicit specific information about the today state the prospect is experiencing. The resulting information will, by its very nature, contain assumed needs.

The key here is to think not in product terms, but in terms of solutions and ideas. Be prepared to let your mind run free. Don't start comparing this situation with others. Keep your mind focused on that particular prospect at this early stage. Resist the temptation to think from past experiences.

The beauty about these today questions is that by converting potential solutions and ideas into questions, you are not *telling*. Instead, by asking questions, you will be perceived as being genuinely interested in finding out about your prospect. For example, imagine your product is a design service for websites. One way it *could* address a problem for some hypothetical client is that a website can provide 24-hour point of contact with the prospect's organisation. The today question developed might be, 'How important is it that your customers are able to access details of your product range outside normal business hours?'. Or an even more basic today question might be, 'What, if any, problems are you experiencing with getting your product information out into the marketplace?'

Today questions are critical in the exploration strategy of more complex sales. Learn the skill of researching your prospect and designing good questions that get to the heart of your prospect's situation through being generated by the potential of you and your product to provide broad solutions that meet the prospect's general challenges.

Questioning type no. 12—Tension-building questions

Tension-building questions are the third of the four primary types of questions that tend both to characterise and differentiate the exploration strategy proposed for the complex sale. Unlike background questions, they are focused specifically on needs. In this respect, they are similar to today questions. Where they differ from today questions is in the type of needs they are designed to uncover. Today questions are specifically designed to explore the prospect's present or current 'wants' with the objective of gaining from the prospect their direct first-hand perceptions of their current reality in the form of their assumed needs. However, these soft assumed needs don't usually include a strong resolve to follow any specific fixed course of action, and often don't convey any particular urgency to work towards the required change to the current situation. At this assumed need stage, the prospect often talks not about 'how' and 'when', but 'what' is required.

Tension-building questions, on the other hand, help the prospect to explore the consequences of their current reality, their today state. That is, they help to explore the real-life implications of the continuing unsatisfactory situation, and in particular work to identify their true specific or dominant needs, based on the previously identified assumed needs.

I talked earlier of the two sides of a solution: the *pleasure* of envisaging a satisfying solution; and the *pain* resulting from the continuing unsatisfactory situation. Tension-building questions are specifically designed to explore the gap between the prospect's today state, or their current reality, and their tomorrow state, or the results needed. Their primary focus is to redefine the soft, non-specific assumed needs identified in response to the today questions. Tension-building questions focus on the specific consequences of the continuing unsatisfactory situation. In other words, their primary focus is to identify dominant needs.

It could be suggested that whereas the today questions were designed to give the seller information *about the prospect's perception of their current reality and to ensure that they accept and appreciate the current reality of their situation*, and provide a measure of awareness of their needs in the form of assumed needs, tension-building questions are designed to take that next natural step. They are designed to provide the seller with information *about the prospect's perceptions of the negative outcomes, the detrimental effects, the unwanted consequences of that today state and to ensure that the prospect fully appreciates the implications of these short-comings and thereby refines their assumed needs into true, specific dominant needs.*

The tension-building form of question clarifies the dissatisfaction of the current situation such that the prospect can clearly see and then articulate the real dominant need—the hard target that the salesperson now must focus on meeting. It might be suggested that these questions help to *identify*, *refine* and then *bridge* the gap that exists between the today and the tomorrow state.

Tension-building questions are foreign territory to the bulk of salespeople who prefer dealing in background information, with some perhaps moving on to exploring non-specific assumed needs via today-style questions. When it comes to the complex sales process, very few appreciate the need to further refine these prospect-generated soft assumed needs. Nor do most salespeople comprehend the immense opportunity available for the taking, when it comes to using tension-building questions to construct their feature benefit ideas and to help them create a *unique* and compelling sales story. These questions include:

- 'Why is that happening?'
- 'How will this affect your . . .?'
- 'What are the major consequences of . . .?'
- 'What other less obvious implications does . . .?'
- 'How is this critical to your operation?'
- 'What are the costs of this . . .?'

If we were to use a tension-building question to explain the importance of using these types of questions, we might ask the following:

Q: Thinking back to your current situation . . . Tell me . . . What are the potential implications of *not using* tension-building questions and *thereby* becoming sidetracked into addressing the prospect's stated soft, non-specific assumed needs?'

A: Without fully exploring the consequences of the prospect's today state, the best you can hope to achieve is to deal in generalities, what are described as 'advantages' in this book. Non-specific or soft assumed needs cannot be used as targets for feature benefit ideas simply because these assumed needs are usually somewhat vague and there often is no real urgency felt by the prospect to change the situation.

By stopping your exploration strategy at today questions, you will be forced to deal in these non-specific assumed needs. With no hard targets to aim at, feature benefit ideas are difficult, if not impossible, to propose. You are therefore restricted to dealing in advantages, which is at best a hit-and-miss operation—the downside of which is that the misses often prompt objections that obscure or obliterate the real needs.

So, how can you design good tension-building questions? There are broadly two related methods that can be used. The first method involves you, the salesperson, working backwards from potential dominant needs to related non-specific assumed needs and thereby back to questions designed to develop the former from the latter.

The second method of designing tension-building questions is to tackle the issue from the problem itself by exploring specifically the consequences of that problem, thereby unearthing potential specific dominant needs.

Don't think that it's a matter of asking only one tension-building question. If it were so easy, everybody would be doing it. Depending on the prospect's response, you may need to probe deeper to build more tension, develop urgency and uncover the dominant needs.

It is interesting to note there does appear, on face value at least, to be a direct correlation between the tension or stress the prospect feels and the surfacing of a specific dominant need and the urgency to act felt by the prospect. The closer you get to uncovering the real dominant need, the more urgency the prospect feels. The corollary to this is also worth considering. If you are dealing with a prospect who exhibits little or no inclination to change or act now, chances are that you are only at the surface, dealing with non-specific or soft assumed needs and have little or no idea of the real issues and consequences associated with the real dominant needs.

Question type no. 13—Tomorrow questions

Tomorrow questions are the fourth and final of the types of questions you need to master to succeed in complex sales. What is their primary purpose? Put simply, tomorrow questions serve to develop the value the prospect will equate with being able to meet a dominant need by buying your product. This is best achieved if the prospects themselves become so involved in responding to questions that they volunteer to *tell you* the benefits they see by using your product. By asking tomorrow questions, it's possible to literally *listen* the prospect into buying. To put this in more prospect-oriented terms, it's possible to *listen* the prospect into enthusiastically selling themselves the product.

If you take a minute to consider the previous three types of questions, you will recall that I started the ball rolling by using background questions to explore background information about the prospect. This provides the general 'wants', including the facts, data and other information about the prospect and their organisation to enable the salesperson to build a solid foundation on which to fully explore the prospect's real needs. And this is exactly what you now proceed to do, employing a variety of well-designed today and tension-building questions, both of which deal with your prospect's perceptions.

Today questions are designed to uncover perceptions of their current situation and provide the prospect's assumed needs as soft targets to explore further. Tension-building questions develop these non-specific assumed needs into specific dominant needs, which are then hard targets for feature benefit ideas. This is implemented by developing *with the prospect* their perception of the real effects or consequences of their current reality, thereby creating a sense of urgency and refining their real needs. This final tomorrow style of question is the first time you invite your prospect to link *your* product to *their* situation via their specific dominant needs. Here we also deal with perceptions, but there is a subtle twist. Here we deal with *positive* perceptions. We are now dealing with those positive perceptions that centre around how your product provides benefits that clearly address the specific dominant needs.

These tomorrow questions are the first time you attempt to discuss your product, albeit indirectly, by discussing the vision of the results your prospect needs and wants. With tomorrow questions comes the switch to positive benefits—to results, to wins, to satisfaction, to pleasure and away from pain—but only when you have effectively explored your prospect's needs and are sure you are dealing with their specific dominant needs.

What are these tomorrow questions? Taking some of our earlier hypothetical sales situations, they might sound something like this:

- 'Given our discussions concerning the cost of operation of your current printer, how might you be able to differently use a machine with a "refill on the run" style of continuously available ink supply?'; or
- 'You mentioned earlier that speed was an issue. How effective would a machine with a much shorter warm-up time be, say something less than five seconds?'; or
- 'When you outlined your operations, the noise issue was something that I believe you felt you must currently accept and work around. Thinking for a minute beyond that barrier, what might happen if you were able to drastically reduce the noise from your compressors, say by about 80%?'

How do you design these questions?

In reality, these are probably the most enjoyable and most rewarding of the four types of questions. Here you draw together the outcomes of the three previous types of questions and lead, inspire or invite your prospect to imagine, think and feel these positive outcomes of their buying decision—but only after setting the stage by using the three previous styles of questions.

The design of these tomorrow questions can be approached by first considering the advantages (potential benefits) your product can provide, then considering potential specific dominant needs that are required to be identified so that your prospect will see unambiguous 'value' in your product. In fact, they will, in all likelihood, view your product as unique simply because it addresses what they believe are *their* unique needs, not at all because your product is necessarily unique.

Once you have determined the prospect's potential dominant needs aligned with your product's benefits, you are in a position to turn them around by simply restating them as a *positive* question, using the specific dominant needs as a lever to trigger the prospect to *tell you the benefits of your particular product's features* without necessarily referring directly to those features—*to, in fact, begin to sell themselves on your product.*

I have witnessed salespeople do just this. The exchange is something worth experiencing. The prospect (*P*), in essence, attempts to convince the salesperson (*S*) why the prospect should have the product, often to the point where they are so excited at the idea of owning and using the product that it can be fun just to suggest some possible obstacles to the prospect acquiring the product and watch the reaction. The exchange might go something like this . . .

S: Of course, it only comes in safety yellow.
P: Terrific, this place could do with some brightening up. When will they be available?

or

S: We probably can't install the package in one go. We'll need to stage the installation to keep you on-line as much as possible.
P: That sounds good. They will be able to directly compare the new and the old equipment and experience these benefits for themselves at first hand.

So, in summary, you need first to spend time collecting adequate and accurate information by asking your background questions. Second, design and deliver quality and relevant questions by using today questions to explore the prospect's current unsatisfactory situations. Third, develop the consequences of the undesirable aspects of their current reality by exploring the implications, thereby clarifying their assumed needs and determining specific dominant needs by using well-designed tension-building questions. Finally, have some fun by asking tomorrow questions to go straight to the heart of the matter. Invite the prospect to imagine a more positive situation—one where the focus is on the vision and pleasure of having overcome their problems and obstacles, a vision of their tomorrow state which concentrates on various parts of your ccompelling sales story where these problems, concerns and difficulties are vanquished in favour of specific concrete outcomes that make the prospect look and feel good.

However, remember, when it comes to this last style of tomorrow questions, don't indulge yourself prematurely. Don't proceed to invite a prospect to explore their perceptions of how a proposed solution or situation *might* be a benefit *unless* you are clear that you have uncovered and are responding to the prospect's real, specific dominant needs.

Figure 27.1 *Outline of successful exploration journey*

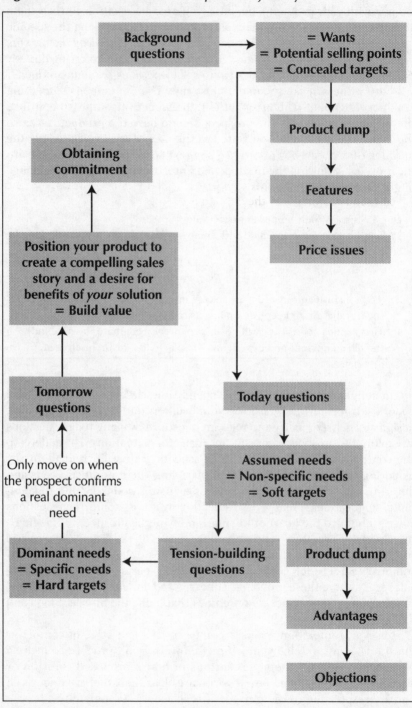

Set out in Figure 27.1 is an outline of the successful exploration journey we have just discussed involving all four questions and the outcomes and dangers of not completing the full journey.

When looking at the diagram, keep in mind the following:

■ *Specific/dominant need*—The buyer states a specific want or intention—*now*—for a solution/change. They talk about *how* and *when* they will deal with the current reality. These are the hard targets you aim for.

■ *Non-specific/assumed need*—The buyer confirms a general problem, concern or difficulty. They don't yet necessarily indicate a need to solve the problem or change the situation, because the real need and its consequences haven't been identified. These are the soft targets that can send you off down the wrong path.

chapter 28

Resolution skills I—dealing with barriers to the sale

You've been talking to your prospect for only a relatively short time, 15 or maybe 20 minutes at most, when they say: 'Look, I really don't see the need to spend that much for a new . . . when a reconditioned one will do what we want for about half the price!' What are you going to do? How will you respond? How will you react? Before you read on, take a minute to think about what you might say in a similar situation.

I certainly can't predict what you are going to say, but let me share with you what would appear to be the 10 most popular responses salespeople use to deal with this objection.

Response no. 1—Product dump

The salesperson's response goes something like this: 'Yes, I understand, but there are a number of reasons why our new Model X machine is far superior to the alternative you suggested. There is the . . . and then the . . . and the . . . not to mention the . . . So you can see that the alternative of a reconditioned machine just doesn't measure up when you consider all these features.'

Here our intrepid salesperson takes the view that the prospect obviously doesn't fully understand the multitude of features and advantages available with the *new* product. Once this is pointed out to our wayward prospect via a good dose of 'product dump', the salesperson feels the prospect is sure to recognise the errors of their ways. The prospect will then see the obvious and understand why the alternative they proposed is inferior to the solution proposed by the salesperson of buying a new 'Product X'.

This is a hit-or-miss approach where the chances of a hit are remote at best, and the consequences of a miss can be catastrophic in terms of the potential damage done to your relationship with the prospect.

Response no. 2—Attempt at empathy

Here you respond by saying something like, 'Yes, I understand that cost is important to you, but I'm confident that once you've understood all the advantages we offer with our new improved Product X, you'll quickly reassess your position.'

Now, think about this approach for a minute. You start by attempting to demonstrate a measure of empathy and then inject a big *but* into your response. This has the effect of completely undermining your attempt at empathy. Your response then goes on to contradict the prospect—not the stuff on which foundations for good interpersonal or professional relationships are built.

Response no. 3—The 'if' technique

The good old 'if' technique just doesn't cut it these days. If you are genuinely trying to maintain a good relationship and believe that manipulating the prospect (that's assuming you can even do so) isn't an acceptable approach to 'overcoming' objections, you won't respond like this: 'If I could show you how the real cost of Product X is less than the alternative you mentioned, will you make a decision to buy Product X today?' In my opinion you would have to be desperate to try this response on your prospect in a complex sale. It clearly telegraphs to your prospect that your objective for the sale doesn't factor in their needs, wants or feelings—just your commission.

Response no. 4—The leading question

This response was used a great deal by financial services salespeople, who would start off their canned presentation or sales patter by saying something like, 'You want to achieve a measure of wealth and security for the future protection of your family, don't you?'

One way to respond to this inane type of question is to answer 'No' and see where they go from there. Most salespeople who receive this 'No' response stop dead in their tracks. They have absolutely no idea what to do next. It's patently obvious that no one has ever answered 'No!' to their leading questions before, so why should this prospect answer 'No'? It's not normal, they think. These are dubious forms of questions that were designed to be answered in only one obvious way— with a 'Yes'. They are insulting, and most of your prospects will rightly feel insulted.

Response no. 5—Switching tracks

Here the salesperson might respond by saying something like, 'Yes, but what do you see as the best solution for the long-term view of the company?', or perhaps, 'How does that view sit with the company's quality assurance goal?'

This is clearly a response that switches from one track to another. In the blink of an eye you have changed the topic, or at least completely diverted it from the real barrier to the sale erected by the prospect.

Response no. 6—The contradiction

This response might go something like this: 'Really, that's interesting, because most of our customers prefer this latest-model Product X.'

This isn't a good look. As a result of such a confrontational and challenging statement, the prospect is almost certainly going to become defensive, if not downright aggressive, in response.

Response no. 7—Reflective statement

Here the salesperson restates what they *believe* to be the barrier, as stated by the prospect, sometimes almost word for word, although usually with a subtle twist. In response to the prospect's objection, they might say something like, 'Oh, so what you are saying is you don't necessarily need new equipment and you would rather look at a much cheaper alternative?', or 'So you think a reconditioned one will do the job?'

Again, why see them as an adversary and challenge their thinking? Why push them into defending a point of view that you have accidentally or even purposefully misconstrued, and which may not be the correct one, let alone one that the prospect could support if questioned skilfully? Why engage in point scoring at the expense of the relationship and, quite possibly, the sale?

Response no. 8—Ignore it

A response like 'Here, let me show you how much quieter this new Product X runs. I think you'll be really impressed!' simply seeks to ignore the real or stated barrier to the sale raised by the prospect. This again is generally not a good strategy to adopt unless you have a distinctly sound reason to do so.

Response no. 9—The assumption

Here the salesperson takes a rather long bow and assumes they understand exactly what the prospect's real concerns are, then compounds the error by jumping to an incorrect conclusion and making a statement based on the incorrect assumption: 'Oh, so what you are really suggesting is that you can't see the benefits of a new Product X over a second-hand piece of equipment?' Now, the prospect didn't say that at all.

Alternatively, the salesperson may misinterpret or mistranslate something the prospect has said, and respond with, 'Ah, so it's a matter of finding how to meet your limited budget constraints?' The prospect also gave no direct indication that they even had budget constraints.

Lazy is the best way to describe both of these responses by the salesperson.

Response no. 10—The challenge

This response is often exhibited following a demand, or what is perceived by the salesperson as a demand, from the prospect. In response to 'Your price is too high', the salesperson challenges the prospect: 'What price did you expect?', or 'What number did you have in mind?' A clash of egos invariably ensues, and in most cases both parties declare the other as 'difficult' (this is the nice way of putting it) and decide never to do business with the other again.

There is absolutely no need to take the initial demand from the prospect, if indeed that is what it was, and then by your response raise it to the next level of all-out personality conflict. It is unprofessional and immature. It's up to you, the salesperson, to avoid rising to the bait, if that is what it is, and to control your behaviour in response. Mind you, I don't suggest it's easy to do at times. However, we all know that it's undoubtedly the best course of action.

One could take the view, and many salespeople do, that there is nothing essentially wrong, bad or even unprofessional about the 10 types of response outlined above. However, I believe that they are potentially damaging to the relationship and show a distinct lack of concern for the prospect's point of view. They also indicate a total obsession by the salesperson with what *they* want to happen. This last point, by the way, is usually not lost on the prospect.

Now I know that most readers, having reviewed these 10 types of response, will be saying, 'Oh, no. That's not me. I wouldn't respond like any of those examples. If I were in that salesperson's shoes, I would ask questions.' They know that the best response when encountering any barrier to the sale is to dig deeper, to ask a question, perhaps a series of questions, designed to flush out the real underlying concerns, problems or objections. But let me suggest that, in observations of salespeople in real on-the-job situations and in training room role-plays or simulations, this doesn't happen. Most salespeople simply don't ask questions in response. And if they do, they don't take them deep enough. They don't persist with their line of questions. They accept another answer as the genuine obstacle and often proceed to respond with one of the 10 types of response described above. They never dig deep enough to uncover the real barrier to the sale.

Very few salespeople, it seems, respond with something like, 'Yes, I can imagine, as you appear to indicate, that cost is an important consideration. May I ask what it is exactly that causes your concern? Is it the actual investment or perhaps something else?', or sometimes something as simple as, 'Why is that?'

This may appear obvious. But it just doesn't happen most of the time. The crux of the matter is that you need to ask 'why' questions until you get to the real barriers to the sale. This failure to respond in 'why' mode almost invariably leads to the salesperson resorting to one or more of the 10 inadequate responses detailed earlier. Which then invariably leads to an overwhelmingly severe dose of product dump at some stage in the future.

Salespeople need to extricate themselves completely from the various props and crutches they use, such as manipulative sales techniques and tricks. They need to get in touch with their naturally inquisitive nature. They need to find out more about how the prospect thinks and feels. They need to display more interest in the prospect than in the outcome of the sale.

As a salesperson, to do this you need to engage the prospect by demonstrating empathy and then proceed to question, listen and position, rather than engage in this multitude of tricky techniques. You see, it is these very same techniques that stop the natural quest for answers, that circumvent the need to understand why the prospect said what they said, and to appreciate what they really mean and really need. These tricky techniques are the natural enemy of the 'why'.

All 10 responses above reflect a view of the sales process by the salesperson as being heavily based in the tell mode of the traditional sales approach. They are rooted in a view of sales as persuading, as convincing, as imposing your understanding and will over that of the prospect.

Barriers to a sale—10 ways to deal with them

Barriers to the sale raised by the prospect need to be carefully responded to. Set out below are 10 major considerations for approaching barriers to a sale expressed by your prospect. Think about each of these and your current view of objections, and how you usually deal with them.

1. Treat barriers as a challenge

Not as a direct personal challenge, but as a challenge to the sales process that you, the salesperson, need to meet. And, let's not kid ourselves: you do have a choice. You can take the challenge or sidestep it. The way to a successful sales career is to treat any and all barriers to the sale as a professional does and realise that they are a part of the sales process. They go with the territory. As such, expect them, if possible prepare for them, and rise to meet them.

2. Understand that it takes two to tango

This simply means it takes two of you, working together, to dissolve these barriers. I don't mean you the salesperson and your assistant or another salesperson. I mean you the salesperson and the prospect. What you should consider is that, when it comes to dealing with barriers to the sale, the resolution or dissolution resides partly in your own head and partly in the prospect's head. You cannot dissolve the objection without the prospect's 'buy-in'. The prospect's 'buy-in' means that they accept your legitimate attempt to resolve the barrier and should assist you in doing so. Which means you cannot work to remove barriers to the sale without understanding just what the prospect believes, wants and needs.

3. Display patience and courage

Both of these personal attributes are essential to addressing your prospect's concerns and working with them to remove barriers to the sale. As you might imagine, without them you won't get very far.

4. Control your frustration

Easier said than done? You would be an unusual salesperson indeed if, from time to time, you didn't need to make a special effort to control your rising frustration. Take a deep breath, count to five, start again, keep the pace and volume of your speech down, and avoid repeating yourself. If you feel you're losing your grip, plan to take a break or seek permission to table the issues at hand for later, then move on to another facet of the prospect's needs.

5. Don't provide ready-made answers

Being prepared is one thing. Trotting out entire generic responses to barriers raised by the prospect is another. Resist the temptation to give 'ready-made', 'off the shelf' or 'one size fits all' answers in response to objections. Wait, listen, question, and tailor your product knowledge, expertise and experience to fit the prospect's circumstances.

6. Avoid defensiveness at all costs

The minute you believe the prospect is questioning you, your product or your organisation and you take it personally, you are bound to become defensive. This defensiveness is the single biggest contributor to people 'digging in'. Defensiveness invariably results in our reinforcing the current negative and unconstructive position. This inevitably leads to our rationalising our current position by reinforcing our current thinking, and spending less time investigating the prospect's position and thinking, which may be worlds apart.

7. Resist arguing and engaging in contradiction

While the temptation may seem great, resist at all costs arguing with or contradicting the prospect. It doesn't do much for the relationship. If you have a different view, or are in possession of facts contrary to those expressed by your prospect, resist the temptation to 'tell' them. Let them continue to talk. Ask specific questions about their views and thoughts. Ask why they think, feel or believe that.

Slowly and strategically, introduce your contrary information and view of things in an objective, cooperative manner. Deal in the facts; if you must disagree openly, do so by disagreeing with the facts, not the person.

8. Understand the sales process

If you understand the sales process you will accept, as I suggested earlier, that barriers are a normal and very natural part of the sales process. In fact, maybe you should start worrying if your prospect *doesn't* raise any objections. Genuine barriers to the sale are considered an expected part of the sales process and generally mean that your prospect is seriously considering your propositions.

9. Don't avoid or ignore them

Prospects know when their concerns and fears are being ignored. Further, when a salesperson ignores their concerns, it is often interpreted by the prospect as an inability by the salesperson to meet their real 'needs', which then reflects poorly on the salesperson, the product or the organisation. The other by-product of ignoring or avoiding objections without permission from the prospect to do so is that they may be less inclined subsequently to take you into their confidence and share their thinking with you again.

10. Don't give up or give in

Never give up or give in. Continue to probe, to question, to listen. If, despite time and effort, you haven't succeeded in dissolving the barrier satisfactorily, it probably means you haven't uncovered the real obstacle. Don't give in. Remember, hang in there: you can bet that your competition is withering on the vine.

The dialogue resolution model—dissolving barriers to the sale

One approach to removing or dissolving barriers to the sale that I have seen generate exceptional outcomes is what I call the 'dialogue approach'. I use this name because the very basis of the model is to create a dialogue, to obtain a better understanding of the prospect and continue to strengthen the 'connection' with them.

The model involves the following five primary elements:

1. *maintain* presence;
2. *demonstrate* empathy;
3. *ask* questions to understand;
4. *position* your response; and
5. *test*.

Let's look at each of these five elements that work together to dissolve barriers to the sale.

1. Maintain presence

Avoid at all costs jeopardising the relationship by becoming arrogant, hostile or impatient. Guard against jumping to conclusions, making subjective judgements, automatically concluding the prospect is wrong, becoming defensive, or interrupting the prospect. All of the above have a major negative impact on the 'presence' you established in your first sales call and the 'connection' with the prospect you subsequently reinforced through the sales process.

Your presence is all about how you project your personal image. It's the 'you' in the sales equation. It's what helps differentiate you from the competition. In an ever-competitive market where the prospect may at least initially perceive all the products on offer, including yours, as essentially the same, it's your personal style that differentiates you. Remain calm and confident. Display sincere interest and a positive approach. Listen, listen and listen again. Concentrate on maintaining even, deep, regular breathing and a positive body posture. Both will help you to remain alert and project a positive image to your prospect. Remember, barriers to the sale should be welcomed and are a positive sign. Think of barriers to the sale as no more than a question, often in the form of a statement, raised by your prospect, and you will find it easier to stay in control, maintain presence and use the barrier as a springboard to lift your relationship to another level, beyond the reach of your competitor.

2. Demonstrate empathy

Most salespeople accept and understand the importance of expressing empathy. However, the real problem here is twofold: first, they often don't do it in a manner that is perceived as 'sincere' by the prospect; second, they often undo all their good work in expressing and demonstrating empathy by using it as a vehicle for concealing or prefacing a gaggle of subsequently inappropriate responses, that range from product dump to contradicting the prospect, through to avoiding the issue or objection by switching tracks entirely.

If you can't convince yourself that *you really care*, it's highly unlikely you will be able to effectively communicate this 'I really care' message to the prospect. Empathy is all about showing interest in the prospect and their situation. It also involves displaying a real concern for their problems and being sensitive to their feelings. The key objective in demonstrating empathy is to effectively *communicate* this empathy to the prospect by encouraging a two-way dialogue. This tends to accomplish three things:

- *It helps to defuse a potentially difficult or stressful situation.* This action is reinforced if followed up by questions aimed at finding out more about how the prospect feels.
- *It reduces the prospect's defensiveness.* By expressing empathy you have crossed to their side of the void that is starting to open between you and the prospect and are seen to be attempting to view and to understand the situation from their perspective.
- *It provides a natural platform from which to explore the objection further.* It achieves this by asking questions. Send them a message that you care about how they look, feel and sound about your propositions and then explore these barriers by asking well-constructed questions.

3. Ask questions to understand

One of the most underrated and misunderstood principles in selling is this. The prospect will give you information and guide you in *how* to sell them if you take the time to ask them the right questions.

So when it comes to barriers to the sale, questions are probably even more important and serve exactly the same purpose. They can give you the information on how to dissolve the barriers, with the help of your prospect.

It is interesting to observe that when well-constructed questions are carefully put to the prospect in response to a stated barrier, the prospect often answers their own objection. It may take a series of competent questions, rather than just one. However, I believe that if you become a practitioner skilled at designing and asking good questions, you can quickly get to the heart of the thoughts and concerns of the prospect and, in the process, help them understand these concerns, which are often just vague feelings. Once they fully understand these barriers themselves, they often see them for what they are—emotional responses—or are in a better position to answer their own 'fears'. At the very least, if you need to go to the next stage in this dialogue model for dissolving barriers, you have a real target to aim at, rather than feelings that you and your prospect will find not to be rooted in fact or reality.

Traditional methods of dealing with problems and objections that are expressed during the sales process concentrate on a resolution model, which invariably includes either knowing *all* the answers or attempting to *change the prospect's mind* about how they view the barriers.

First, you don't and cannot have all the answers. As I said earlier, you need to work with your prospect. You cannot and should not attempt to work in isolation. Together, you and the prospect will have the answers if you ask the right questions.

Second, changing your prospect's mind may appear to be a laudable objective, but in reality it's a ridiculous notion. You cannot change your prospect's mind. Only they can do that. Your mission is to work with the prospect and position your response to their stated barriers so that they view your product in a totally new light and, in so doing, remove all of their stated concerns and objections.

4. Position your response

Positioning is covered in an earlier section of this book, where I introduced it as one of the critical elements of the sales process. Positioning your response to an objection is no different from the concept of positioning your product in the first instance. The concepts and mechanisms are identical.

In positioning your response to a barrier to the sale, you encourage the prospect to consider and focus on the appropriate features and benefits of your product. And you can only do that when, in terms of dissolving barriers, *you and the prospect* have a clear, concise and shared perception of the real barriers to the sale. The rest is relatively easy. The prospect will tell you what they really need. It's up to you to narrow down the real issues and concerns and focus your technical knowledge and sales expertise on providing the information that responds directly to your prospect's real dominant needs. Sounds just like the approach to value-based selling described in the early sections of this book, doesn't it? And so it should. Dissolving barriers is no more than a sale within a sale. When you are using this dialogue model to dissolve barriers, all you are doing is concentrating on specific prospect-raised barriers that you have probably failed to address as part of the needs and positioning elements or that perhaps the prospect failed to appreciate or understand.

So, dealing with objections is nothing more than a sale within a sale. Instead of dealing with a range of needs and wants and positioning your dominant needs propositions, your prospect is drawing your attention to one or two specific concerns that they believe weren't covered, or weren't covered effectively, or require further discussion or explanation.

5. Test

We use testing as an element in the dialogue resolution model to:

- avoid needing to assume that the concern or barrier has been dissolved. Why assume, guess, interpolate when all you need to do is ask? As the Bible says, 'Ask and ye shall receive.' So ask for the prospect's thoughts and feelings once you believe you have positioned your response. Confirm that they are satisfied with the response; and
- determine exactly where you are at with the prospect. Gather information about other issues and concerns as well as with the status of the current barrier. You don't need to wait until you believe the barrier has been dissolved. Feel free to test at any time when you feel you need an indication from the prospect that they are with you, that you are on the right track, that you are both on common ground.

So, how do you test when you are in dialogue resolution mode? Simple—just ask for feedback to determine how your prospect feels about the issues at hand or your response. It could be feedback on a conclusion you have reached, or on your understanding of what the prospect has just said. It could be as simple as asking:

- 'What do you think about . . .?' or, simpler still, just 'What do you think?', or
- 'Does that help?'

Obviously your relationship to the prospect, the environment, the product in question and a host of other factors tend to dictate the way in which you choose to test. No matter how you choose to test, make sure you do it and receive a green light to proceed before you leave those barriers to the sale behind.

One other important point worth raising is this: when it comes to price or cost barriers, you might consider *not* testing immediately after you have stated the price or terms. Doing so is often perceived by the prospect as a lack of confidence and can be seized on to continue with the barrier when no real objection exists in the prospect's mind.

chapter 29

Resolution skills II—the dialogue approach (the before and after story)

T o help bring perspective to some of the ideas and suggestions I made in Chapter 28 on dissolving barriers to the sale, it might be constructive to review a number of hypothetical sales situations and look at the responses both bad and good. I have called this the *before and after story*. I submit the following scenarios as examples of how I have observed salespeople respond before and after they have come to realise, accept, understand and then implement a more value-based methodology to deal effectively with barriers to the sale.

First, in reviewing the hypotheticals, see what you think of the 'before' responses. How do these compare with what you might have said or done yourself in a similar circumstance? Then have a close look at the 'after' responses. Can you see a different approach, a different style and focus? Do you see it as one that is targeted at promoting a dialogue as a means of understanding the prospect's thoughts and feelings and reinforcing the relationship at all times?

Dissolving barriers to the sale—the before and after story

It may be helpful to review a number of typical sales scenarios that demonstrate some of the things salespeople *shouldn't* do and then provide an example of what salespeople might do as they address barriers to the sale. I've chosen what I will loosely term a 'before and after' format, to clearly demonstrate that salespeople do have options and that choosing the best option is neither difficult nor risky. It's a matter of making an effort to change some of the 'old ways'. You might take the time to quickly review the 10 most frequently observed responses to barriers used by traditional salespeople listed in Chapter 28. In these before and after scenarios, the before examples use forms of these 10 responses.

You will, I hope, see that each of the hypothetical sales scenarios demonstrates the different approach of the 'before', or traditional salesperson's, response from that of the 'after', or value-based salesperson's, response. This latter salesperson is a value provider who is aware of and uses the elements of the dialogue resolution model to deal effectively with the prospect's concerns, fears, objections, and, ultimately, work to dissolve the barriers to a sale.

So what do the 'before' responses share as common approaches? They each incorporate in some fashion one or more of the 10 basic salesperson-focused or product-focused responses talked about in Chapter 28. You may recall these were:

1. product dump;
2. attempt at empathy;
3. 'if' technique;
4. leading question;
5. switching tracks;
6. contradiction;
7. reflective statement;
8. ignore it;
9. the assumption; and
10. the challenge.

What outcome do all the 'before' approaches have in common? They are all dialogue killers. They terminate or block any chance of opening or continuing a meaningful discussion and thereby establish a conduit into the prospect's thinking which allows the salesperson to receive and send messages and ultimately work together with the prospect to dissolve the barriers to the sale.

Regardless of how these negative responses are phrased, they will almost definitely trigger defensive answers from the prospect, which will see them digging in their positions, which will result in little or no chance of movement from their entrenched views.

Learn to promote and to keep the dialogue going. Learn to use the questioning approaches discussed earlier.

Sales scenario no. 1

BEFORE—*product dump*; AFTER—*dialogue: maintain presence and demonstrate empathy*

Prospect: *'I'm not sure we really do need to spend that much money to fix our problem.'*

BEFORE

Traditional salesperson response: *'I can see why you might think that . . .'*—an attempt at empathy that, depending on delivery, may fall flat and sound patronising . . . *'but let me tell you about the host of advanced features that make this one of the most unique new products in this line for decades. First, there is . . ., then there is . . .'* Rather than detour and investigate what appears to be a clear obstacle to the sale, the salesperson attempts to 'overcome' the objection by sheer weight of numbers of product features.

AFTER

Value-based salesperson response: *'Frankly, Mr Smith, given the relatively short time we have spoken and given that we haven't investigated your problem to any depth, it could well be that you are absolutely right'*—demonstrating empathy. *'With just this in mind, perhaps it would be prudent to discuss your current situation so that we can make sure all the bases are covered before even considering solutions'*—setting the stage to ask questions to understand.

Sales scenario no. 2

BEFORE—*product dump*; AFTER—*dialogue: maintain presence and demonstrate empathy and position themselves to ask questions*

Prospect: *'We have been buying this product from our preferred supplier for more than 10 years—I can't see any real need to change that arrangement!'*

BEFORE

Traditional salesperson response: *'Far be it from me to want you to jeopardise your relationship with your current supplier.'* This has the potential to be interpreted as an insincere remark, if not straight-out sarcasm. Then the big *but*: *'But let me tell you what you would be missing . . . With 50 years of business behind us, over 100 staff, in seven locations Australia-wide, no one can compete with our service'*— followed by bragging and probable exaggeration that does nothing to maintain presence and build empathy.

AFTER

Value-based salesperson response: *'Loyalty is something I admire and something our company works hard at developing. So I certainly understand, appreciate and admire your comments concerning your current supplier.'* This begins by maintaining a strong professional presence and building a foundation of empathy on which to open a continuing dialogue. *'If you could possibly spare me 15 or 20 minutes, what I would like to do is simply explore what areas of your business we may be able to assist you with in the future. Perhaps in the event that your current supplier is temporarily out of stock or can't respond as quickly as you would like. There may even be opportunities to supply competitive product in areas you are sourcing elsewhere.'* Here the salesperson, having acknowledged the prospect's reservations, is attempting to continue the dialogue with the sole purpose of establishing a strong presence and receiving permission to continue to ask questions to understand the prospect's situation.

Sales scenario no. 3

BEFORE—*attempt at empathy*; **AFTER**—*dialogue: demonstrate empathy and ask questions to understand*

Prospect: *'I don't really think I like the colour.'*

BEFORE

Traditional salesperson response: *'I think I understand what you mean, but . . .'* (the infamous *but . . .*) *'this colour really is very popular this year. We are selling more of this colour than all the other colours combined.'* Here the salesperson negates the attempt at empathy with a *but*. In other words, they run the risk of their attempt at empathy being overbalanced by their desire to push their view and that of others on the prospect's barrier, at the expense of the prospect's view.

AFTER

Value-based salesperson response: *'The colour is important. I know it would be for me and it certainly is for other customers in some circumstances. Could I ask why you don't like it?'* What is behind the barrier to the sale of colour? Is it personal preference or is it a work-related issue? Ask why to find out more, rather than latch onto the colour issue and attempt to push the prospect to reconsider.

Sales scenario no. 4

BEFORE—*attempt at empathy*; **AFTER**—*dialogue: maintain presence; nothing is impossible; ask questions to understand.*

Prospect: *'Your standard response time is far too slow.'*

BEFORE

Traditional salesperson response: *'You are right,* but *there really isn't anything I can do',* or *'I can see how that might be a problem* but *that's the system. You will find that no one else can do it any faster',* or *'Others have also expressed that concern* but *they tell me that's because most of the parts need to be imported so that's the problem.'*

AFTER

Value-based salesperson response: *'I can well imagine that response time is important to you. Let me get a better picture of your situation. Generally when must you get a response by? For instance, how would it be if we could get the parts for you by 10 a.m. the day after', or 'What if I take some details about your real needs in this area now, then look into it and get back to you on Tuesday with a suggested course of action that meets your requirements? Is that okay?'* Resist the temptation to undermine your attempt at empathy by introducing the big *but*. Instead, be creative. Find out what is required and work to make it happen.

Sales scenario no. 5

BEFORE—*the 'if' technique*; **AFTER**—*dialogue: ask questions to understand*

Prospect: *'I simply don't believe I really need it!'*

BEFORE

Traditional salesperson response: *'Ah! So you are saying you are concerned about the cost not justifying the expense and hence you don't see a need for it. If I can demonstrate cost savings and why I believe you simply do need it, would you make a decision now to buy it?'* Here the salesperson is making an enormous leap of deduction (which is closer to a leap of faith and in this case turns out to be totally incorrect), and goes on to paraphrase the prospect. Then, to compound the error, the salesperson attempts to manipulate the prospect into a closing situation using the 'if' technique.

AFTER

Value-based salesperson response: *'It's certainly not hard to understand that you wouldn't want something you view as unnecessary. Given that it seems to meet your overall objectives, may I ask why you feel you don't need it?'* If you believe that it is genuinely in the prospect's best interests to reconsider, ask for more information. Why do they feel that way?

Sales scenario no. 6

BEFORE—*the 'if' technique*; **AFTER**—*dialogue: demonstrate empathy and ask questions to understand*

Prospect: *'I don't believe your organisation has the experience and track record to help us with this particular project.'*

BEFORE

Traditional salesperson response: *'You've mentioned what appear to be your two key criteria—experience and track record . . .'* This is almost certainly an incorrect assumption. *'If'*—this translates to 'are you prepared to wager with me?'—*I can demonstrate clearly how we do indeed have both the experience and the expertise, would you be prepared to recommend us for the project?'* This is very premature, especially as this approach is usually followed by a barrage of product-dump features and leading questions designed to trap the prospect.

AFTER

Value-based salesperson response: *'I understand from your comments that experience and track record are important to you. And, quite frankly, so they should be—there is quite a bit at stake.'* Support the prospect's thinking; why argue, especially if their concerns are misconstrued in the case of your company? Cross to their side and consider their concerns with them. *'So that I can better appreciate the overall scope of this project, could you tell me . . .'* Ask questions to understand just where the prospect is coming from in arriving at their stated perceptions, or *'I honestly believe our company has a considerable degree of experience and an enviable track record'.* This is simply a statement of confidence . . . *'And* (not *but*) . . . *because these two issues are so central to your needs I would appreciate the opportunity to explore them a little further with you. Tell me, what . . .?'* Invite the prospect to tell you more, to explain and freely discuss with you their goals and fears. Listen and ask well-designed questions aimed at understanding.

Sales scenario no. 7

BEFORE—*leading question*; AFTER—*dialogue: ask to understand*

Prospect: *'Your price is just too high!'*

BEFORE

Traditional salesperson response:

'Well, we assumed you were interested in quality . . .' or *'You are interested in quality, aren't you?'* While it is generally a good strategy to link price and quality, this is most definitely *not* the way to go about it. This could easily insult the prospect and at the very least damage the relationship. These are leading, self-serving questions that are challenging and confrontational to the prospect. Translated, these questions really say: *'You dummy, surely you're aware that if you pay peanuts, you get monkeys?'*

AFTER

Value-based salesperson response:

'I know we have discussed budget constraints several times. And so that we can objectively compare the relevant factors . . . can you tell me how or what you are comparing us to when you suggest you feel the price is high?' Once you know how you are perceived relative to other constraints, you will be in a much better position to discuss price relative to quality, which is the best way to demonstrate value and, ultimately, preserve price. Remember, quality is a relative term, so find out how your prospect is measuring it.

Sales scenario no. 8

BEFORE—*leading question*; **AFTER**—*dialogue: demonstrating empathy and asking to understand*

Prospect: *'We just can't see your proposal working for us at this time!'*

BEFORE

Traditional salesperson response: *'Our analysis of your situation indicates, to us at least, that your major concerns would be cost and availability, wouldn't they?'* This is a leading question, not a tested and agreed need. *'As this is one of your selection criteria, we would like to show you how we propose to deal with this issue so that you will be prepared to recommend our bid.'* The leading question was designed to lock the prospect into a course of action favourable to the salesperson.

AFTER

Value-based salesperson response: *'Given the time and resources that both of us have committed to the project so far, I imagine you are disappointed with that outcome. I know I certainly am . . .'* Maintain your professional presence, avoid displaying frustration and move towards demonstrating empathy by centring responses on how the prospect might feel. *'Could you tell me a little about why it is you don't see our ideas working for you?'* Ask 'why' questions to understand before you even consider positioning your response to the barrier.

Sales scenario no. 9

BEFORE—*switching tracks*; AFTER—*dialogue: begin positioning your response testing by feedback*

Prospect: '*Unfortunately, you're not considered a preferred supplier to this organisation.*'

BEFORE

Traditional salesperson response: '*I realise that we may not be thought of as a major product supplier or even be considered as the best, but let me tell you exactly why it is that you should look at our new Model X . . .*' Learn to deal with the barrier presented and avoid the temptation to switch tracks by introducing new variables into the equation.

AFTER

Value-based salesperson response: '*I suspected that this just might be an issue for you. I would be interested in exploring exactly what concerns you have about us.*' Why let the barrier build by reinforcing it, then completely avoiding it as the traditional salesperson did above? '*I believe we may be able to allay your fears in most, if not all, cases. But, of course, you can be the judge of that . . . !*' Recognise the importance of the barrier to the prospect and confirm your view that the barrier could be effectively dealt with to their satisfaction. '*If I understand your position, it appears that . . .*' Test to see where you really stand in this particular concern and test your understanding of it prior to positioning your response.

Sales scenario no. 10

BEFORE—*switching tracks*; **AFTER**—*dialogue: maintain presence and ask questions to understand*

Prospect: *'I have a couple of problems with the proposal that you provided for our next board meeting. It simply doesn't address all the major issues we discussed in our last meeting and for which, if you recall, we specifically requested answers.'*

BEFORE
Traditional salesperson response:

'When is your next meeting?' Here the salesperson *may* be trying to help and this is a pertinent question, *but* it is asked at the wrong time. It avoids the issue at hand by diverting or switching the topic to another track. The focus at this point should be on finding out more about the particular problems raised by the prospect.

AFTER
Value-based salesperson response:

'Yes, I am aware it doesn't deal with all the major issues and I am certainly disappointed that we were unable to completely cover all of your issues at this time. Perhaps I should have brought that to your attention. What exactly is the concern you have regarding those particular major issues not included?' Use a key word in the objection, 'major issues', to test for clarification and increase your understanding of the situation. Get to the heart of the concern. Ask 'why'. Later, when it's more appropriate to do so, you can get to discussing the prospect's real timeframes.

Sales scenario no. 11

BEFORE—*contradiction*; **AFTER**—*dialogue: maintain presence and ask questions to understand*

Prospect: *'The numbers just don't seem to add up!'*

BEFORE

Traditional salesperson response:

No? Well I checked them myself so I am fairly sure they are right', or perhaps *'Well, let me explain them again so that you can see exactly how they work.'* What, in fact, you are doing is simply suggesting to the prospect that you don't believe them or, worse, they must be stupid if they can't understand, which does little to enhance a value-based approach to selling.

AFTER

Value-based salesperson response:

'As you know, we are both committed to a successful outcome, which means, quite simply, we really do need to get the very best result we can. Could you spare a couple of minutes now and show me exactly where you see the problem so that I can better understand why you are thinking the numbers might be wrong?' This translates to: 'Let's work together towards what we both see as a shared common objective by talking through the differences.' It emphasises the common ground and doesn't elevate the prospect's perceptions of the problem to a major hurdle that will then have the potential to cripple the sale.

Sales scenario no. 12

BEFORE—*contradiction*; **AFTER**—*dialogue: position a response, test by feedback and ask questions to understand*

Prospect: *'I don't think we can wait 12 weeks for delivery.'*

BEFORE

Traditional salesperson response:

'Mr Brown, the wait will be well worth it, I can assure you! The reduced power consumption of the new machine alone will pay for the wait.' The salesperson patronises the prospect by dismissing their concerns out of hand, even going so far as to contradict them and, worse, appearing to assume what they will find valuable.

AFTER

Value-based salesperson response:

'Perhaps if we could spend a couple of minutes reviewing your timeframes, I could better understand how to meet your needs.' The salesperson is positioning a possible

shift to investigating the prospect's particular situation. *'It seems to me, at least on the basis of a preliminary analysis, that . . . and . . . In order to gain a better appreciation, tell me . . . how does your organisation . . .?'* The salesperson is now starting to test by providing feedback and asking specific questions in order to understand the prospect's thinking and feelings behind the perceived delivery time barrier to the sale.

Sales scenario no. 13

BEFORE—*reflective statement***; AFTER—***dialogue: demonstrate empathy and ask questions to understand*

Prospect:	*'I need to achieve a specific number of copies per minute and I'm afraid your system just won't do that!'*

BEFORE

Traditional salesperson response: *'Oh, so if I understand you correctly, what you're suggesting is that you need to achieve a specific copy output per minute and you are afraid that our system won't do that?'* This form of response, reflective listening, has been taught to many salespeople over the years as an effective questioning technique. The technique is not in itself inherently bad, although in most sales situations it has been greatly overused and abused due to laziness on the part of the salesperson.

AFTER

Value-based salesperson response: *'I certainly understand you are concerned about achieving a fast copy rate. So that I can be absolutely clear about your needs, may I ask what are your concerns about our system, in particular our ability to meet your specific output targets?'* Again, as in the previous scenario, this translates to: 'Let's work together to achieve the specifics you need in order to meet your targets.'

Sales scenario no. 14

BEFORE—*reflective statement*; **AFTER**—*dialogue: demonstrate empathy and ask questions to understand*

Prospect: *'I think we would probably prefer to stick to our current supply arrangements. After all, from what I am told, they seem to have done a good job to date.'*

BEFORE
Traditional salesperson response: *'So, based on what you have said, your current supplier has done a good job so far and on this basis you will continue to stick with them.'* This reflective form of question in response is usually used as a platform to set the prospect up for a fall. It's the type of approach a barrister might use in cross-examining a witness in court. The subtle twist of the prospect's own words can completely alter the meaning of the original message.

AFTER
Value-based salesperson response: *'I can certainly understand your view that if your current supply arrangements were working well you might be tempted to leave them in place . . .'* Why not agree with what appears, at least on the surface, to be a reasonable line of thinking by the prospect? *'. . . and if our positions were reversed I'm not sure I wouldn't be inclined to take a similar course of action . . .'* Reinforce the reasonable nature of the response—build empathy *'Tell me, could we spend a little time today looking at some of the criteria that are important, if not critical, to your supply needs? In fact, can we spend a couple of minutes exploring those supply issues that are important to you in any contract?'* Why not, by encouraging further dialogue, stimulate the prospect to evaluate their true position by exploring their real needs and thereby agreeing with them exactly what constitutes a 'good job'? Then, and only then, armed with this information, can you position your response to this barrier to the sale.

Sales scenario no. 15

BEFORE—*ignore it*; AFTER—*dialogue: maintain presence and ask questions to understand*

Prospect: *'To tell the truth, I'm quite satisfied with my present system!'*

BEFORE

| Traditional salesperson response: | *'Well, let me explain to you why this new system we are offering today is the latest and greatest piece of equipment of its type, and second, just what it can do for you that your present system can't.'* |

AFTER

Value-based salesperson response: *'I know a little about your current system and, quite frankly, it's a good one. In fact, it was our most widely sold model. Perhaps you could tell me a little about it . . .? For instance, with your particular use in mind, what is it that you like about your current system and how, if at all, could it be improved?'* Get a dialogue going. Ask questions that get behind the prospect's statements. There isn't one single hard target to aim at in the prospect's response. You will need to dig much deeper or risk separating from the prospect at this point in the sale and finding yourselves on separate roads.

Sales scenario no. 16

BEFORE—*ignore it*; AFTER—*dialogue: maintain presence*

Prospect: *'Thanks for the offer, but I just bought one.'*

BEFORE

| Traditional salesperson response: | *'Fine! I hear that a lot, but I think you would find it worthwhile to spend five minutes looking at the features of this new model'*, or *'In that case, when should I call again to see about another one?'* Ignoring the prospect's response, and thereby the opportunity to work with them, does little to indicate competence and professionalism. Some forms of ignoring the response will be perceived by the prospect as giving up or being just plain belligerent or stupid. |

AFTER

Value-based salesperson response: *'That's certainly a coincidence. Tell me, out of professional interest, what did you buy?'*, or *'Really . . . from whom did you purchase it?'*, or *'When did you buy it?'*, or *'How do you find it?'* Keep asking questions. Look for opportunities to learn more about the prospect's situation and to commence building an enduring interpersonal and professional relationship at every opportunity.

Sales scenario no. 17

BEFORE—*assumption***; AFTER—***dialogue: maintain presence and ask questions to understand*

Prospect: *'I believe I need much more flexibility in approach than you are currently offering.'*

BEFORE

Traditional salesperson response: *'I know you need to stay reasonably fluid and that the freedom to adapt to changes in your industry is an important factor.'* This assumes why the prospect needs flexibility. What in fact it actually does is put words in the prospect's mouth. Don't make assumptions, don't attempt to interpret statements or guess the meaning of what the prospect says. Ask why! You might be very surprised at their reasons.

AFTER

Value-based salesperson response: *'That's perfectly understandable and, if I may suggest, very forward-thinking. When you say you need to be more flexible, may I ask what kind of specific features or outcomes you are looking for to give you this flexibility?'* After all, what does 'flexibility' really mean? You have absolutely no option other than to ask the prospect to tell you more. Without more 'specifics', you aren't even dealing with soft targets, you are dealing with no targets. Yet it's surprising just how many salespeople will fail to ask!

Sales scenario no. 18

BEFORE—*assumption*; AFTER—*dialogue: maintain presence and ask questions to understand*

Prospect: *'Thanks anyway . . . but I have a friend in the business who usually looks after me.'*

BEFORE

Traditional salesperson response:

'Well, I would really appreciate the opportunity of competing against your friend's price. I think you will be surprised at our attractive low prices.' First, why assume the 'friend' supplies exactly what it is you sell? Second, why compound this mistake by assuming they buy whatever it is they do buy, which the salesperson didn't bother even to investigate, for price. Don't make silly leaps of interpretation. It will ultimately embarrass you, the prospect or both of you, and lead to a failure to establish presence—the first part of developing a relationship.

AFTER

Value-based salesperson response:

'Well, that should make the process of ordering new products easier, and it's certainly not the first time I've come across this situation. In fact, it happened last year over at XYZ Corporation . . .' Let the prospect know that you have no intention of challenging their relationship with their 'friend', if that is in fact who they are dealing with. *'In that situation, what we ended up doing was working with that person to investigate options to improve the performance of their packaging division quite considerably . . .'* Reinforce that you are there to work with the prospect on their needs. *'To do that we looked at their current operations and provided a preliminary assessment of potential key areas for review. Could you tell me a little about how you . . .?'* Demonstrate that you are not there to threaten their current situation. Encourage them to begin to talk about themselves and their organisation. Experience has proven time and time again that dialogue is the only way of uncovering opportunities to help the prospect to help you.

Sales scenario no. 19

BEFORE—*the challenge*; **AFTER**—*dialogue: maintain presence, position a response and ask questions to understand*

Prospect:	*'The rate is simply too low. Can't you provide something better?'*

BEFORE

Traditional salesperson response:

'Well, please tell me exactly what rate you are looking for.' This perpetuates a demand spiral that goes from one demand to another. Use this question later (although much better framed) to uncover from the prospect a specific number or range with which to work. For example, just before you leave you might ask, *'In order to give me a better idea of your thinking, what rate are you thinking you might accept?'* This way you can get a sense of where the prospect's perception is.

AFTER

Value-based salesperson response:

'I can certainly understand that the rate is an important consideration. In fact, all our best customers express exactly that sentiment. Could you please tell me what you are comparing us to when you suggest that our rate is too low?' Briefly express empathy, then confidently move on to confirm that the prospect's response is reasonable and is, in fact, shared by other successful businesses. The question that follows is designed to explore the prospect's real needs rather than react to one non-specific need masked in the form of a vague demand. *'What is behind the rate issue? Why might it be a barrier to the sale?'* You must find the answers to questions like these if you are to deal effectively with this type of barrier to the sale.

Sales scenario no. 20

BEFORE—*the challenge*; AFTER—*dialogue: maintain presence, position a response*

Prospect: *'That may be all well and good for your other customers, but we need a two-day turnaround.'*

BEFORE

Traditional salesperson response: *'Quite frankly, that is an unreasonable condition, given the quantity and complexity of the job. Why would you need two days?'* Why don't you just tell the prospect that they are unreasonable and be done with it? There is nothing wrong with wanting to know—*'Why two days?'*— but putting it in the form of a challenge elevates the discussion to a personal level that questions the prospect's reasonableness, competence and understanding of reality.

AFTER

Value-based salesperson response: *'Our arrangements with each and every one of our customers tend to be a response to each of those customer's particular needs . . .'* Put your comments in context. Resist challenging the prospect, but don't be afraid to set the record straight; refuse to be misquoted or to have your statements taken out of context. Position your desire to know why the prospect needs a two-day turnaround. *'If you would be willing to work with us in reviewing the current situation, both yours and ours, I am very confident we can give you exactly what you want.'* From the previous positioning statement, now move into asking questions to understand why. Note that rather than *need*, the salesperson used the more emotive *want* to underscore the strength of what they were proposing.

chapter 30

Negotiating skills—negotiating your way through tricks and traps

N ow might be a good time, having outlined the major competing approaches to the negotiating element in Chapter 20, to turn our attention to the negotiating tricks and traps used often in negotiating complex sales. In this chapter it is intended to discuss the behaviours and perspective a salesperson needs to adopt in order to recognise them, and to implement strategies to meet and circumvent the threats these tricks and traps may pose to a cooperative win/win outcome.

Negotiating tricks and traps

This chapter is not intended to moralise or to discuss the various merits, or indeed ethics, of the various tricks or traps identified. I leave it to the reader to make their own value judgements. I merely present a simple overview of some of the various tricks and traps that may be used, sometimes quite unconsciously although usually consciously, by other parties in the negotiating process.

Needless to say, you can expect to come across many of these tricks and traps if you find yourself down the bargaining end of the negotiating continuum most of the time in your negotiating. The tricks and traps can be divided into three board categories:

1. *Externally imposed 'control tactics'*—designed primarily to appear as if a separate objective external source is setting the fixed parameters for the negotiation. The ultimate objective of these allegedly externally imposed control tactics is that of severely limiting your options and thereby your room to manoeuvre.
2. *Applied manipulative 'pressure tactics'*—designed to allow the other party to grasp the initiative very early in the negotiation process and maintain it throughout the negotiation, providing you with little opportunity to gain your balance and actively resist.
3. *Hidden 'traps' set along the path*—designed to entice you into giving concessions and thereby eroding your margins and reaching your

bottom line quickly, while in the process the other party makes little or no meaningful concessions themselves.

Let's have a closer look at each of these three types of negotiating tricks and traps, starting with control tactics.

1. Agenda control

One of the most commonly used tactics to control the scope of the negotiation to your disadvantage is to control the agenda. This includes controlling:

- *content*—what gets included, sometimes even more importantly excluded, from the agenda of negotiation issues on which the negotiation will focus;
- *procedures*—which might appear as insignificant or very minor items, such as who is responsible for minute-taking, distribution, security and scheduling, and chairmanship of the various meetings; and
- *participants*—who participates, which may or may not be important. Pay attention when and if it is discussed, especially as it relates to any experts or specialists you may wish to include in future meetings.

While they may appear to some as inapplicable to their sales environment, the impact of each of these controls will be immediately obvious to salespeople who have experienced any number of complex sales negotiations. Let's look quickly at the counter to each of the three types of agenda control tactics above.

The only way to overcome agenda control is to carefully review the agenda and request clarification of any terms you are unsure of. You should also strenuously insist that items be included that you believe are legitimate and exclude items you believe are not reasonable. Silly as this may sound, you will often need to be prepared to negotiate the agenda prior to commencing the negotiation proper. However, this tactic of agenda control is likely to be an issue only in more complex negotiations. The bulk of sales negotiations are unlikely to require an agenda and even more unlikely to require procedural issues or programs to be worked out in advance of the negotiation per se.

2. Limit control

Unusual though it might at first sound, self-imposed limits by a party as to this party's stated ability to negotiate beyond a preset limit can be an advantage in the negotiation. The most common limit control tactic you will hear in negotiations is one of authority: 'I don't have the authority to agree to that; however, . . .' is a well-worn tactic. Also well used are the related limits of policy: 'I'm afraid that would contravene our purchasing policy . . .'; and financial limits: 'I can only approve contracts up to $10 000. Above that I will need to involve the finance committee and possibly . . .'

Less common self-imposed limits include technology: 'I don't believe we have the capacity at present to . . .'; and legal position: 'I would certainly like to do that, but my legal division has just sent around a memo advising all of us that . . .' When it comes to these stated limits, which are often self-serving and, more importantly, very often self-imposed, you might keep two things in mind:

- Consider asking, before the negotiation gets formally under way, if there are any limitations, policies or procedures that the other party is aware of that would be likely to impede a resolution of the issues to be negotiated by the parties involved during the negotiation.
- Don't necessarily accept the stated limitations. Ask for clarification and, if you suspect that the limitations will seriously jeopardise the conduct of the negotiations, request a recess; or don't commence the negotiation until the limitation, real or imagined, can be dealt with.

3. Options control

This form of control, as the name suggests, is designed to severely limit your negotiation options. This control is usually implemented by the other party referring to past practices, with you directly, with your organisation or with other third parties, which seem to adversely affect your preferred outcomes and severely limit your choices.

Using this form of control tactic, the other parties will use past practices or precedents to suggest things like, 'But we have never been asked for . . . before', or 'Our verbal confirmation has been accepted by your predecessor in the past', or 'We are currently finalising a deal with our other suppliers and I know this wouldn't be an issue with them.' You need to be careful here. If you feel they are deliberately limiting their ability to be flexible and meet reasonable conditions and terms on your part by referring to their past practices or their history, with either you or others, you can counteract this tactic by clearly demonstrating that the 'precedents' as expressed in the cases they are referring to are not relevant in the current situation.

4. Time control

Perhaps time control is the most famous of all controls in negotiations. Stories are legion about negotiating partners finding out your deadlines and leaving the real meat of the negotiations until the last minute, when they realise they will be placing you under extreme pressure; possibly you will feel there is no choice but to agree to their terms in order to do the deal by the deadline. Here the other parties may reduce or even extend the timeframes in which they say they have to make a decision, probably being apologetic as they do so. Counter this by insisting on a timeframe that suits you. Don't accept unrealistic or open-ended timeframes.

In each of the above four control tactics the other parties may legitimately, although in my experience it is usually a case of manipulatively, seek to impose controls on both you and themselves, thereby restraining you or constraining you in terms of limiting your:

- freedom to act to your full capacity; and/or
- room to manoeuvre.

Both may work to severely limit your available options.

These tactics are designed to box you in, and they do so in a very subtle way. They do so by allegedly constraining the freedom of movement of the other party, not you. You must be careful in accepting these controls. Realise, if confronted by them, that they are part of the negotiation itself and as such are in themselves legitimate issues to be negotiated prior to commencing the real business at hand.

Frequently used manipulative pressure tactics

Pressure tactics, you will recall, were primarily introduced by the other party to allow them to seize the initiative usually quite early in the proceedings. There are five pressure tactics you need to be aware of and sensitive to, as you will almost certainly come across them at some stage in your negotiation career, and probably quite often at that. They are:

1. large demands;
2. threats;
3. deadlock;
4. shock; and
5. bypass.

Let's look at them one by one.

1. Large demands

Right at the outset, your opposite number in the negotiation drops an amount on the table (figuratively speaking), perhaps simply in the course of conversation or even as a direct opening offer. This amount is either many times greater or, depending on the situation, considerably less than you were expecting. What is your response?

Sometimes the sheer surprise of the demand, be it large or small, shakes your self-confidence to such an extent that you are at a loss for words. Worse, your negotiating strategy seems to disappear before your very eyes. You feel you are left with no option but to quickly reassess your position and lower your sights.

The counter to this is not to respond directly to the prospect's suggestions or opening bids but rather to probe with questions. Find out *how* they arrived at the stated position, assessment or viewpoint. Don't be afraid to ask:

- 'What makes you suggest . . .?'
- 'Why do you think that . . .?'
- 'How did you reach the conclusion that . . .?'

2. Threat

Threats by the other party can come in all shapes and sizes, from quite direct, such as 'If you can't agree to this, we are going to have to talk to our other suppliers . . .' to more indirect, such as 'Well I don't see this leaves us any alternative but to consider our options . . .'

Then there are the personal threats: 'I'm afraid we just don't feel we can continue to deal with you if . . .' and 'We intend to ask for someone else. You don't seem to be acting in a professional manner consistent with someone of your position and standing . . .'

These are often designed to make you rethink and regret your actions and take a much softer line. They do this by making you question your own behaviour, your self-image and self-esteem, and ultimately shake your self-confidence.

The counter to this tactic depends largely on the type and frequency of the threats and an assessment of what is at stake. You might elect to call their bluff and ask them to call you when they have 'reviewed their options'. You may consider showing a complete lack of concern by, for example, treating it as a joke and acting as if you expect them to laugh with you and acknowledge their tactic. Or you may appear to take serious exception to the threats and strenuously insist on the elimination of them as a precondition of a continuation of the negotiation process.

There is one other response that is often effective, and that is to simply ignore it. This response is often the best first response, with other more direct response options left in reserve.

3. Deadlock

The other party suggests they can go no further—apparently an impasse has been reached! When the negotiation seems to reach this stage and, as a result, stalls and appears to have reached a deadlock, which in your view has been engineered to place pressure on you to concede or backtrack, carefully weigh your options before doing so.

Deadlock can often be overcome by reminding the other parties what is at stake for both of you. Having done this, reinforce your common ground in the current situation and reiterate any agreements already reached in the negotiation process thus far.

Respond to this pressure tactic by continuing to explore options and to table and reassess proposals. Another response would be to consider calling a recess, if only for an hour or for a lunchbreak. This often gives the other party time to come back with another proposal based on their 'time to think through . . .' or 'after checking with . . .'. Which may or may not be the case.

4. Shock

Shockingly 'unrealistic' ambit claims are suggested to have many strategic advantages. Among them are:

- creating manoeuvring room;
- catching the other party off balance;
- having the other party revise their expectations; and
- shaking confidence.

Statements made or actions taken by the other party designed to surprise or even shock you generally have one of two major objectives in mind: either to severely shake your confidence; and/or to disorganise and disorient you by requiring you to quickly reassess your strategy and objectives in favour of the other party.

The surprise can take the form of an allegedly simple statement of fact—perhaps a statement which just happens to include material you considered confidential to your organisation, and which causes you to wonder what else they know. It could be the tabling of revised selection criteria by the prospect that now appear to require a total rethink of your approach to the sale. To effectively 'shock' the other party, the offer, demand or response must come out of the blue during the course of the negotiation. This is often carried out by appearing to appreciate your position, and praising you, the company and the product. This lulls you into a false sense of security.

Beware of 'Greeks bearing gifts'. A shock may be just around the corner. 'I'm sorry to say that, rather than continue to deal with one supplier, our board is considering advertising for expressions of interest from other potential suppliers', is dropped on the table like a bombshell. You're stunned. After all the encouraging talk and work to date, they open the third meeting with you with a statement that appears to pull the rug out from under your feet.

You feel angry, betrayed and frustrated at having wasted your time. Sometimes the other party will mask their shock offer or statement in a cloak of legitimacy by, just before making the offer, offering what may seem a reasonable ground for the offer or statement. It may be that the offer is the highest to which they can 'stretch their budget'. It may be that they 'don't need all the extras', they just want to pay for the base model. It may be that 'your professional approach has alerted them to other more urgent priorities . . .'. It could be a fact, such as 'Our investigations suggest that your cost of purchase of . . .', that is slipped, apparently quite innocuously, into the conversation with the specific intention of unnerving you. It could be an action, such as cancelling the next meeting at very short notice or introducing new players to the negotiation without warning.

As with the large demands tactic above, probe with questions. Ask *why* questions. Find out what the stated reason is for the other party mentioning or doing whatever it is that has generated the element of surprise. The surprise tactic is nothing more than a token ambush aimed specifically at reducing your resistance. Ask for an adjournment, check out the facts, and respond appropriately only when you are sufficiently prepared.

The counters to this tactic are:

- *Prepare for it.* Especially if you are being praised beyond reason.
- *Do your homework.* Know what your position is in regard to realistic opportunities available to the other party.
- *Prepare your own position to such a tactic in advance.* Do so in such a way that it cannot be manipulated by this tactic.
- *Stick to your game plan.* Don't let your negotiation strategies become 'unhinged'. Be flexible and realistic, but not so flexible that you bend with little pressure.
- *Ask questions.*

This tactic is often used by experienced negotiators who are used to testing and probing your negotiation experience and character at the outset.

5. Bypass

When someone you are negotiating with suggests, perhaps pleasantly enough, that they would like to take up one of their concerns or requests directly with someone else, perhaps the installer of the product in your organisation or perhaps your finance people, beware. It could be a tactic designed to isolate you and undermine your support. They may not even warn you that they want to do so. They may just go ahead, leaving you to find out later or maybe not at all.

Be prepared for the bypass, especially when negotiating with other parties who have had previous dealings with your organisation or where there are other existing relationships in place with which you are not directly concerned in that particular negotiation.

The best counter here is a strong, well-prepared defence through anticipating the bypass, alerting others in your organisation to the possibility of a bypass, and spelling out a suggested course of action for them to follow should it eventuate.

You see this tactic used often in real estate negotiations, where the more forceful prospective purchaser may attempt to bypass the agent and negotiate directly with the seller in an attempt to secure a better deal. Professional agents circumvent this by telling the seller *before* the property is placed on the market what events might unfold, including requests by prospects to inspect the property without the agent and attempts by potential buyers to negotiate directly. The skilled negotiator explains these situations in advance, including reasons for the contacted party not to respond to the other party's direct advances. This skilled negotiator keeps close to their principals and colleagues and gives them a procedure, in advance, to follow if they are bypassed.

Hidden traps along the path

There are quite a number of traps you will find set along the negotiation path. Most of them you will find have been set deliberately, although some might be a result of the dynamics of the communication process rather than any conscious attempt to manipulate a situation for one party's particular convenience.

I leave you to debate the ethical and moral questions associated with these traps. One thing I do suggest, however, is that you familiarise yourself with these practices to protect your own interests, even if you don't ever intend to use them yourself. The fact is that, like it or not, these traps are used in everyday negotiations, so be prepared and recognise them when you encounter them.

Generally, these negotiation traps have one objective in common: they are designed to trap or entice one party into making concessions or giving something away at little or no cost to the other party. The overall method is also one that you will commonly find. This is simply that of presenting a situation where one party, you, feels pressured to do something—usually to give in, to reduce or preferably remove the applied pressure. The best overall counter to these traps is to understand that they work only *if* you accept the premise on which they are based. Don't accept these traps at face value. Question, at least in your own mind initially, their validity, and under no circumstances allow them to be positioned so that they can be used as a lever to exert pressure on you. In fact, what often happens is that these traps are set, and as a result cause you to place the pressure on yourself. In these cases, you end up being your own worst enemy.

So let's look at some of the common negotiating traps that may be set along the negotiating path.

Trap no. 1—Comparison

This trap is dependent on the opening offer or proposal tabled by the other party being very much above the negotiating range they have in mind. They then use 'comparison' as a basis on which to pressure you into accepting, for example, a considerably lower offer, which is still somewhat unreasonable.

For example, suppose the other party proposes to pay a unit price of $100. After you quickly reject this first offer as unreasonable or unrealistic, they very quickly offer to raise it to $180. However, you know that this offer, described by the other party as a 'special incentive' or whatever, is still nowhere near the price of the $250 per unit that is a fair and equitable market price for the product.

Guard against allowing this situation to place pressure on you. Resist the temptation to allow the emotion of the situation to hold sway. Resist at all costs allowing the contrast between their first and subsequent offer, in this case an increase of 80%, lull you into a false sense of compliance or acceptance. If you believe that $250 per unit is closer to the mark, stick to your strategy. Respond by suggesting a much higher price, somewhere at the top end of your negotiating range, and negotiate from there.

Don't accept ownership of the comparison trap and thereby place yourself under pressure to accede to what, by comparison, may appear a very reasonable second or subsequent offer. Maintain your stand.

Trap no. 2—Simplicity

There are several forms of the simplicity trap, and quite a few of them would be known to most negotiators. Simplicity is driven by an attempt by one party to simplify the situation and then offer a solution to what they see as the problem. Two common forms of this trap are 'splitting the difference' and 'rounding off'. You will be aware of both these traps, although perhaps not of the psychology behind them.

Splitting the difference may go something like this: 'Look, we're $1000 apart in this thing. It would be a shame if all our work and effort to date were to go unrewarded. What say we split the difference . . .?' I would bet you have heard this one before. The party simplifies the whole negotiation process by suggesting it's all a matter of meeting in the middle.

Rounding off works the same way except that it's a matter of rounding something up or down. Simple, really: 'Let's agree on $1500 a month at say $30 each. They are nice round numbers we can both agree on and, let's face it, it will save all the aggravation of using an unwieldy number like calculating the supply of 1487 boxes a month at $33.07, as suggested.'

The simplicity tactic is generally applied towards the closing stages of a negotiation, on the basis that these 'simple solutions' make it easier for both parties to simply say 'yes' and to avoid uncertainty and potential conflict given the considerable common ground and progress made by the parties up to this point. It's the 'let's just agree, and get on with life' approach.

The counter to this tactic is to stick to your guns and resist the temptation to 'simplify' the negotiation, unless it's to your advantage. I have seen the parties agree to split the difference only to have one party come back, claiming he could not get his manager to agree and then attempt to again split the difference between his original position and the previously agreed amount that resulted from splitting the difference in the first instance.

Trap no. 3—Nibbling

The tactic here is to wait until the other party has agreed to a proposition and then 'nibble' for something extra. This trap is often also referred to as 'nibbling' or the 'last-minute demand'. The psychology behind this behaviour is that the agreement, having been reached, causes the parties to relax and feel more confident. And just when this happens, when they are feeling good about themselves and the agreed outcomes and are anxious to do the deal, one party requests something extra, something seemingly inconsequential in the scheme of things: 'Of course you will install it at no extra cost?', when installation is an extra charge, or perhaps 'Just to clarify our agreement, it does come with a three-year warranty?', when they know a one-year warranty is standard.

Nibbling succeeds because in this end-of-the-deal euphoric state the nibble is often viewed as such an inconsequential request it's easier to go along than appear to be the killjoy who jeopardises all the good work to date and threatens the spirit of cooperation that has grown. You have just negotiated the sale of your product, or so you believe, and as you start to bask in the glory of your success your prospect says, 'Oh, by the way, this does include delivery, doesn't it?' You know you're being nibbled. Delivery was never discussed or, more to the point, the other party knows that it would normally involve an additional cost. In which case, you should be very clear that this is definitely no clarification. This is a direct attempt to negotiate a further concession by having you place pressure on yourself after agreement has supposedly been reached.

The counter to this tactic is first to curb your frustration, and then either ask for a trade-off or offer to go back to the table to negotiate the request in light of the other facets of the agreement reached to date. In a trade-off response you may initially respond, after a pregnant pause, perhaps with a wince thrown in for good measure, by saying, 'Look, it might be possible somehow to consider delivery in the overall package we discussed. If we can, what can you do for me?' The other response, which centres on an offer to go back to the table, may go something like this: 'I don't believe we discussed delivery in our negotiations to date. However, if this really is an important issue for you, we need to renegotiate aspects of our agreement. Can you tell me . . .?' Ask questions, thereby commencing to renegotiate the issues and see what response you get.

One other counter, which needs to be used selectively and carefully, is to treat the nibble as a joke. Be off-hand and dismiss it as a legitimate try-on and reinforce the good deal for the other party that has been agreed to. Something like 'Delivery? Next you'll be asking us to install it in the price as well! You know you have a good deal, let's leave it there.'

Trap no. 4—Slicing

This tactic is often considered to be related to nibbling. In my view this is incorrect, given the objective implicit in this trap. Nibbling, as discussed, is usually undertaken at the last minute, to gain extra concessions in the form of something additional for no extra cost. Slicing, on the other hand, is used as part of a much bigger and more insidious tactic, where the other party attempts to gain something seemingly inconsequential from you without letting you become aware of their bigger, real objective. The method on which slicing is founded is to avoid stating all the demands but dealing with them one at a time by making lots of much smaller, almost inconsequential demands. Soon, by continuing to accumulate lots and lots of very thin slices, when the other party puts them all together they have done a very good deal to your detriment. And no matter how thinly you slice a salami, if someone gets enough of those thin slices they can end up with most of the salami.

When your prospect appears to want to fully negotiate small chunks of the overall deal piece by piece, one at a time, you must resist. If they want to negotiate the price, then move on to negotiate delivery, then perhaps negotiate payment terms, then quantity, you are probably on the receiving end of the slicing negotiating tactic designed to make you the loser. Before you know it, your prospect holds all the cards, which they have carefully negotiated, a little at a time, until they have almost the full deck. What is happening is that each part or slice of the deal is being aggressively negotiated without knowing what the other concessions demanded will be.

Counter this tactic by refusing to finally negotiate on any one issue without knowing what all the issues are up front. Resist the temptation to negotiate specifics until you are aware of all the demands. You cannot and should not attempt to negotiate piecemeal, taking issues in negotiation one at a time, otherwise pretty soon and usually too late you will find out you have been guilty of giving the shop away.

As a response to this slicing tactic, you need to make your prospect aware that you know about the tactics and ask them diplomatically to stop. If this tactic of theirs continues or even escalates, you need to demand, as a condition of the negotiation continuing, that they desist. Point out that they are jeopardising all the positive outcomes the parties have achieved up until now. As soon as the other party attempts to cut off another slice by placing another demand on the table, let them know their new demand will 'change everything' and threaten to 'renegotiate all concessions' you have made thus far if they don't desist in pursuing their new demands. If all else fails, say clearly, firmly and in a steady voice, 'No!' Don't get personal—stick to the issues.

Finally, a word of advice concerning concessions, which is probably most applicable, given that we are discussing the trap of slicing here. First, try very hard never to give a concession unless you get one in return. Second, you must at all times keep track of all your concessions. Third, take the time to frequently summarise your concessions to keep you in control of the totality of the give-and-take of negotiation. Otherwise, before you know it, you will have given away much more than you think.

Trap no. 5—Almost true

This trap may be a conscious attempt to distort the facts or perhaps even tell complete untruths. It may also be a totally innocent mistake made in ignorance of the true facts. Generally, however, I see this in the form of half-truths, the other party leaving deliberately unsaid those positive things that show the product or situation in another light. It is a manipulative tactic designed to engineer a shift in your perceptions of the issues and the power you believe you enjoy.

I recently witnessed just such a tactic in ongoing negotiations for computer software. The prospect let the salesperson know that an alternative supplier was offering a better deal and selectively went on to outline some of the advantages of the other competing supply proposal.

How do you think this tactic should be handled? You guessed it: don't react one way or the other initially—you have two choices.

First, if you are unaware of the facts as suggested by the other party, don't accept them on face value. Rather than respond by answering the challenge, seek more information, evaluate, question, find out all you can—make sure you are in possession of all the facts before you respond directly.

The second option for dealing with this tactic depends on having done all your homework in advance, such that you know the facts behind those selective tidbits you are being fed. You can then fill in the gaps with those unstated facts that have been deliberately ignored by the other party because they don't enhance the other party's position, and thereby turn the tables on them. You can then make sure they are comparing apples with apples and draw the discussion to a close on that issue.

In the situation I referred to above, the salesperson had already made it his business to find out everything he could about his competitor's offerings. This included details about not only the product but also the usual terms of the offers themselves. When his prospect referred selectively to a 'better offer', the salesperson knew all about it. He chose to deal with it tactfully by asking the prospect questions that made it clear he knew of the offers, including the disadvantages or downside of the offer that was being selectively ignored by the other party. The prospect accepted this and, after a little further discussion, signed the order. They were simply trying it on by highlighting only the points in the competing offer that were favourable to them to see if they could create a situation where the other party accepted this on face value and thereby put himself under pressure to match the offer.

Trap no. 6—Take it or leave it

The 'take it or leave it approach', unless the party employing it does happen to hold all the cards, can lead the other party to choose to 'leave it'. I suggest you never use these exact words, as they inevitably signal a challenge of ego and will almost certainly lead to resentment and frustration and, possibly, irrational behaviour.

When faced with a 'take it or leave it' ultimatum, you need to investigate the situation further and decide whether it is a trap or a legitimate, though perhaps ill-conceived, statement of the other party's position. It will cost nothing to test the other party's intent and resolve prior to your making a decision as to how you wish to respond.

One simple way to test it is to ignore it completely—continue with the negotiations as if you haven't heard the words. If, on the other hand, you suspect, after testing their resolve, that it is a genuine ultimatum, seek to keep the negotiations moving by suggesting you set that particular issue aside and move on to other issues. You might be surprised at how much softer the other party appears once the pressure has abated and significant progress on other issues has been made.

Trap no. 7—Intimidation

This is generally a conscious tactic employed by win/lose bargainers who seek to bully, threaten, cajole and manipulate other parties in the negotiation. There are numerous means by which the other party may seek to intimidate you. These vary from keeping you waiting, cancelling appointments at the last minute, and not doing what they agreed to do, to seating you in an uncomfortable chair. The list of ways of intimidating people in negotiating situations is endless. Arguing, raised voices, displaying anger, insults are all designed to intimidate you into agreeing to or accepting their position, usually to your detriment.

When faced with intimidation, refuse to react emotionally. Be assertive, insist on an improvement or a change of situation before you allow the negotiation to proceed. Consider that the usual reason for intimidation is that the other party is simply testing you, and wants to see just how far you can be pushed and how much you will take.

Counters

There are many tricks and traps employed by experienced parties in negotiations. I have touched on only the dozen or so of these I see used most often in one-on-one sales negotiations. In discussing each, I have suggested simple, specific counters to be considered.

However, as a general rule, counters to these tricks and traps could be by one or more of the following proactive initiatives. If used together they might be considered in an almost descending order of priority, as follows:

- *Anticipate.* Half the battle is being aware of and recognising these tricks and traps. You are then well prepared to counter them by knowing how to respond to them specifically when you see them. If armed with this knowledge, anticipating them in advance is generally the best course of action, especially if the other party has a history of such behaviour. This generally accomplishes three things: first, they don't get very far before you call on them to reconsider their patently obvious tactic; second, you have a counter ready and waiting; and third, and perhaps most importantly, their tactic has absolutely no effect on your overall negotiation strategy.
- *Ask questions.* Asking the other party 'Why?' often knocks the wind out of their sails. This is sometimes the last thing they expect. They usually expect an ill-conceived, highly emotional response that is, they feel, in their best interests and not yours. They least expect a calm, rational, questioning approach—one they may have trouble answering satisfactorily given their manipulative approach to the negotiating process by the use of these tactics.
- *Ignore.* I suggested this as a counter to several of the specific tactics above. This is often difficult to do for many negotiators, as they feel that any and all comments or statements require a response. You may need to practise this one. Don't be afraid to ignore what you feel is a tactic designed to trick or trap you: if it continues, you might even let the other party know that you have consciously chosen to ignore it, but that this will not necessarily continue if they insist on pursuing these unhelpful tactics.

- *Humour*. One of the best strategies for dealing with potential conflicts of personality is the use of humour. Sometimes this will diffuse the situation before the responses escalate to levels that unleash irretrievable damage to the relationship. Humour requires some skill to use effectively and is often most effective when self-deprecating. Nothing is quite so disarming in tense situations as sharing a joke or a humorous anecdote at your own expense, although with an unmistakable message to the other party to desist.

- *Hard line*. This response demands that you directly assert your intention to the other party not to put up with, and not to be manipulated by, their tactics. You make it clear that you won't stand for their behaviour, having drawn their attention to the fact that you are aware of it. For example, indicate clearly that you have no desire to continue the negotiation process in light of the other party's behaviour and start to gather up your papers.

- *Retaliate*. While generally not a strategy that will achieve a great deal, retaliation may be what is required to surprise the other party into reassessing their own strategy and signalling clearly that you won't be intimidated or manipulated. The best form of retaliation is an objective, unemotional response to a tactic that clearly indicates that if they want to play hardball, you are willing to do so also and demonstrate this by using their own tactic against them. But a warning: if you do employ this response, don't back down. You must be prepared to carry out what you said you would do, or you will do yourself far greater damage.

- *Renegotiate*. Faced with some particular manipulative practices, one option is to respond by suggesting that, given the current situation, any and all agreements, concessions and trade-offs previously agreed to are now null and void and are therefore now up for renegotiation. Be firm, clearly indicating that if the other party continues to engage in these practices you have no intention of being bound by previous agreements. Again, stick to your guns.

- *Adjourn*. When situations in negotiations reach an impasse, deadlock, or threaten to boil over into open interpersonal conflict, don't be afraid to call a halt to proceedings by adjourning the negotiation to another time and place, perhaps after lunch or a short recess. Sometimes it will be best to adjourn so that others may join the negotiation to help defuse the problem issue. If you see merit in continuing at some future date, agree then and there on the next suitable time and place, and then leave.

- *Withdraw*. If all else fails, or you believe no positive responses to the tactics used by the other party are appropriate, you may withdraw from the negotiation either personally, by appointing a replacement to sit in your place, or by abandoning negotiations with the prospect altogether. While this may seem unrealistic, please understand that this is definitely an option. In some instances, no deal is better than the deal you might end up with if you continue to plug away.

I hope I have provided some insight into the negotiation attitudes and skills you will need to employ to counter some of the more commonplace tricks and traps you will undoubtedly come across in negotiating a sale.

Bear in mind that the more complex the sale, with its longer sales style, the greater the potential for manipulative negotiation tactics from the other party. Be aware of them and resist a spontaneous, emotional response. Consider your options, especially the available counters you could use to get the negotiation back on the rails.

Index